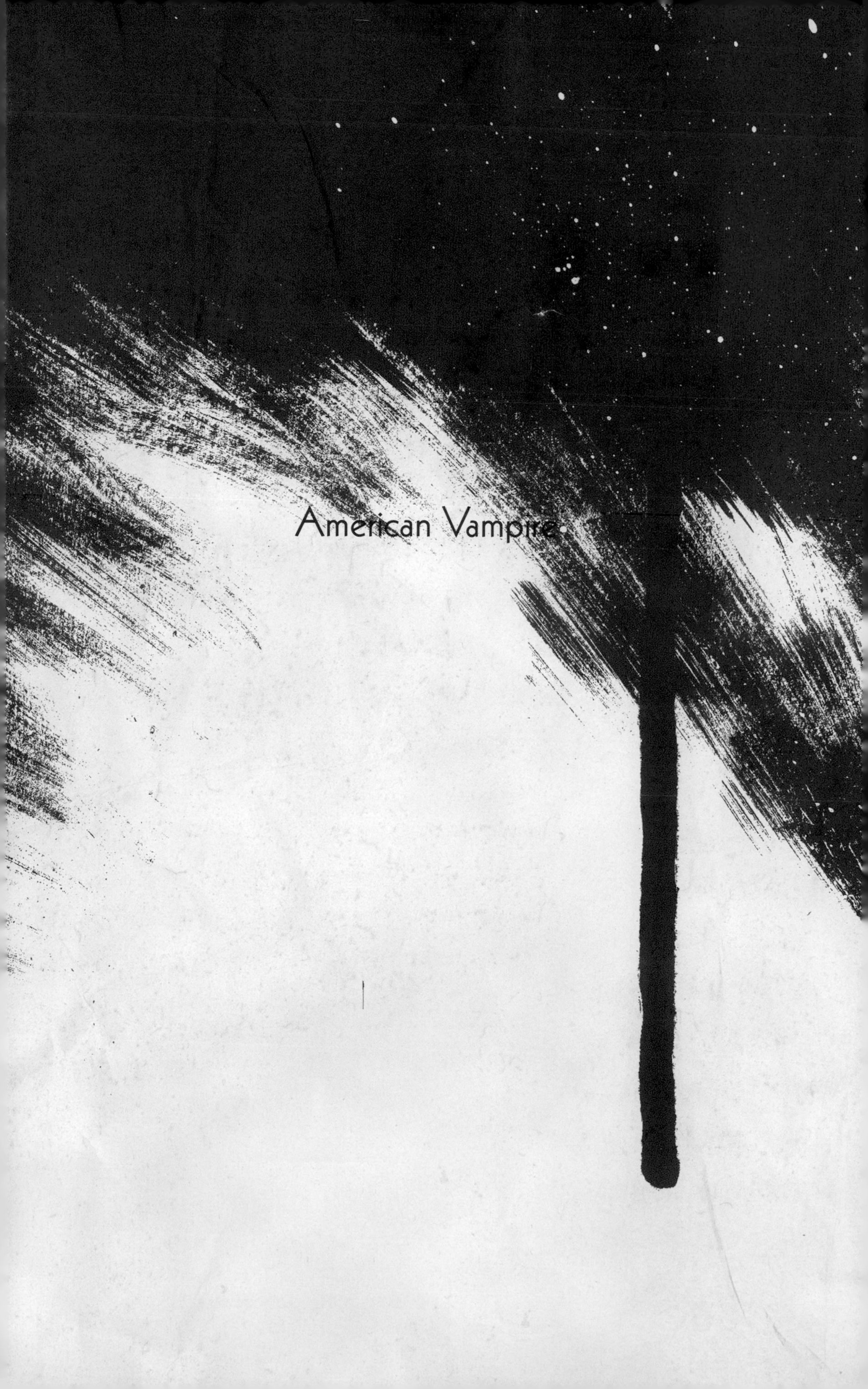
American Vampire

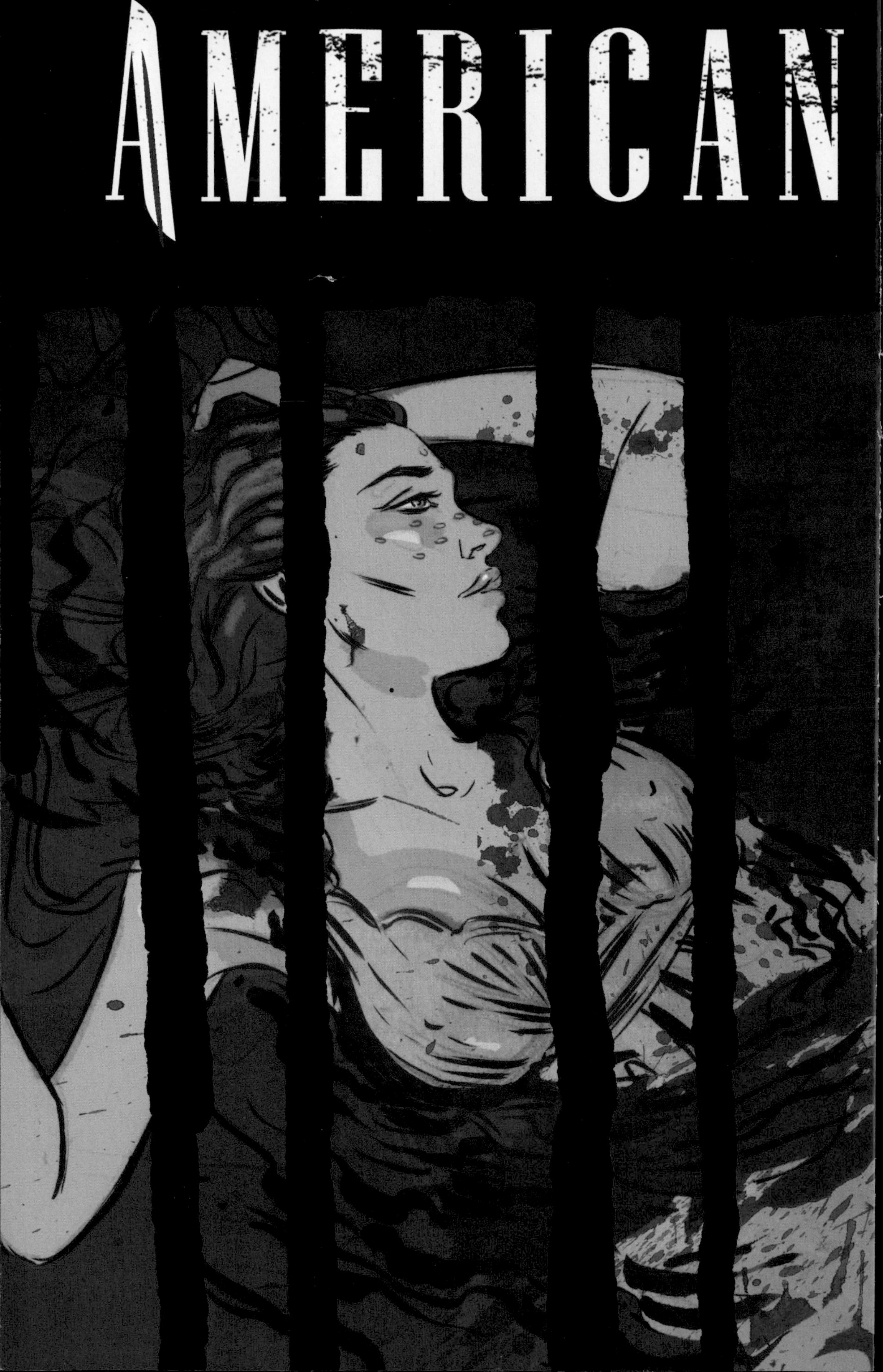
AMERICAN

VAMPIRE

VOLUME SIX

Scott Snyder

Becky Cloonan Francesco Francavilla Jason Aaron

Jeff Lemire Gail Simone Gabriel Bá Fábio Moon Greg Rucka Writers

Rafael Albuquerque

Becky Cloonan Francesco Francavilla Ivo Milazzo Ray Fawkes

Tula Lotay Gabriel Bá Fábio Moon JP Leon Artists

Dave McCaig Jordie Bellaire Colorists

Jared K. Fletcher Steve Wands Taylor Esposito Travis Lanham Dezi Sienty Letterers

Rafael Albuquerque Collection cover art

American Vampire created by Scott Snyder and Rafael Albuquerque

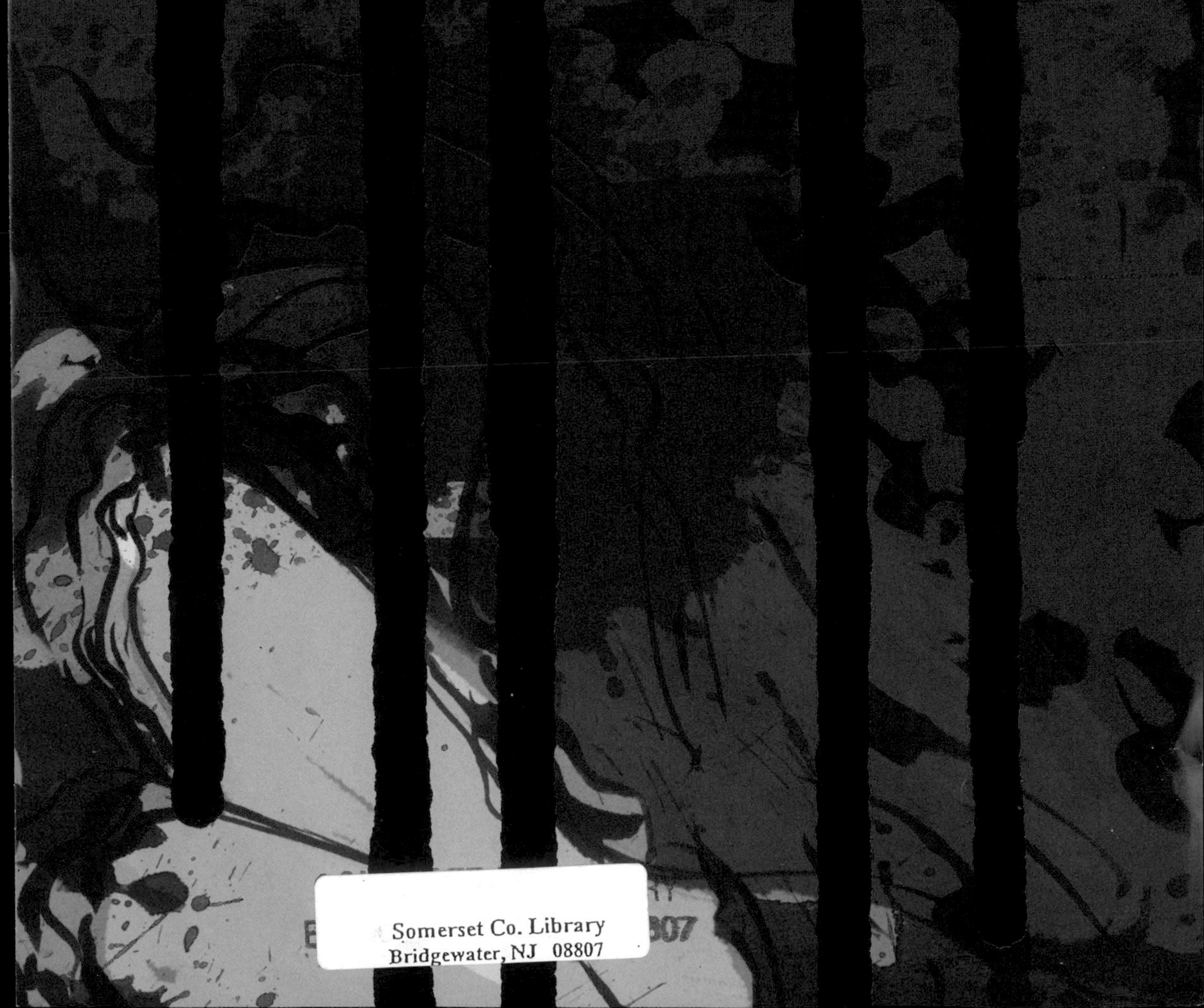

AMERICAN VAMPIRE VOLUME 6
Published by DC Comics. Copyright © 2014 Scott Snyder and DC Comics.
All Rights Reserved.

Originally published in single magazine form in AMERICAN VAMPIRE: THE
LONG ROAD TO HELL 1; AMERICAN VAMPIRE ANTHOLOGY 1 ©
2013 Scott Snyder and DC Comics. All Rights Reserved. All characters, their dis-
tinctive likenesses and related elements featured in this publication are trademarks
of DC Comics. Vertigo is a trademark of DC Comics. The stories, characters and
incidents featured in this publication are entirely fictional. DC Comics does not
read or accept unsolicited ideas, stories or artwork.

DC Comics, 1700 Broadway, New York, NY 10019
A Warner Bros. Entertainment Company.
Printed by RR Donnelley, Salem, VA, USA. 2/21/14. First Printing.
ISBN: 978-1-4012-4708-9

Library of Congress Cataloging-in-Publication Data

Snyder, Scott, author.
  American Vampire volume six / Scott Snyder ; [illustrated by] Rafael
Albuquerque.
    pages cm
  Summary: "You are cordially invited to a party–to die for! This volume
of American Vampire collects eight amazing stories set in the world
of American Vampire, with "lost tales," new characters and old
favorites. Don't miss these stories brought to you by series creators
Scott Snyder and Rafael Albuquerque, as well as other awesome
comics talent like Becky Cloonan (BATMAN), Gabriel Ba and
Fabio Moon (DAYTRIPPER), Jeff Lemire (SWEET TOOTH),
Greg Rucka (The Punisher, BATWOMAN), Gail Simone
(BATGIRL) and many more! Also collected here is the stand
alone tale of Fan-favorite character Travis Kidd–the vampire
hunter who likes to "bite them back" in AMERICAN
VAMPIRE: THE LONG ROAD TO HELL"– Provided
by publisher.
  "Originally published in single magazine form as
AMERICAN VAMPIRE: LONG ROAD HOME 1,
AMERICAN VAMPIRE ANTHOLOGY 1."
    ISBN 978-1-4012-4708-9 (hardback)
  1. Vampires–Comic books, strips, etc. 2. Graphic
novels. I. Albuquerque, Rafael, 1981- illustrator.
II. Title.
  PN6727.S555A48 2014
  741.5'973—dc23

2013049635

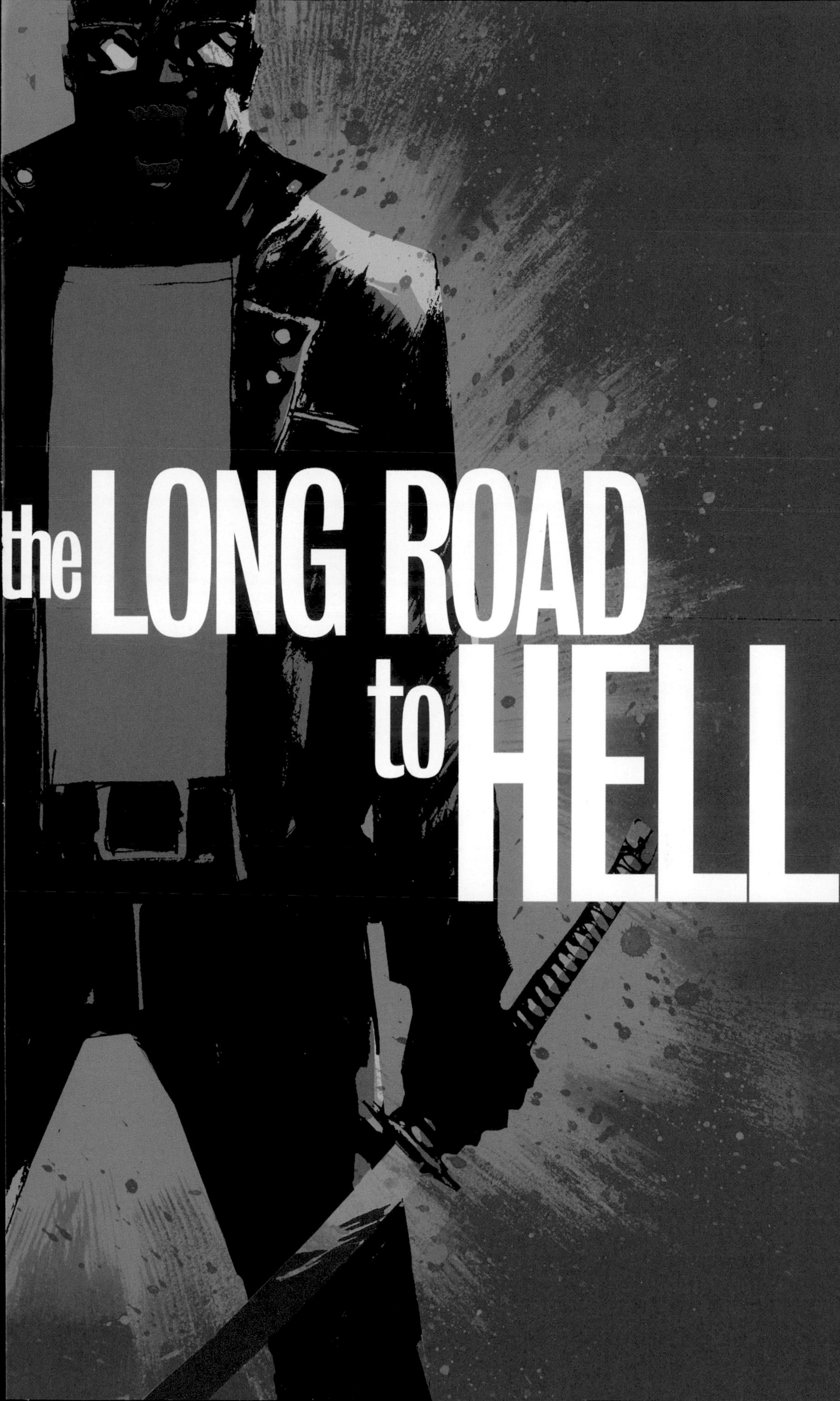
the LONG ROAD
to HELL

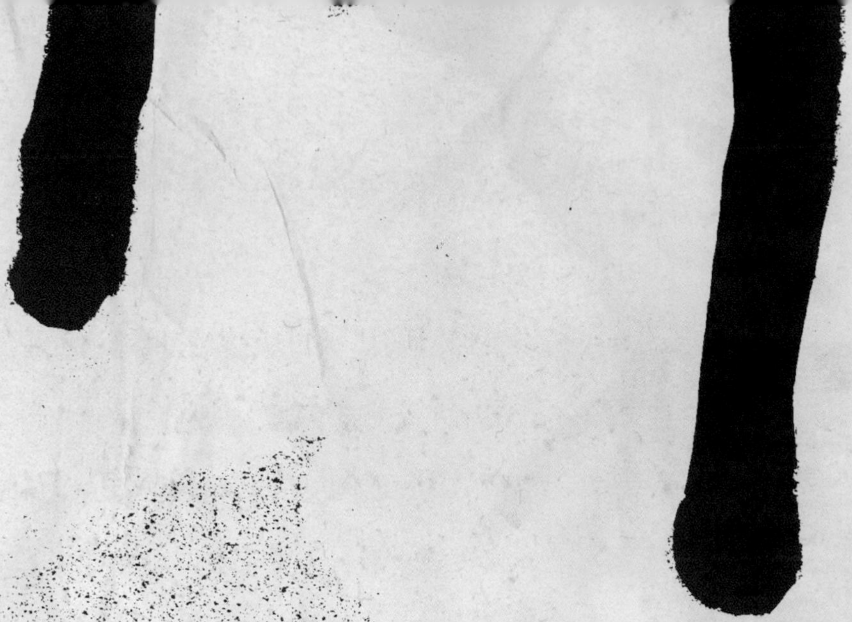

THE LONG
ROAD TO HELL

Story by
Scott Snyder &
Rafael Albuquerque

Script and Art by
Rafael Albuquerque

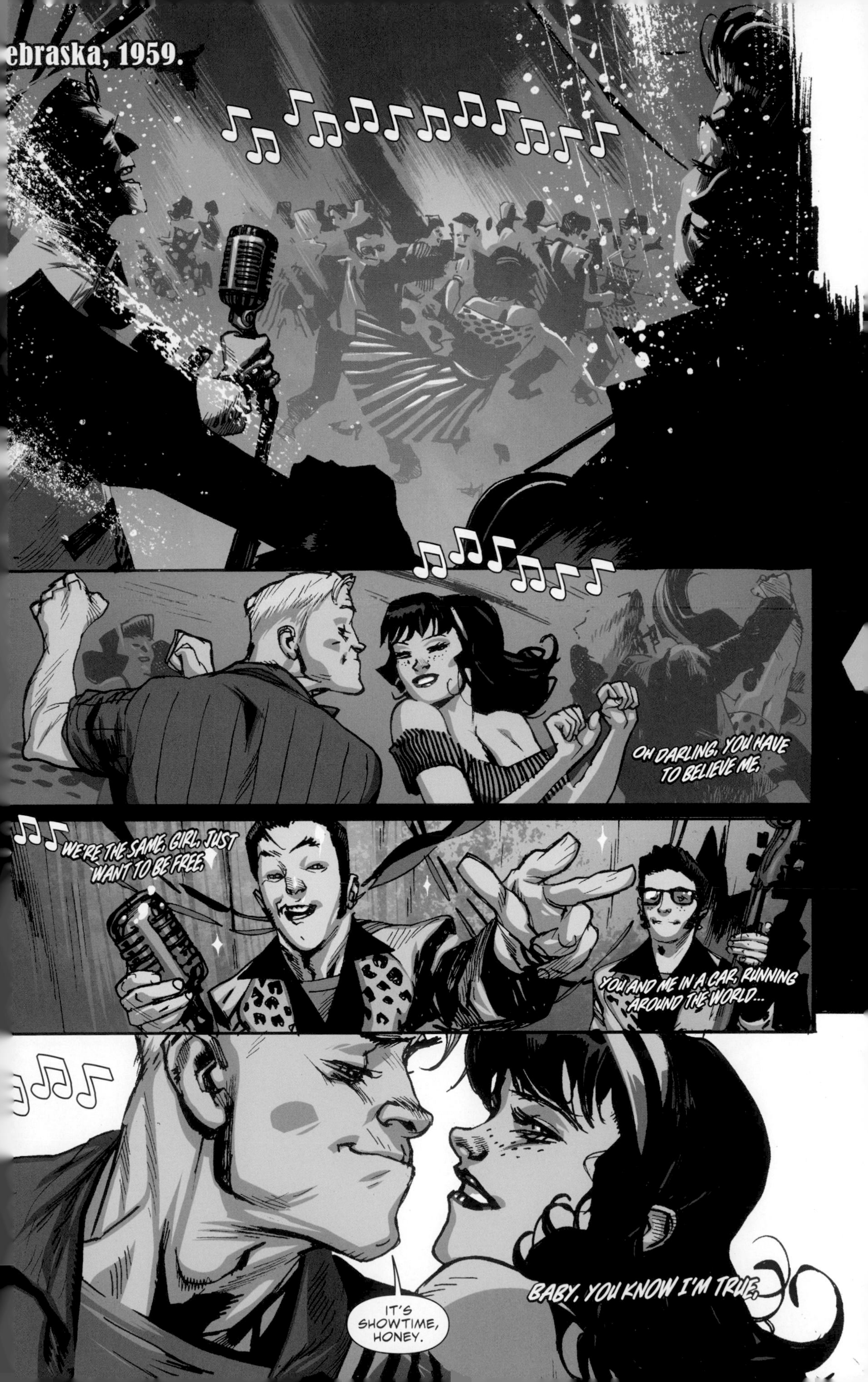
ebraska, 1959.
OH DARLING, YOU HAVE TO BELIEVE ME,
WE'RE THE SAME, GIRL, JUST WANT TO BE FREE,
YOU AND ME IN A CAR, RUNNING AROUND THE WORLD...
IT'S SHOWTIME, HONEY.
BABY, YOU KNOW I'M TRUE,

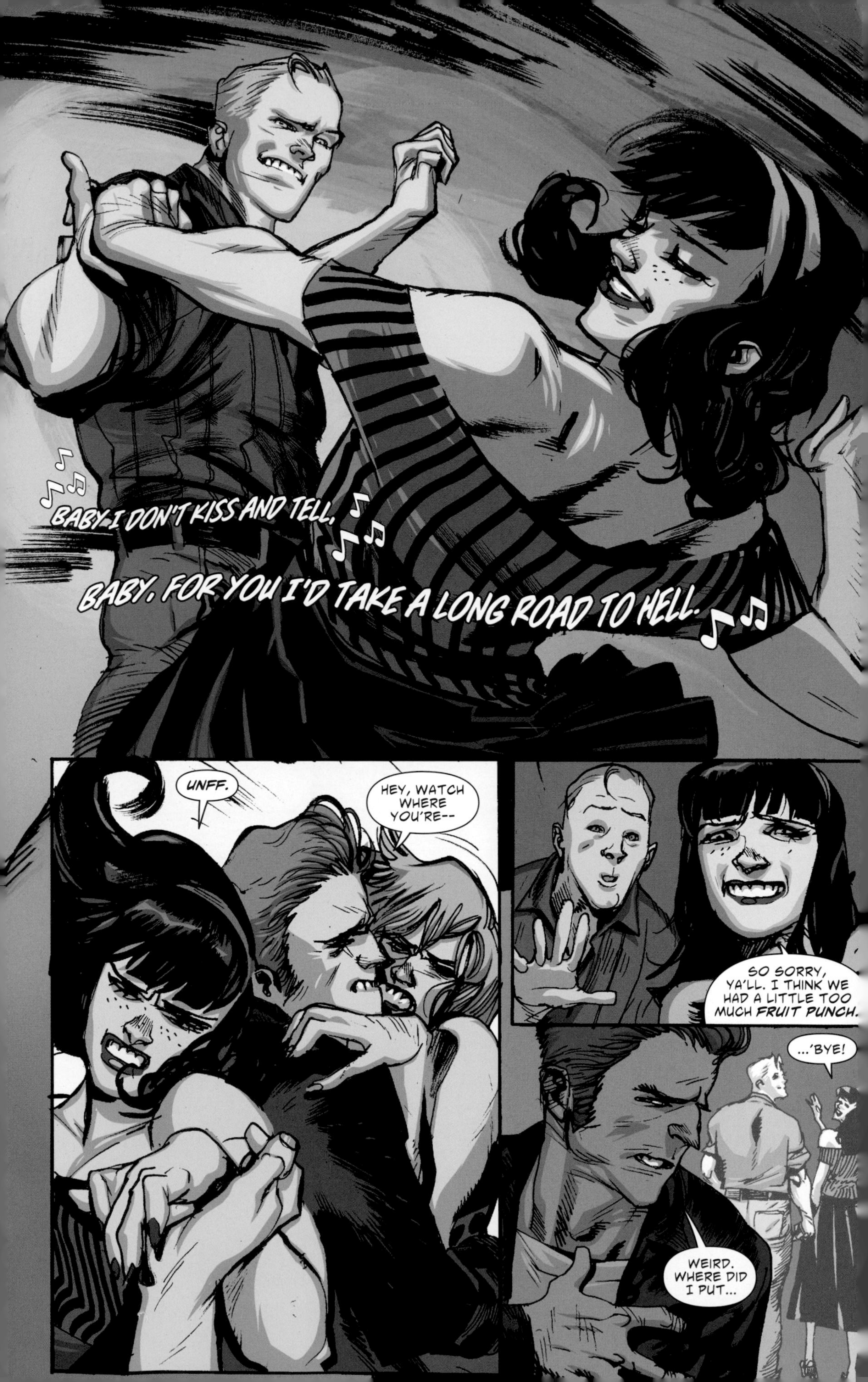
BABY I DON'T KISS AND TELL,
BABY, FOR YOU I'D TAKE A LONG ROAD TO HELL.
UNFF.
HEY, WATCH WHERE YOU'RE--
SO SORRY, YA'LL. I THINK WE HAD A LITTLE TOO MUCH FRUIT PUNCH.
...'BYE!
WEIRD. WHERE DID I PUT...

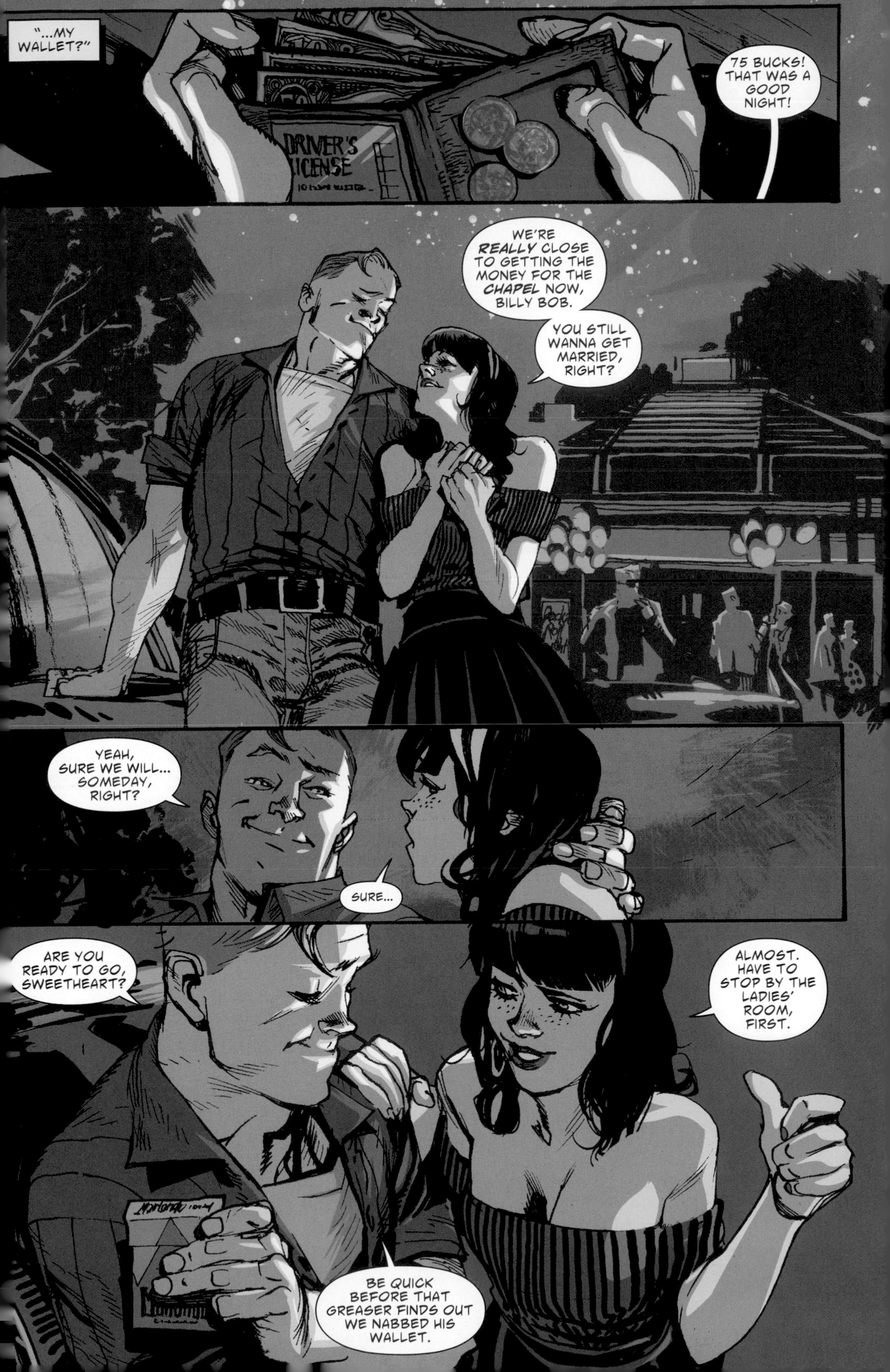
"...MY WALLET?"
DRIVER'S LICENSE
75 BUCKS! THAT WAS A GOOD NIGHT!
WE'RE REALLY CLOSE TO GETTING THE MONEY FOR THE CHAPEL NOW, BILLY BOB.
YOU STILL WANNA GET MARRIED, RIGHT?
YEAH, SURE WE WILL... SOMEDAY, RIGHT?
SURE...
ARE YOU READY TO GO, SWEETHEART?
ALMOST. HAVE TO STOP BY THE LADIES' ROOM, FIRST.
BE QUICK BEFORE THAT GREASER FINDS OUT WE NABBED HIS WALLET.

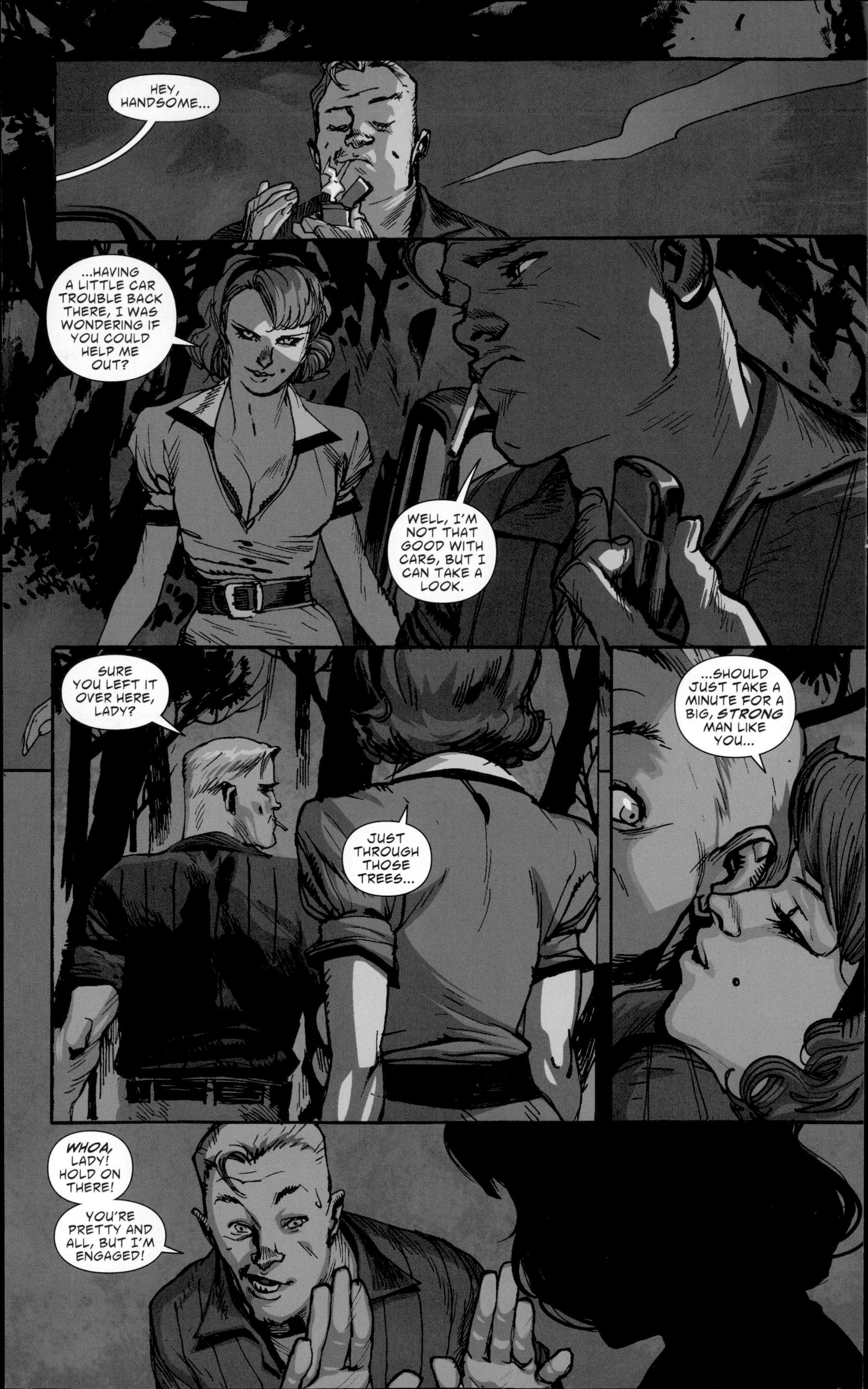
HEY, HANDSOME...
...HAVING A LITTLE CAR TROUBLE BACK THERE, I WAS WONDERING IF YOU COULD HELP ME OUT?
WELL, I'M NOT THAT GOOD WITH CARS, BUT I CAN TAKE A LOOK.
SURE YOU LEFT IT OVER HERE, LADY?
JUST THROUGH THOSE TREES...
...SHOULD JUST TAKE A MINUTE FOR A BIG, STRONG MAN LIKE YOU...
WHOA, LADY! HOLD ON THERE!
YOU'RE PRETTY AND ALL, BUT I'M ENGAGED!

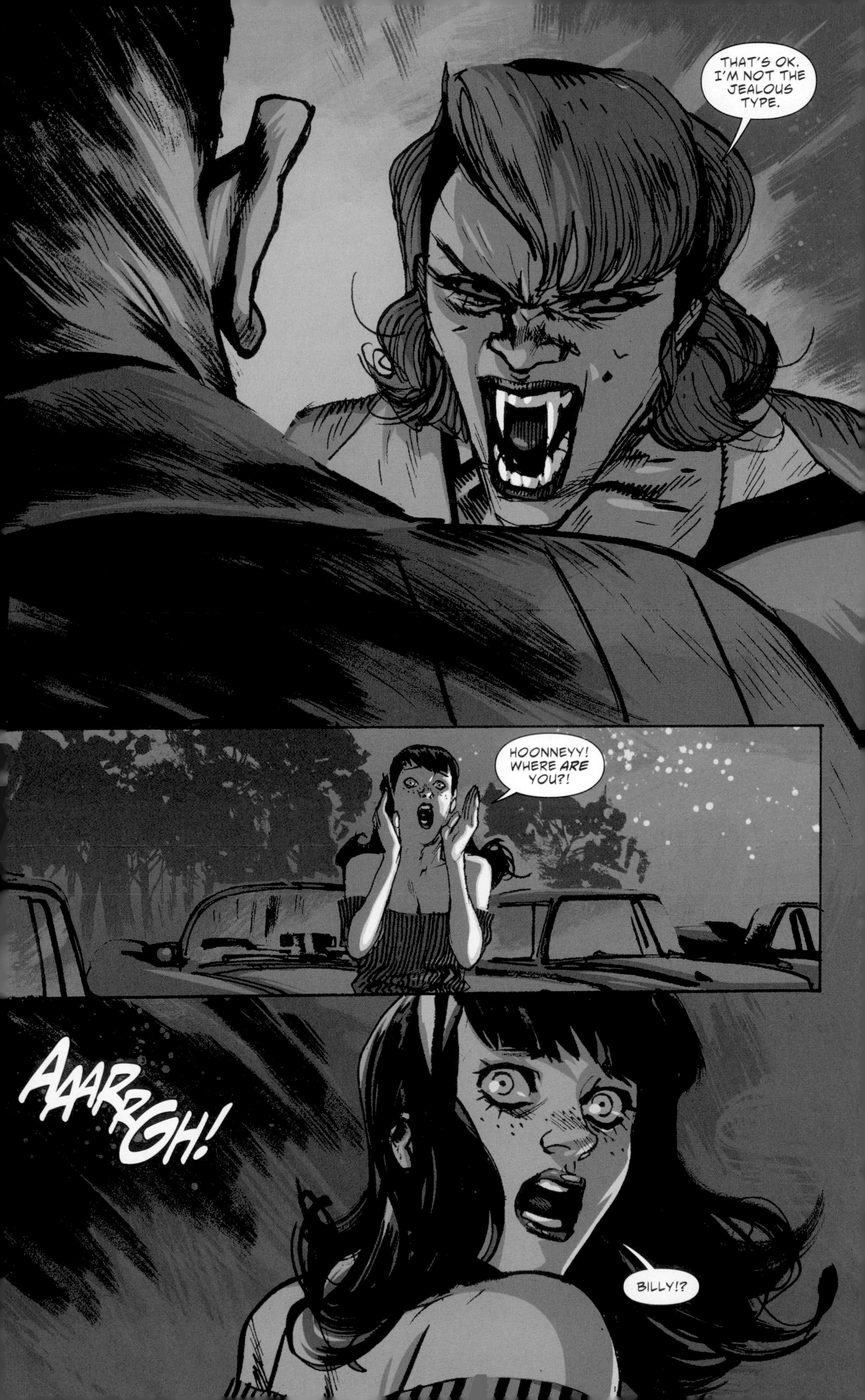
THAT'S OK. I'M NOT THE JEALOUS TYPE.
HOONNEYY! WHERE ARE YOU?!
AAARRGH!
BILLY!?

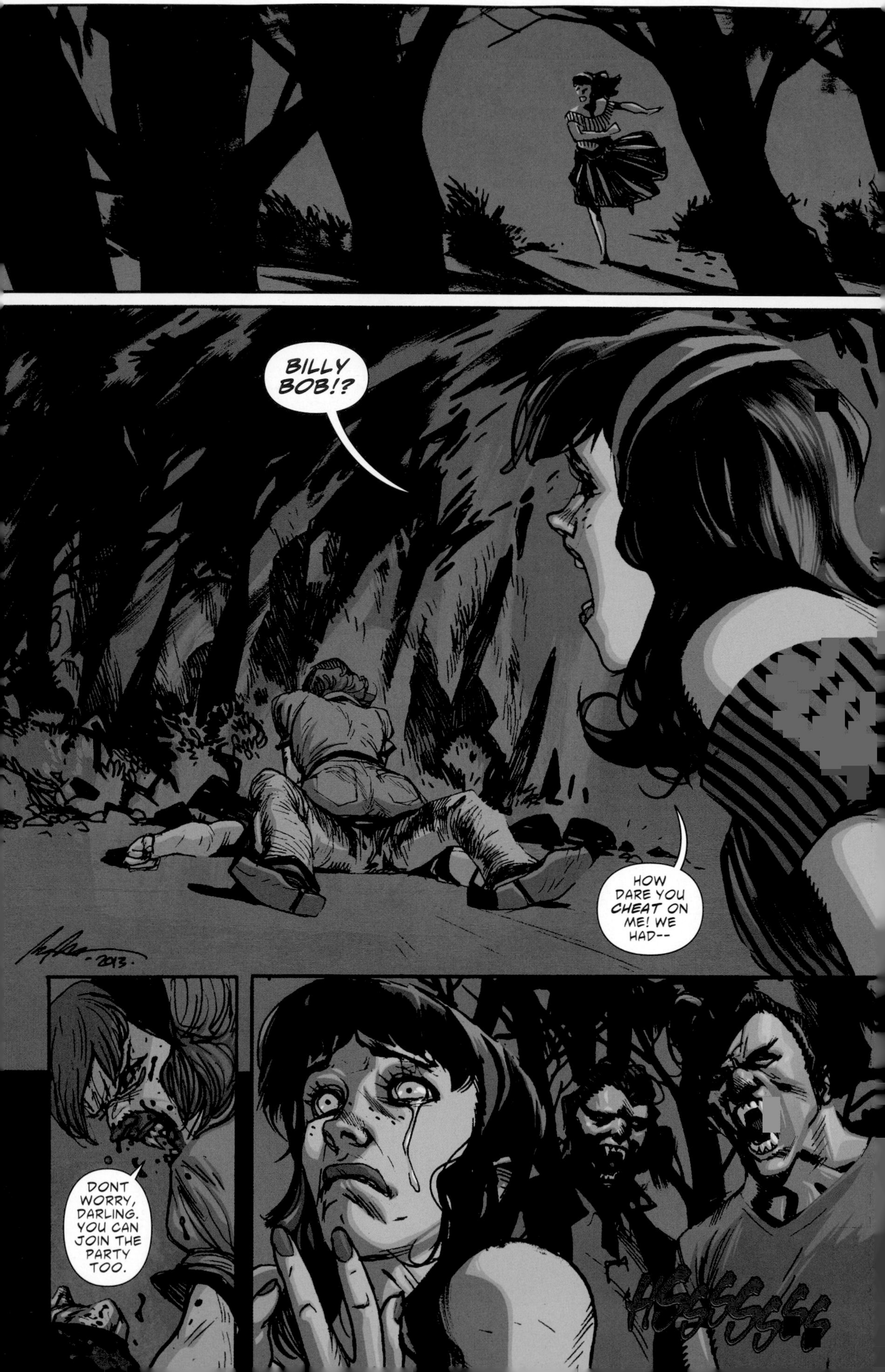
BILLY BOB!?
HOW DARE YOU CHEAT ON ME! WE HAD--
DONT WORRY, DARLING. YOU CAN JOIN THE PARTY TOO.

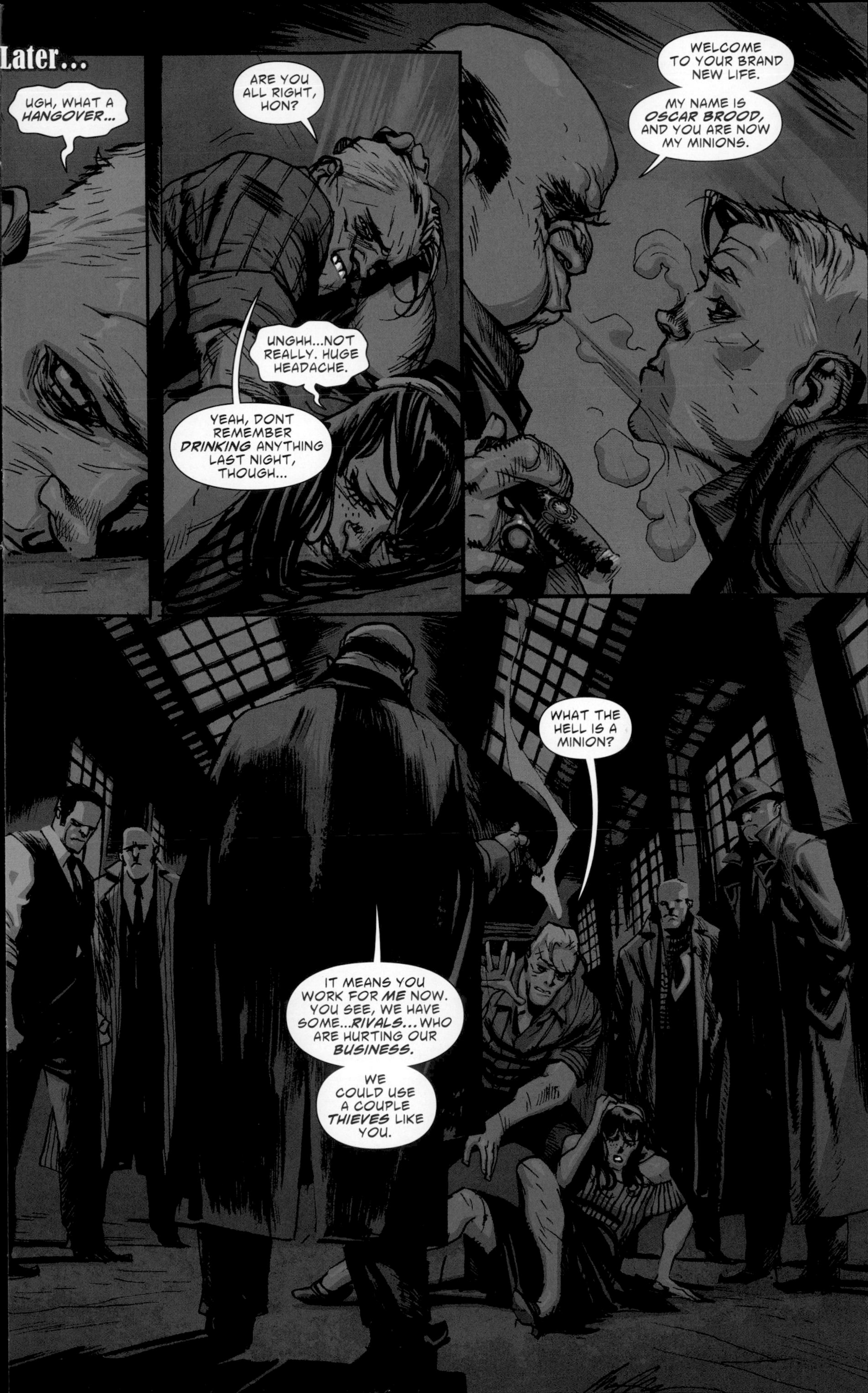
Later...
UGH, WHAT A HANGOVER...
ARE YOU ALL RIGHT, HON?
UNGHH...NOT REALLY. HUGE HEADACHE.
YEAH, DONT REMEMBER DRINKING ANYTHING LAST NIGHT, THOUGH...
WELCOME TO YOUR BRAND NEW LIFE.
MY NAME IS OSCAR BROOD, AND YOU ARE NOW MY MINIONS.
WHAT THE HELL IS A MINION?
IT MEANS YOU WORK FOR ME NOW. YOU SEE, WE HAVE SOME...RIVALS...WHO ARE HURTING OUR BUSINESS.
WE COULD USE A COUPLE THIEVES LIKE YOU.

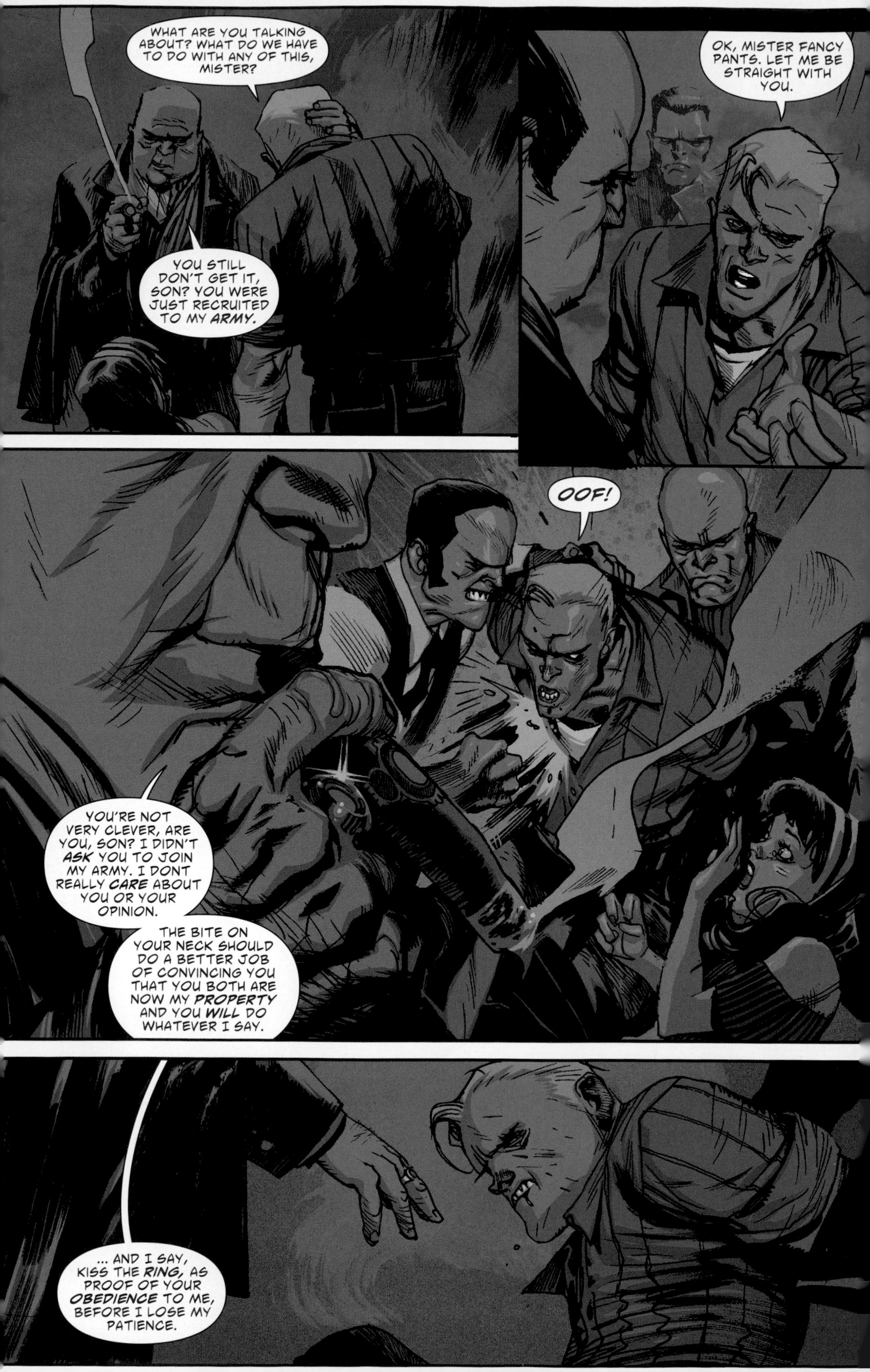
WHAT ARE YOU TALKING ABOUT? WHAT DO WE HAVE TO DO WITH ANY OF THIS, MISTER?
YOU STILL DON'T GET IT, SON? YOU WERE JUST RECRUITED TO MY ARMY.
OK, MISTER FANCY PANTS. LET ME BE STRAIGHT WITH YOU.
OOF!
YOU'RE NOT VERY CLEVER, ARE YOU, SON? I DIDN'T ASK YOU TO JOIN MY ARMY. I DONT REALLY CARE ABOUT YOU OR YOUR OPINION.
THE BITE ON YOUR NECK SHOULD DO A BETTER JOB OF CONVINCING YOU THAT YOU BOTH ARE NOW MY PROPERTY AND YOU WILL DO WHATEVER I SAY.
... AND I SAY, KISS THE RING, AS PROOF OF YOUR OBEDIENCE TO ME, BEFORE I LOSE MY PATIENCE.

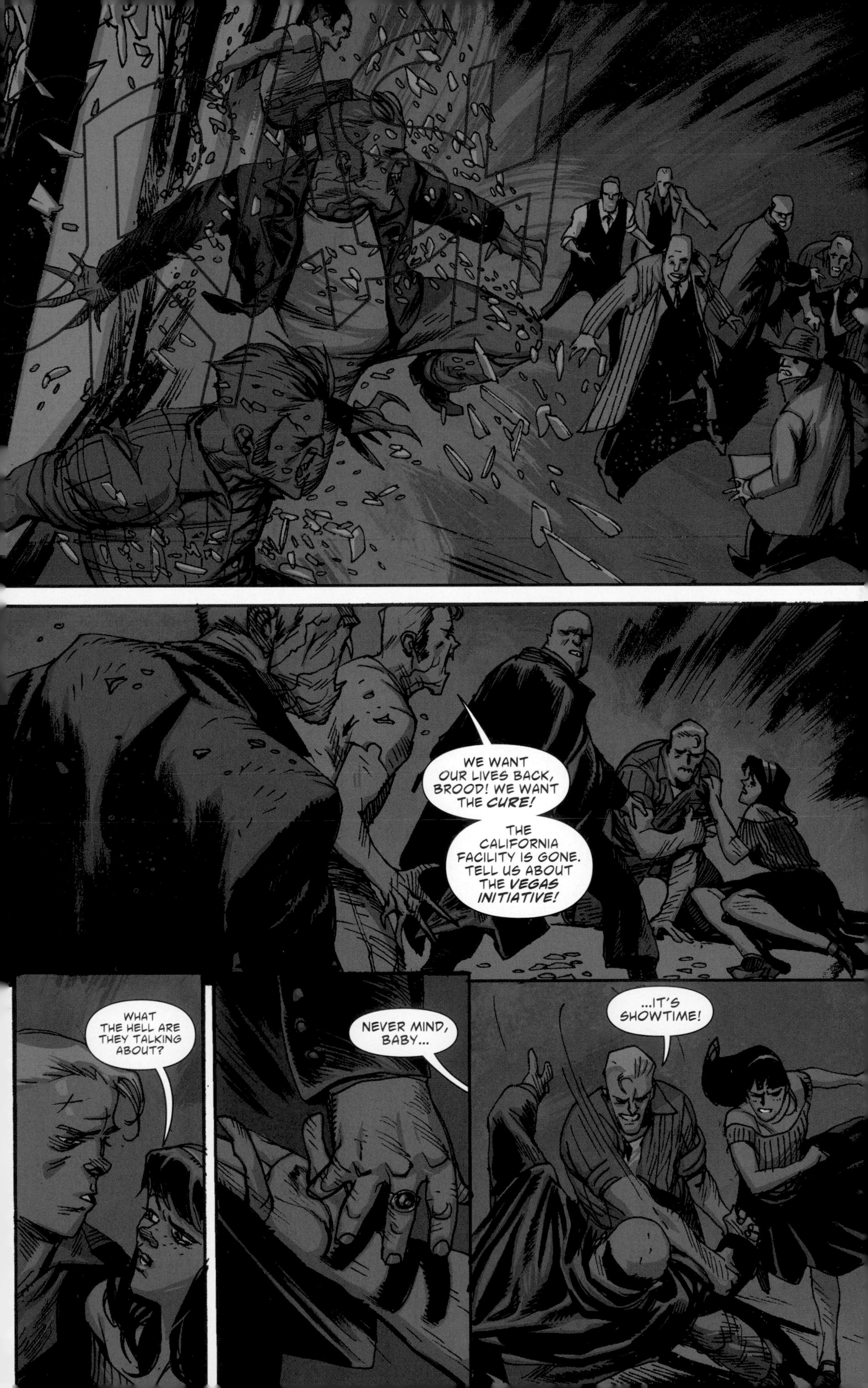
WE WANT OUR LIVES BACK, BROOD! WE WANT THE *CURE!*
THE CALIFORNIA FACILITY IS GONE. TELL US ABOUT THE *VEGAS INITIATIVE!*
WHAT THE HELL ARE THEY TALKING ABOUT?
NEVER MIND, BABY...
...IT'S SHOWTIME!

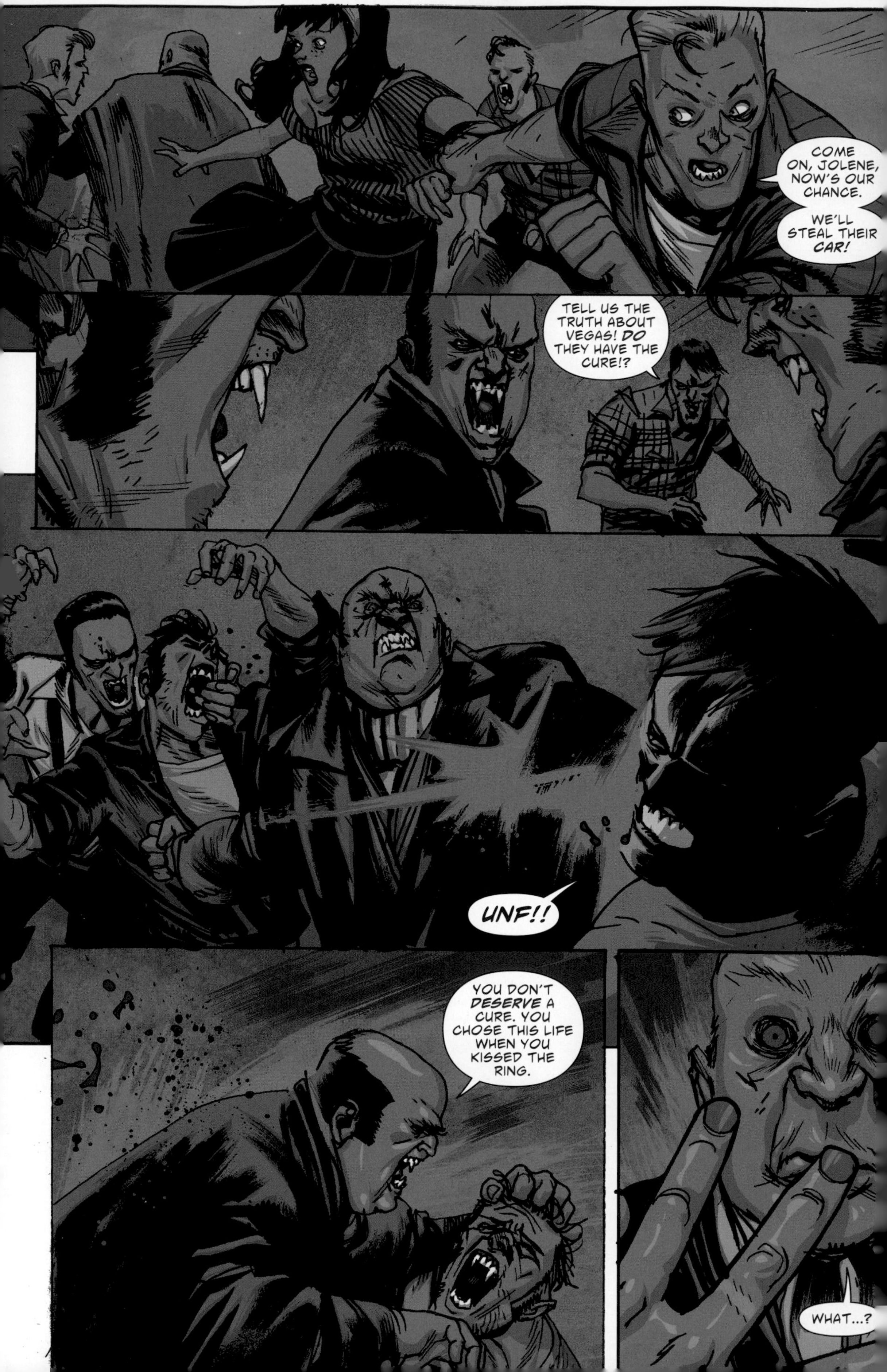
COME ON, JOLENE, NOW'S OUR CHANCE.
WE'LL STEAL THEIR CAR!
TELL US THE TRUTH ABOUT VEGAS! DO THEY HAVE THE CURE!?
UNF!!
YOU DON'T DESERVE A CURE. YOU CHOSE THIS LIFE WHEN YOU KISSED THE RING.
WHAT...?

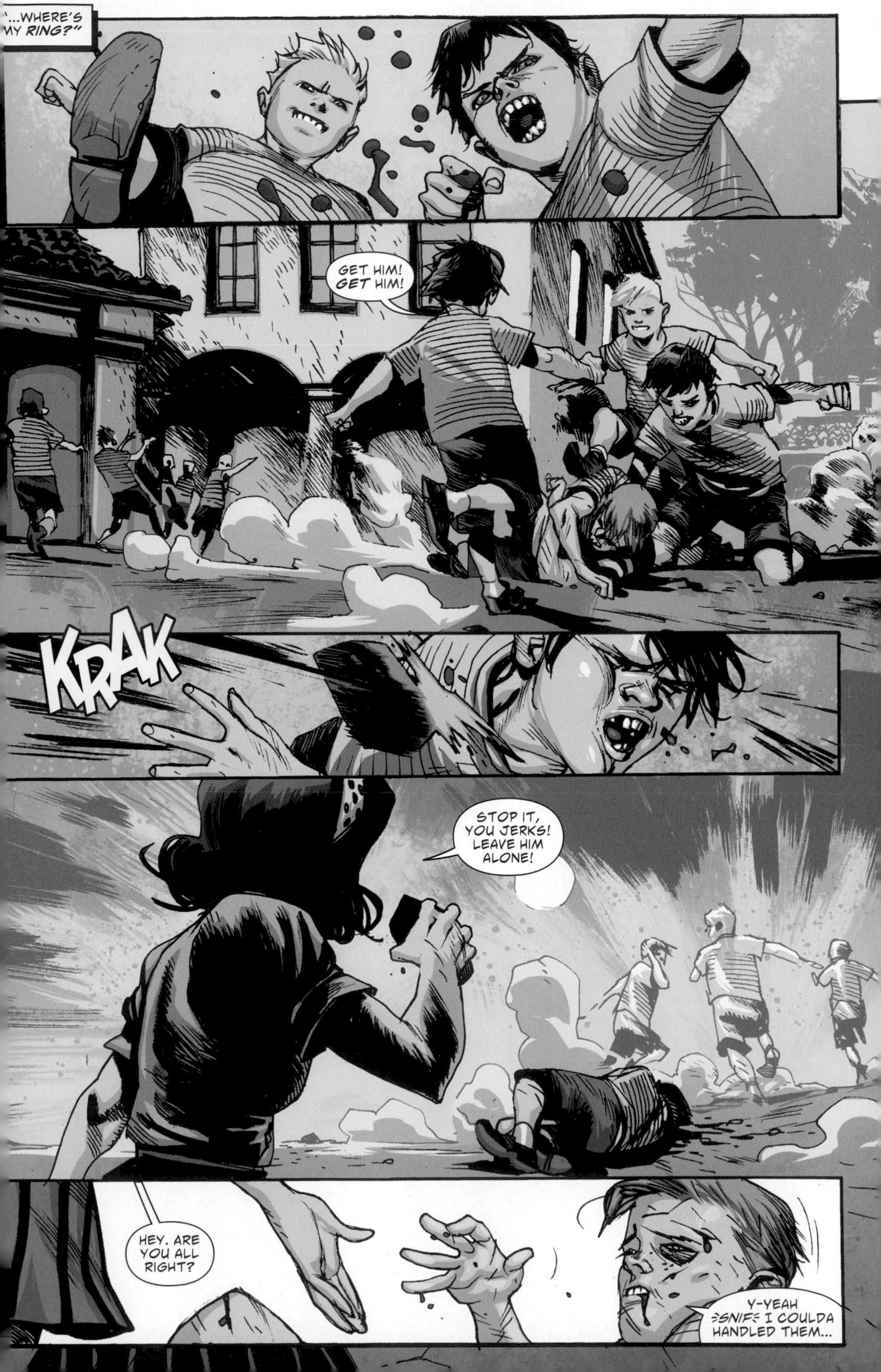
"...WHERE'S MY *RING?*"
GET HIM! *GET* HIM!
KRAK
STOP IT, YOU JERKS! LEAVE HIM ALONE!
HEY. ARE YOU ALL RIGHT?
Y-YEAH *SNIF* I COULDA HANDLED THEM...

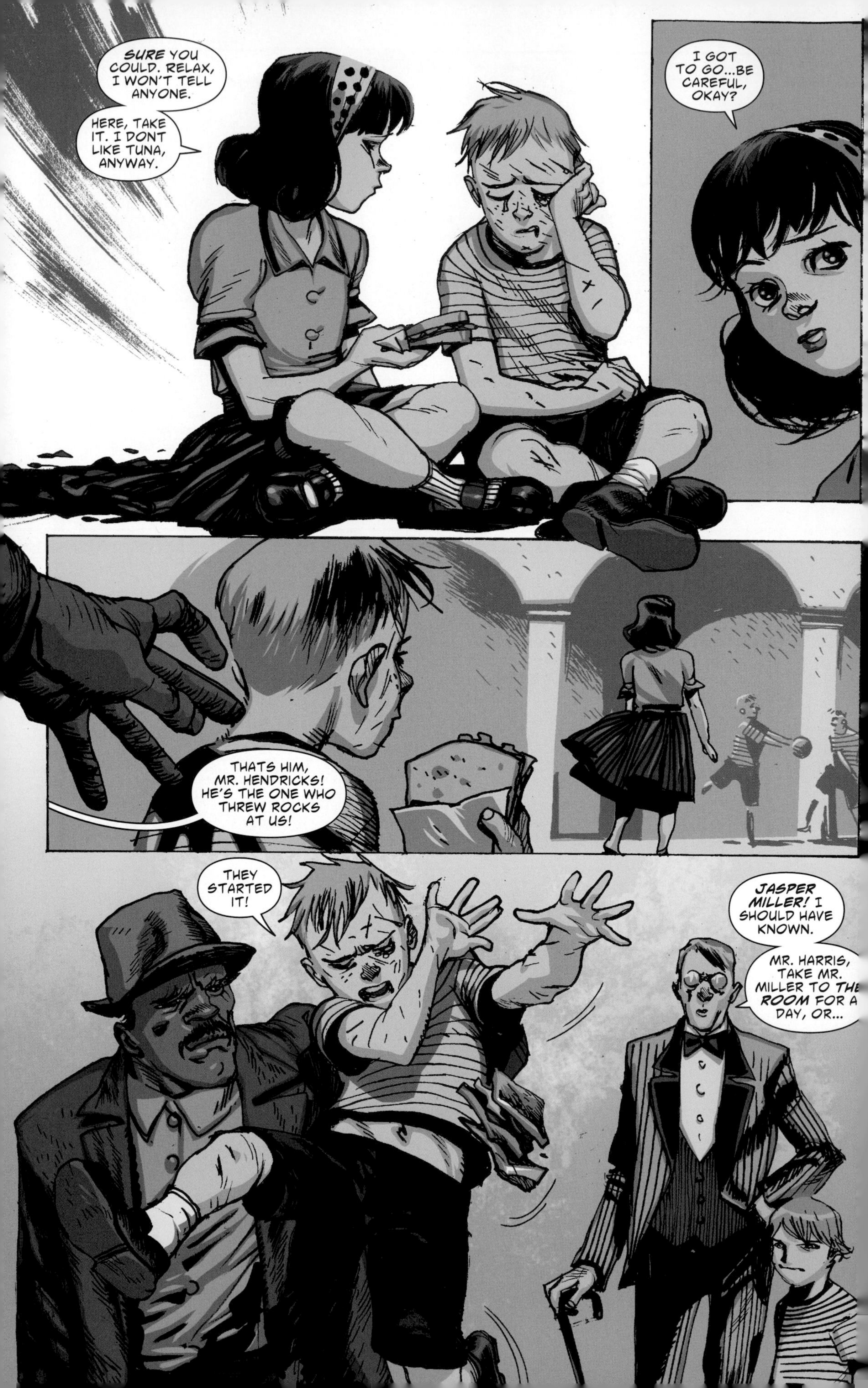
SURE YOU COULD. RELAX, I WON'T TELL ANYONE.
HERE, TAKE IT. I DONT LIKE TUNA, ANYWAY.
I GOT TO GO...BE CAREFUL, OKAY?
THATS HIM, MR. HENDRICKS! HE'S THE ONE WHO THREW ROCKS AT US!
THEY STARTED IT!
JASPER MILLER! I SHOULD HAVE KNOWN.
MR. HARRIS, TAKE MR. MILLER TO THE ROOM FOR A DAY, OR...

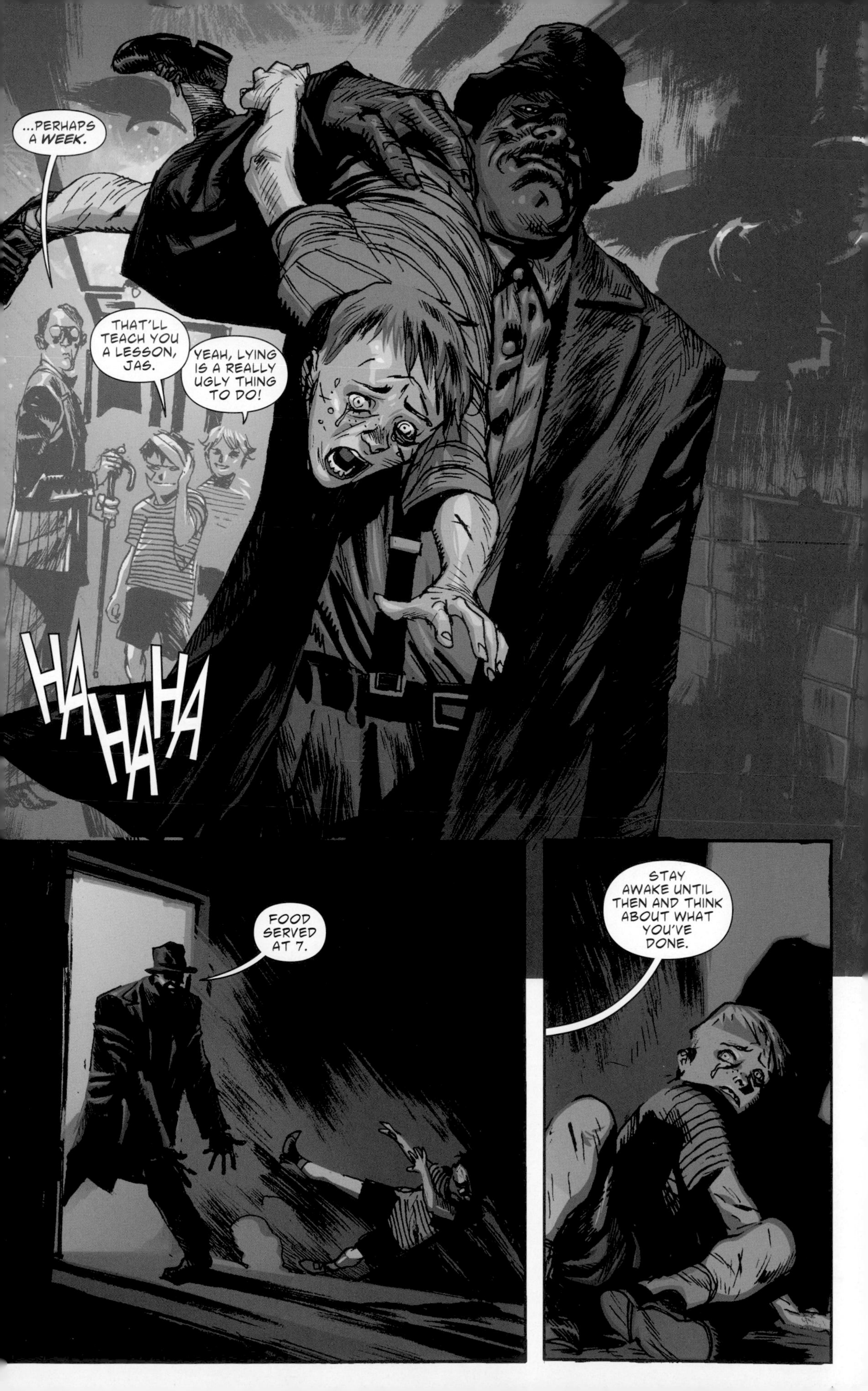
...PERHAPS A WEEK.
THAT'LL TEACH YOU A LESSON, JAS.
YEAH, LYING IS A REALLY UGLY THING TO DO!
HAHAHAHA
FOOD SERVED AT 7.
STAY AWAKE UNTIL THEN AND THINK ABOUT WHAT YOU'VE DONE.

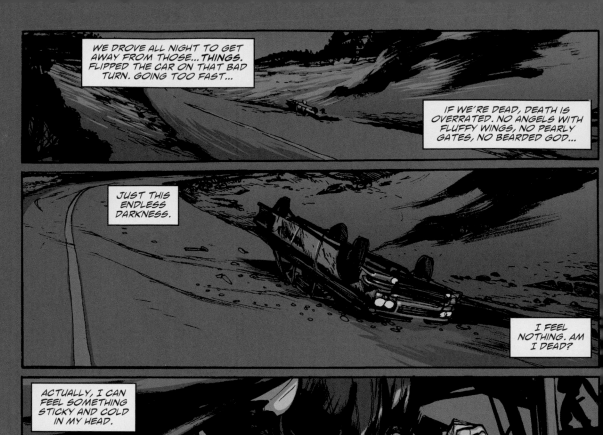

WE DROVE ALL NIGHT TO GET AWAY FROM THOSE...THINGS. FLIPPED THE CAR ON THAT BAD TURN. GOING TOO FAST...

IF WE'RE DEAD, DEATH IS OVERRATED. NO ANGELS WITH FLUFFY WINGS, NO PEARLY GATES, NO BEARDED GOD...

JUST THIS ENDLESS DARKNESS.

I FEEL NOTHING. AM I DEAD?

ACTUALLY, I CAN FEEL SOMETHING STICKY AND COLD IN MY HEAD.

UGH... I CAN FEEL MY GUTS TOO.

I FEEL LIKE I'M COMPLETELY DRY INSIDE, LIKE THERE'S A BIG DESERT IN BETWEEN MY STOMACH AND MY INTESTINES.

AND I'M VERY, VERY THIRSTY.

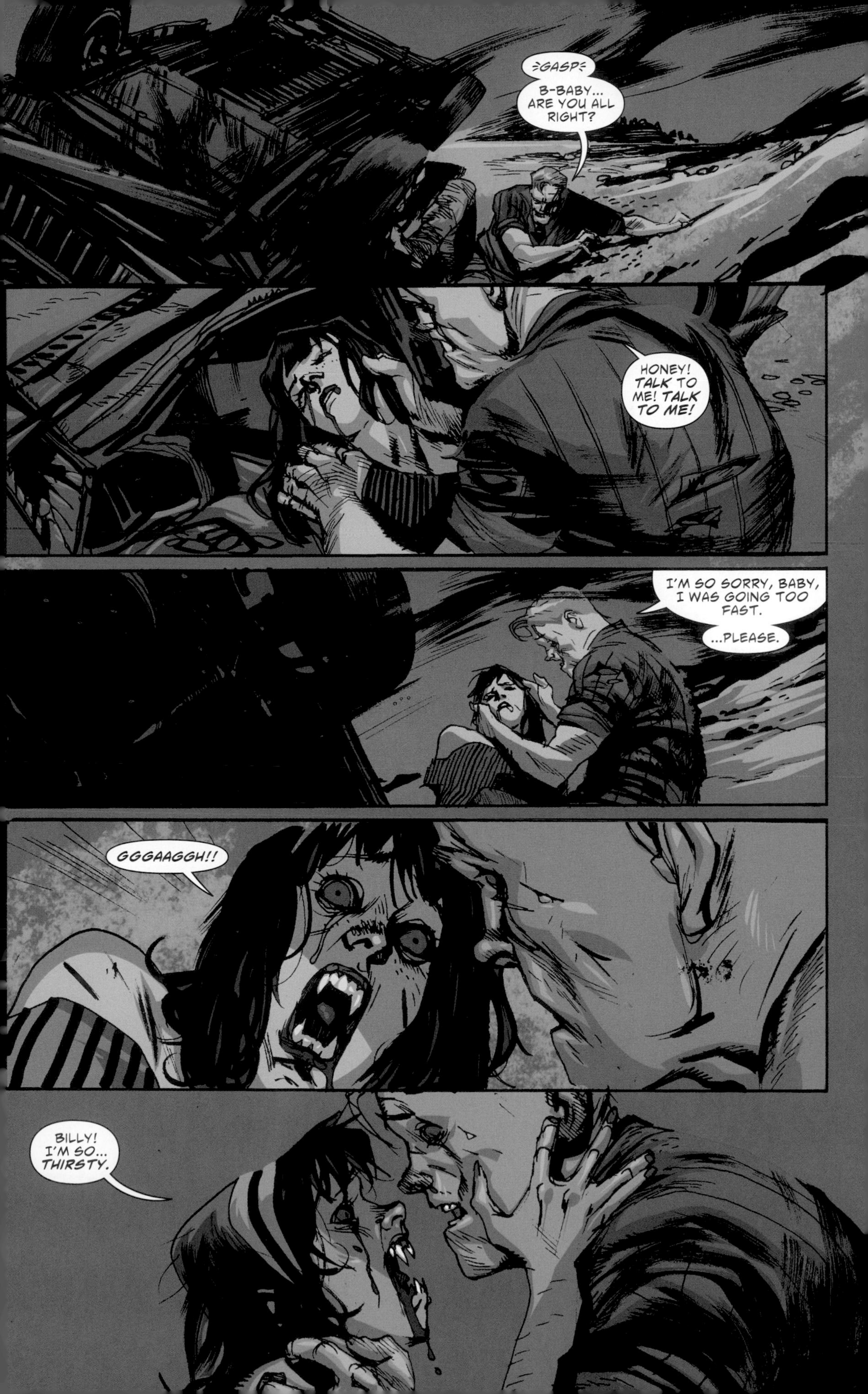
GASP
B-BABY... ARE YOU ALL RIGHT?
HONEY! *TALK* TO ME! *TALK TO ME!*
I'M SO SORRY, BABY, I WAS GOING TOO FAST.
...PLEASE.
GGGAAGGH!!
BILLY! I'M SO... *THIRSTY.*

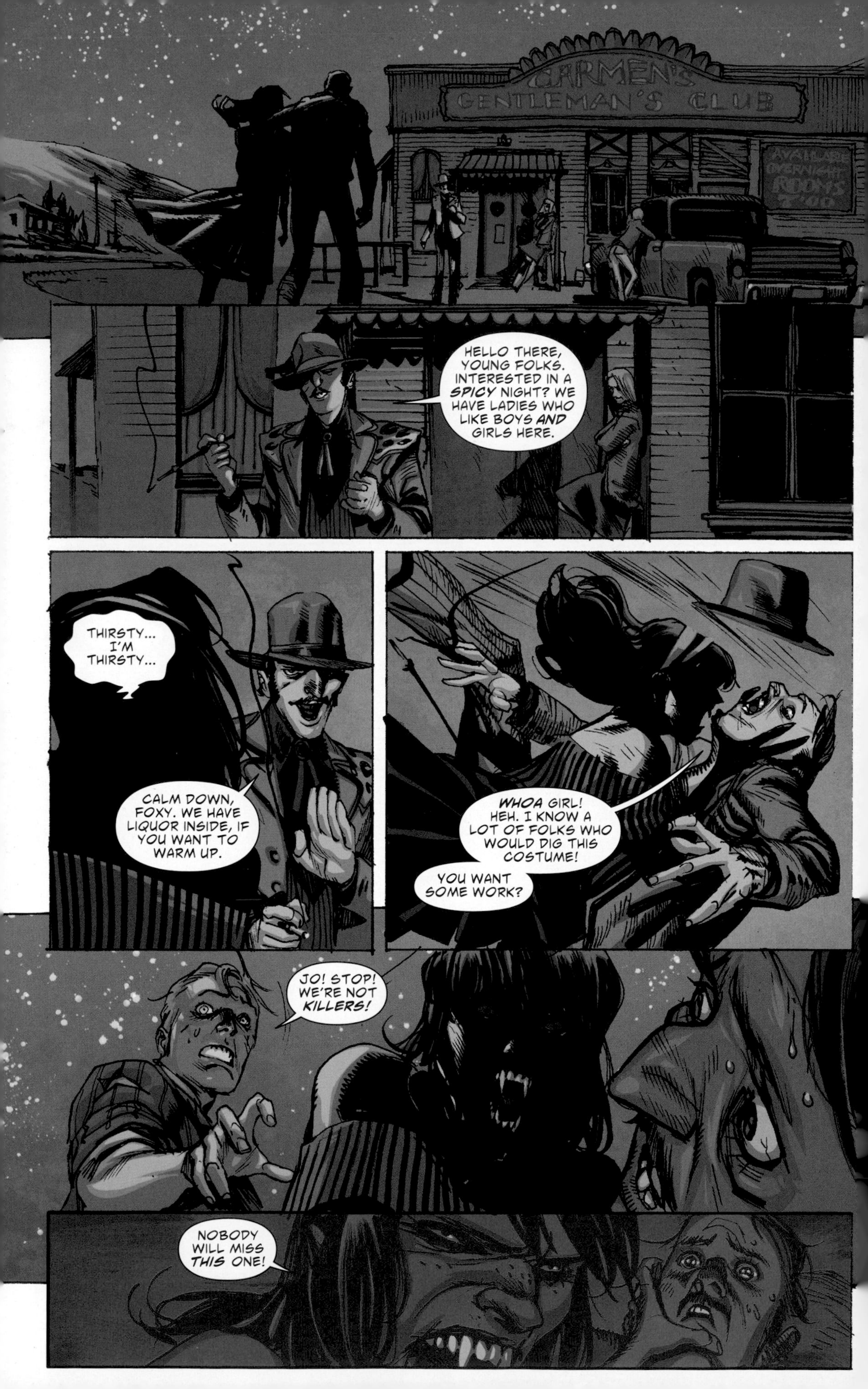
CARMEN'S GENTLEMAN'S CLUB
HELLO THERE, YOUNG FOLKS. INTERESTED IN A SPICY NIGHT? WE HAVE LADIES WHO LIKE BOYS AND GIRLS HERE.
THIRSTY... I'M THIRSTY...
CALM DOWN, FOXY. WE HAVE LIQUOR INSIDE, IF YOU WANT TO WARM UP.
WHOA GIRL! HEH. I KNOW A LOT OF FOLKS WHO WOULD DIG THIS COSTUME!
YOU WANT SOME WORK?
JO! STOP! WE'RE NOT KILLERS!
NOBODY WILL MISS THIS ONE!

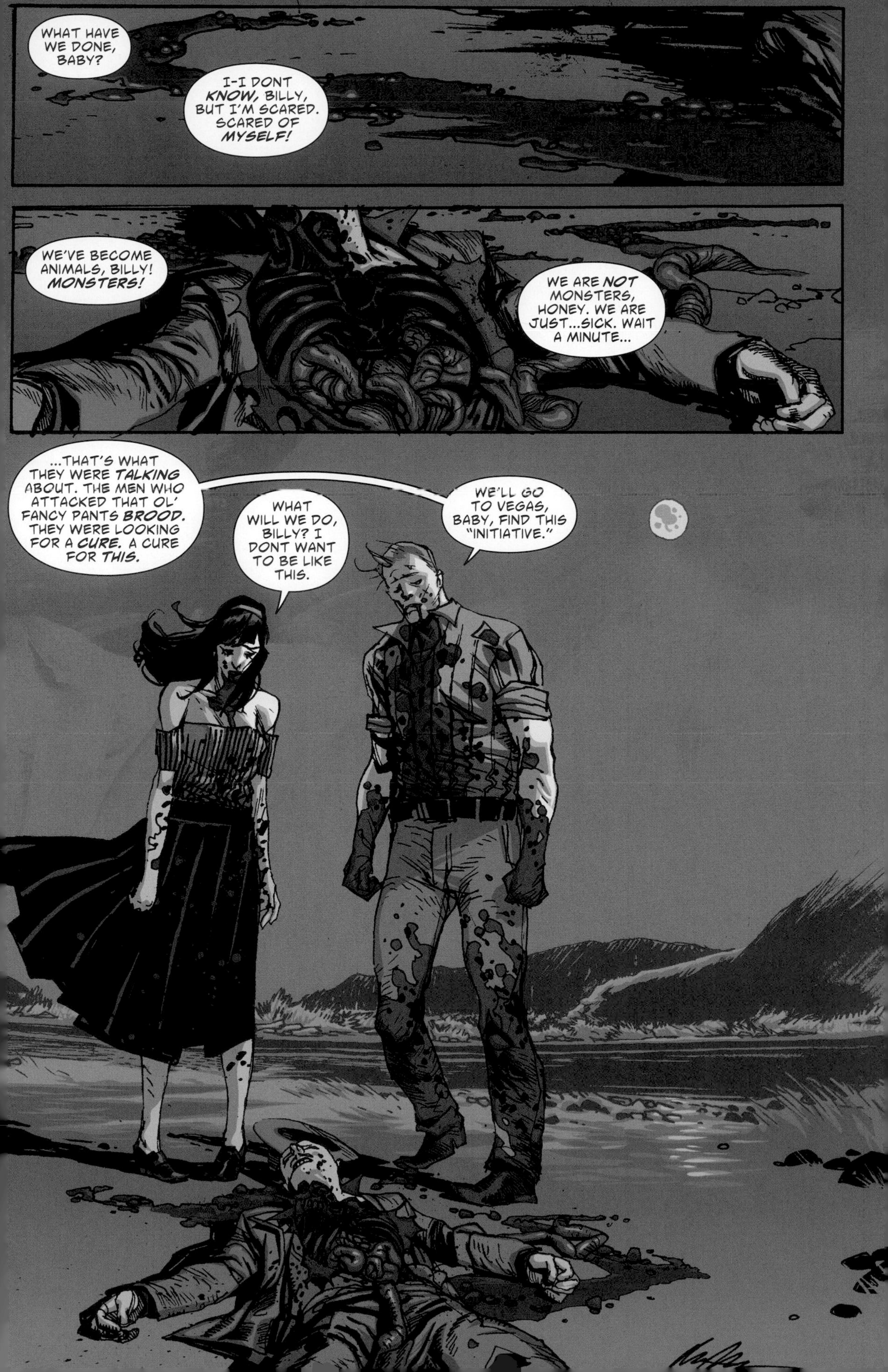
WHAT HAVE WE DONE, BABY?
I-I DONT *KNOW,* BILLY, BUT I'M SCARED. SCARED OF *MYSELF!*
WE'VE BECOME ANIMALS, BILLY! *MONSTERS!*
WE ARE *NOT* MONSTERS, HONEY. WE ARE JUST...SICK. WAIT A MINUTE...
...THAT'S WHAT THEY WERE *TALKING* ABOUT. THE MEN WHO ATTACKED THAT OL' FANCY PANTS *BROOD.* THEY WERE LOOKING FOR A *CURE.* A CURE FOR *THIS.*
WHAT WILL WE DO, BILLY? I DONT WANT TO BE LIKE THIS.
WE'LL GO TO VEGAS, BABY, FIND THIS "INITIATIVE."

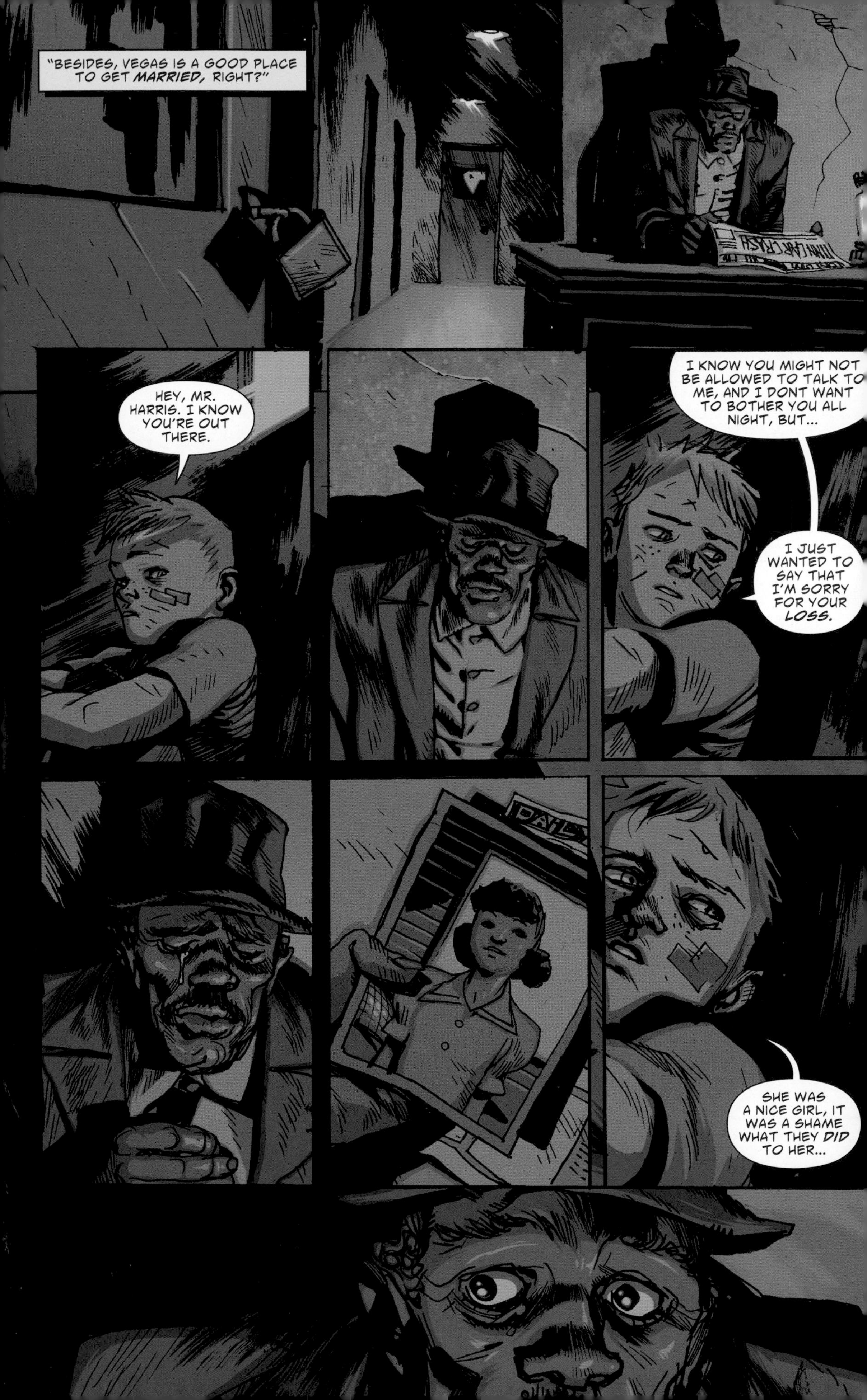
"BESIDES, VEGAS IS A GOOD PLACE TO GET *MARRIED,* RIGHT?"
HEY, MR. HARRIS. I KNOW YOU'RE OUT THERE.
I KNOW YOU MIGHT NOT BE ALLOWED TO TALK TO ME, AND I DONT WANT TO BOTHER YOU ALL NIGHT, BUT...
I JUST WANTED TO SAY THAT I'M SORRY FOR YOUR *LOSS.*
SHE WAS A NICE GIRL, IT WAS A SHAME WHAT THEY *DID* TO HER...

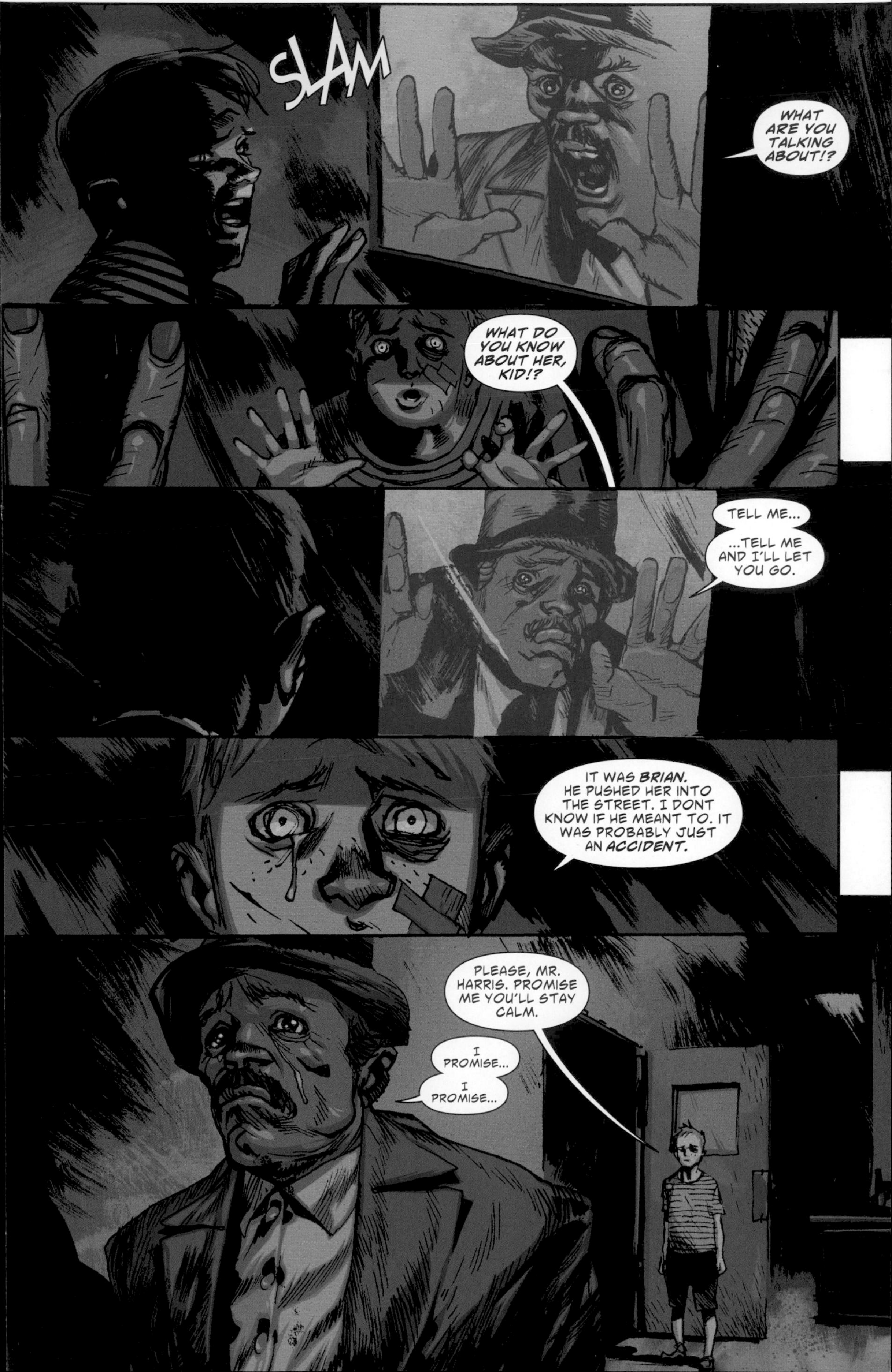
SLAM
WHAT ARE YOU TALKING ABOUT!?
WHAT DO YOU KNOW ABOUT HER, KID!?
TELL ME...
...TELL ME AND I'LL LET YOU GO.
IT WAS BRIAN. HE PUSHED HER INTO THE STREET. I DONT KNOW IF HE MEANT TO. IT WAS PROBABLY JUST AN ACCIDENT.
PLEASE, MR. HARRIS. PROMISE ME YOU'LL STAY CALM.
I PROMISE...
I PROMISE...

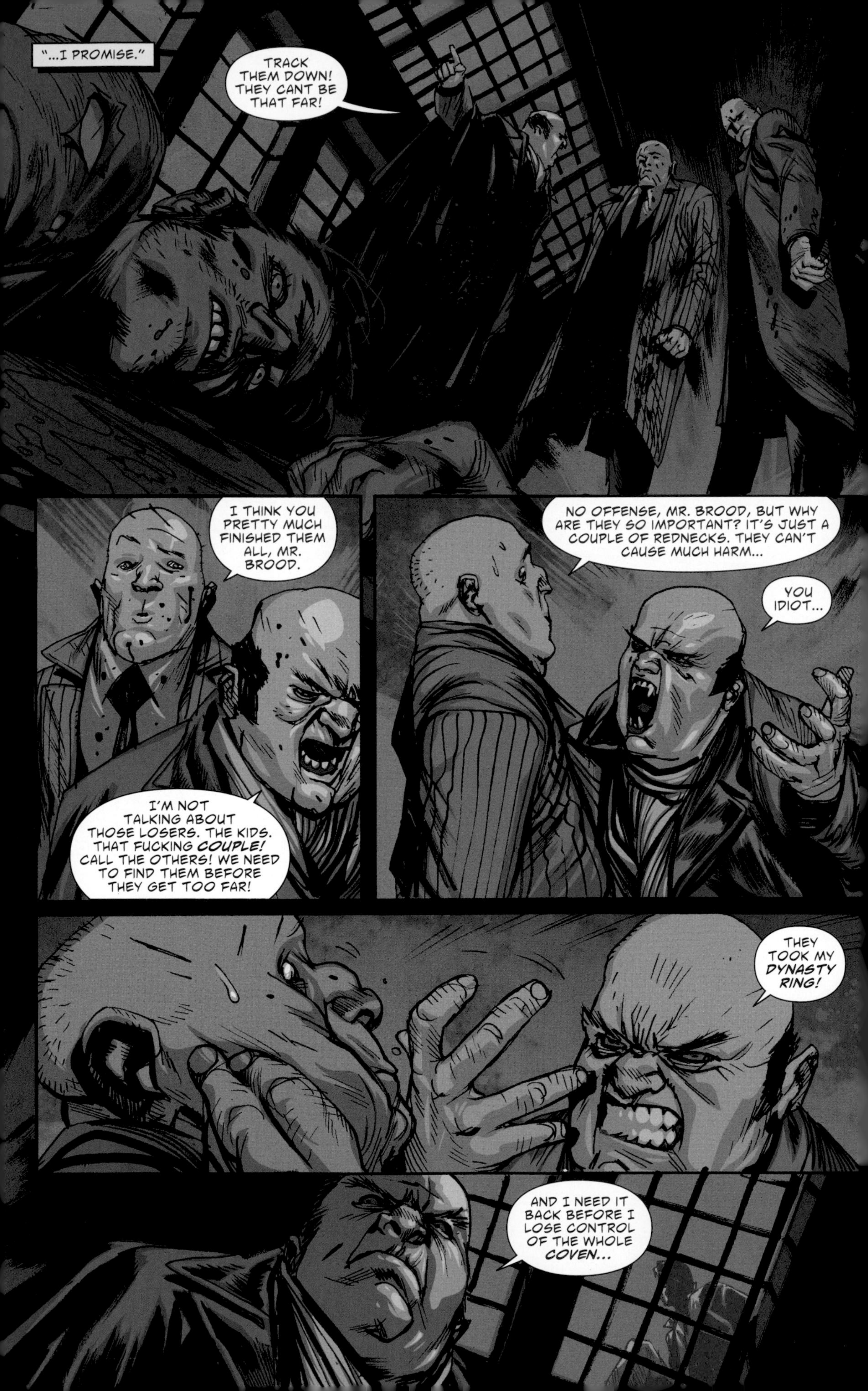
"...I PROMISE."
TRACK THEM DOWN! THEY CANT BE THAT FAR!
I THINK YOU PRETTY MUCH FINISHED THEM ALL, MR. BROOD.
I'M NOT TALKING ABOUT THOSE LOSERS. THE KIDS. THAT FUCKING COUPLE! CALL THE OTHERS! WE NEED TO FIND THEM BEFORE THEY GET TOO FAR!
NO OFFENSE, MR. BROOD, BUT WHY ARE THEY SO IMPORTANT? IT'S JUST A COUPLE OF REDNECKS. THEY CAN'T CAUSE MUCH HARM...
YOU IDIOT...
THEY TOOK MY DYNASTY RING!
AND I NEED IT BACK BEFORE I LOSE CONTROL OF THE WHOLE COVEN...

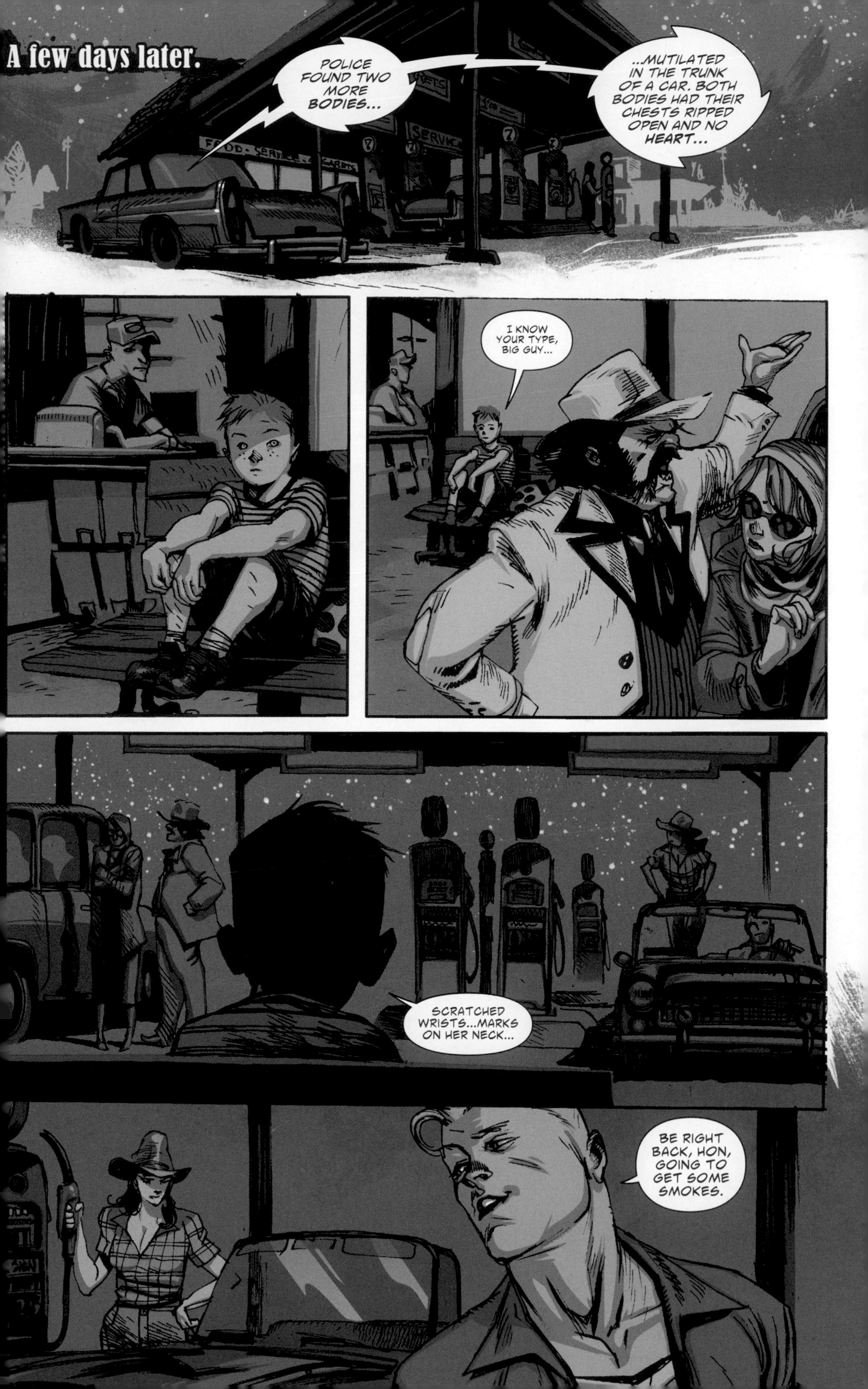
A few days later.
POLICE FOUND TWO MORE BODIES...
...MUTILATED IN THE TRUNK OF A CAR. BOTH BODIES HAD THEIR CHESTS RIPPED OPEN AND NO HEART...
I KNOW YOUR TYPE, BIG GUY...
SCRATCHED WRISTS...MARKS ON HER NECK...
BE RIGHT BACK, HON, GOING TO GET SOME SMOKES.

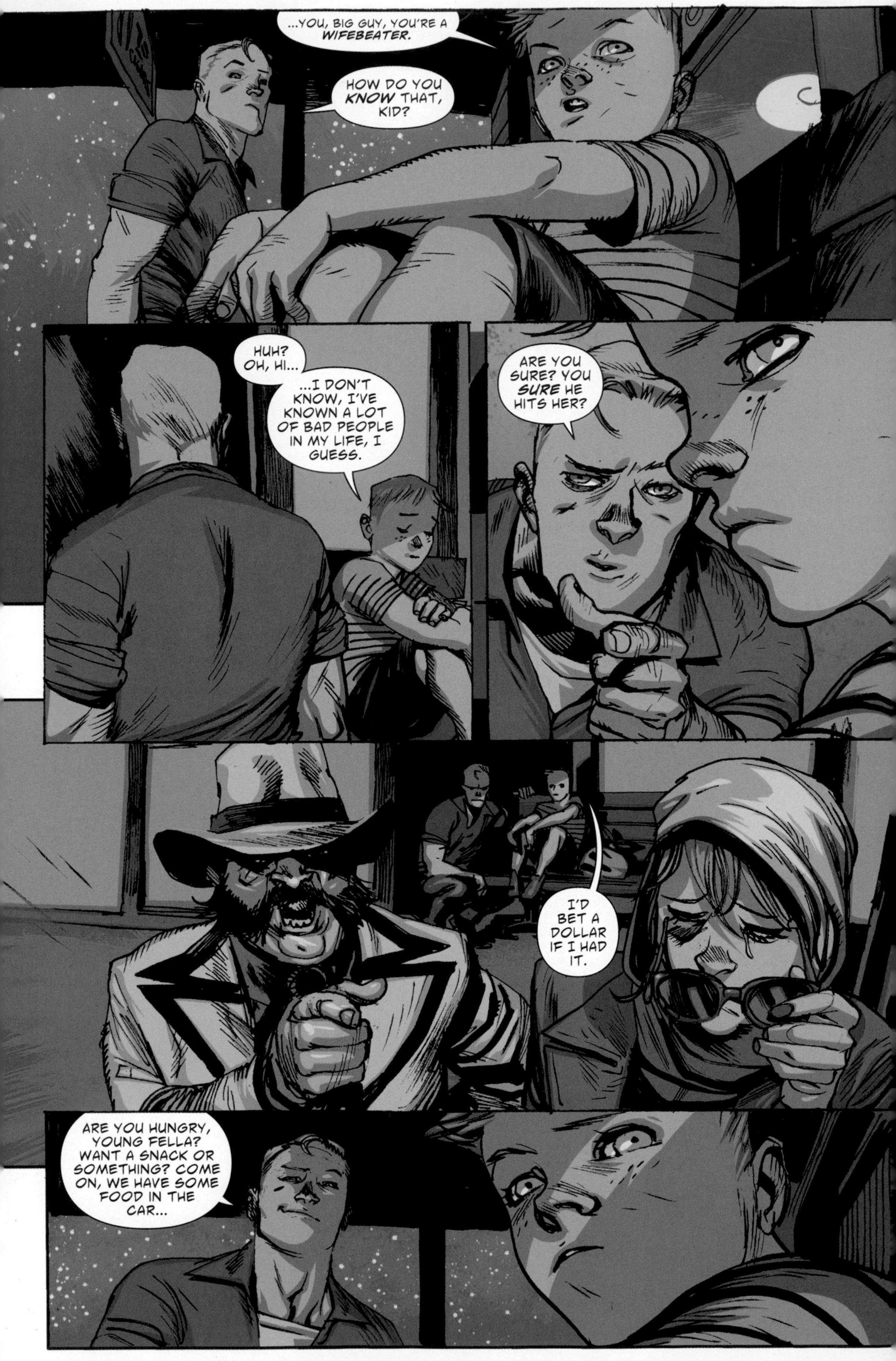
...YOU, BIG GUY, YOU'RE A *WIFEBEATER.*
HOW DO YOU *KNOW* THAT, KID?
HUH? OH, HI...
...I DON'T KNOW, I'VE KNOWN A LOT OF BAD PEOPLE IN MY LIFE, I GUESS.
ARE YOU SURE? YOU *SURE* HE HITS HER?
I'D BET A DOLLAR IF I HAD IT.
ARE YOU HUNGRY, YOUNG FELLA? WANT A SNACK OR SOMETHING? COME ON, WE HAVE SOME FOOD IN THE CAR...

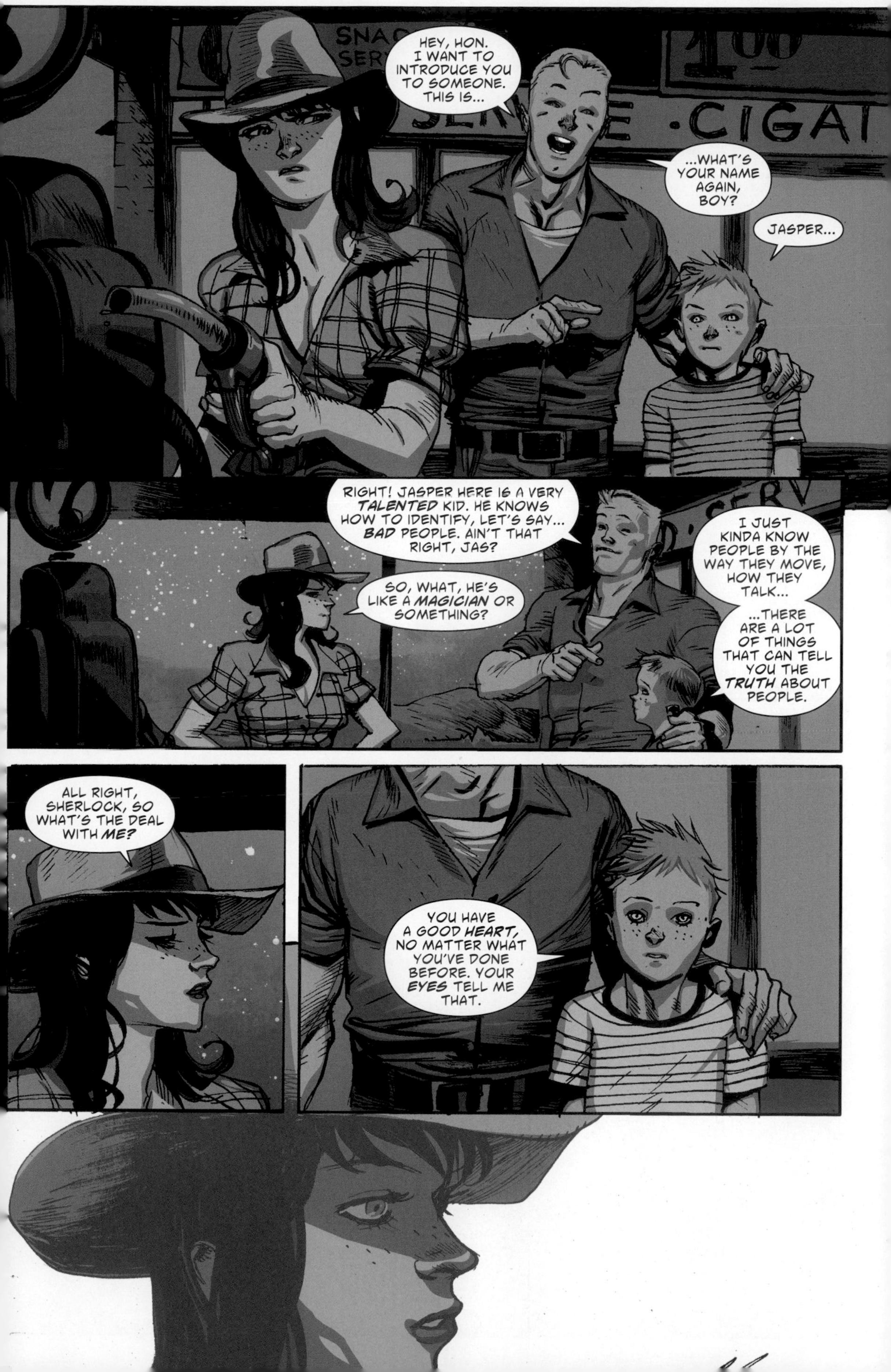
HEY, HON. I WANT TO INTRODUCE YOU TO SOMEONE. THIS IS...
...WHAT'S YOUR NAME AGAIN, BOY?
JASPER...
RIGHT! JASPER HERE IS A VERY TALENTED KID. HE KNOWS HOW TO IDENTIFY, LET'S SAY... BAD PEOPLE. AIN'T THAT RIGHT, JAS?
SO, WHAT, HE'S LIKE A MAGICIAN OR SOMETHING?
I JUST KINDA KNOW PEOPLE BY THE WAY THEY MOVE, HOW THEY TALK...
...THERE ARE A LOT OF THINGS THAT CAN TELL YOU THE TRUTH ABOUT PEOPLE.
ALL RIGHT, SHERLOCK, SO WHAT'S THE DEAL WITH ME?
YOU HAVE A GOOD HEART, NO MATTER WHAT YOU'VE DONE BEFORE. YOUR EYES TELL ME THAT.

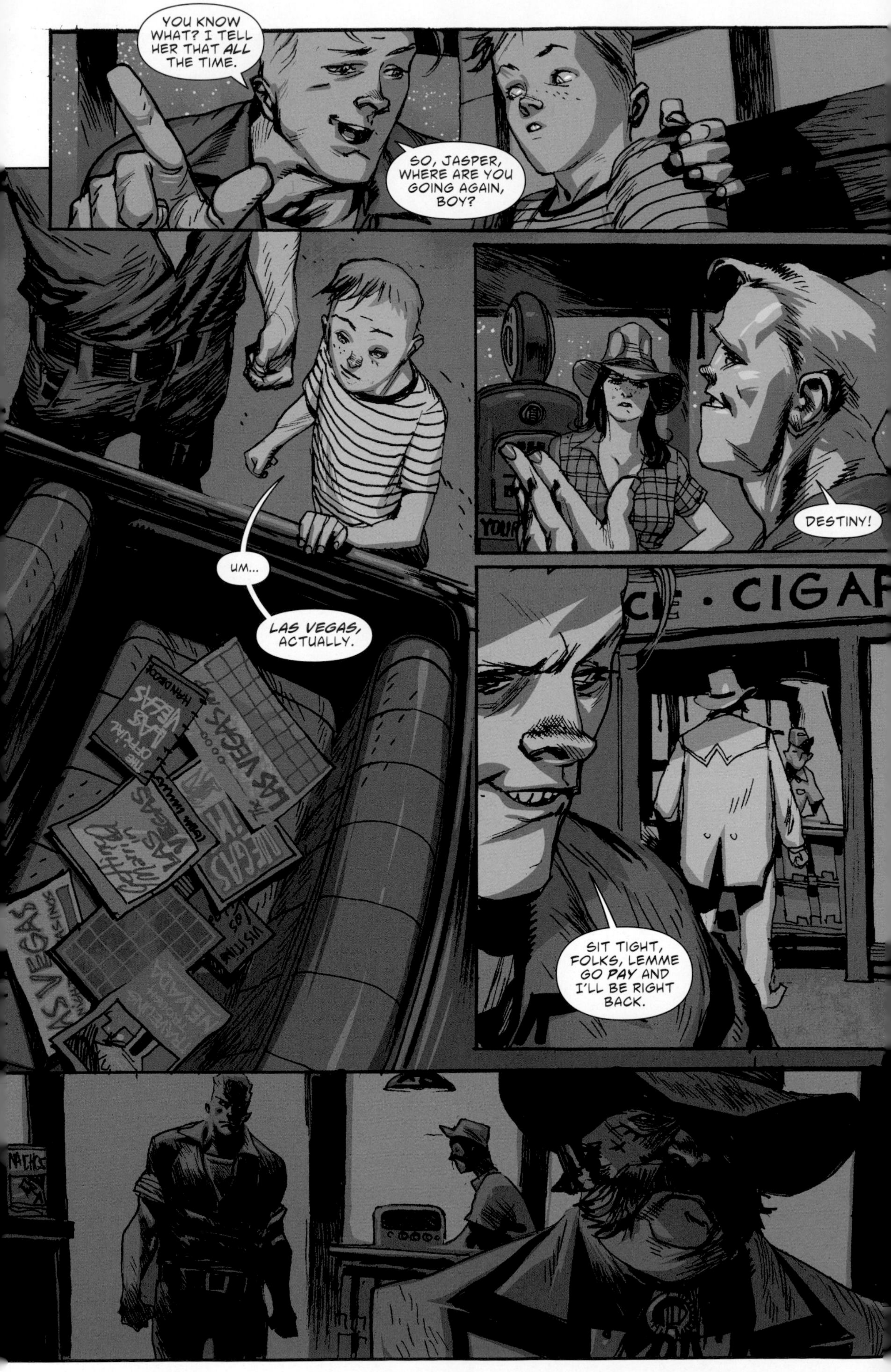
YOU KNOW WHAT? I TELL HER THAT ALL THE TIME.
SO, JASPER, WHERE ARE YOU GOING AGAIN, BOY?
UM...
LAS VEGAS, ACTUALLY.
DESTINY!
CIGAR
SIT TIGHT, FOLKS, LEMME GO PAY AND I'LL BE RIGHT BACK.
LAS VEGAS
NACHOS

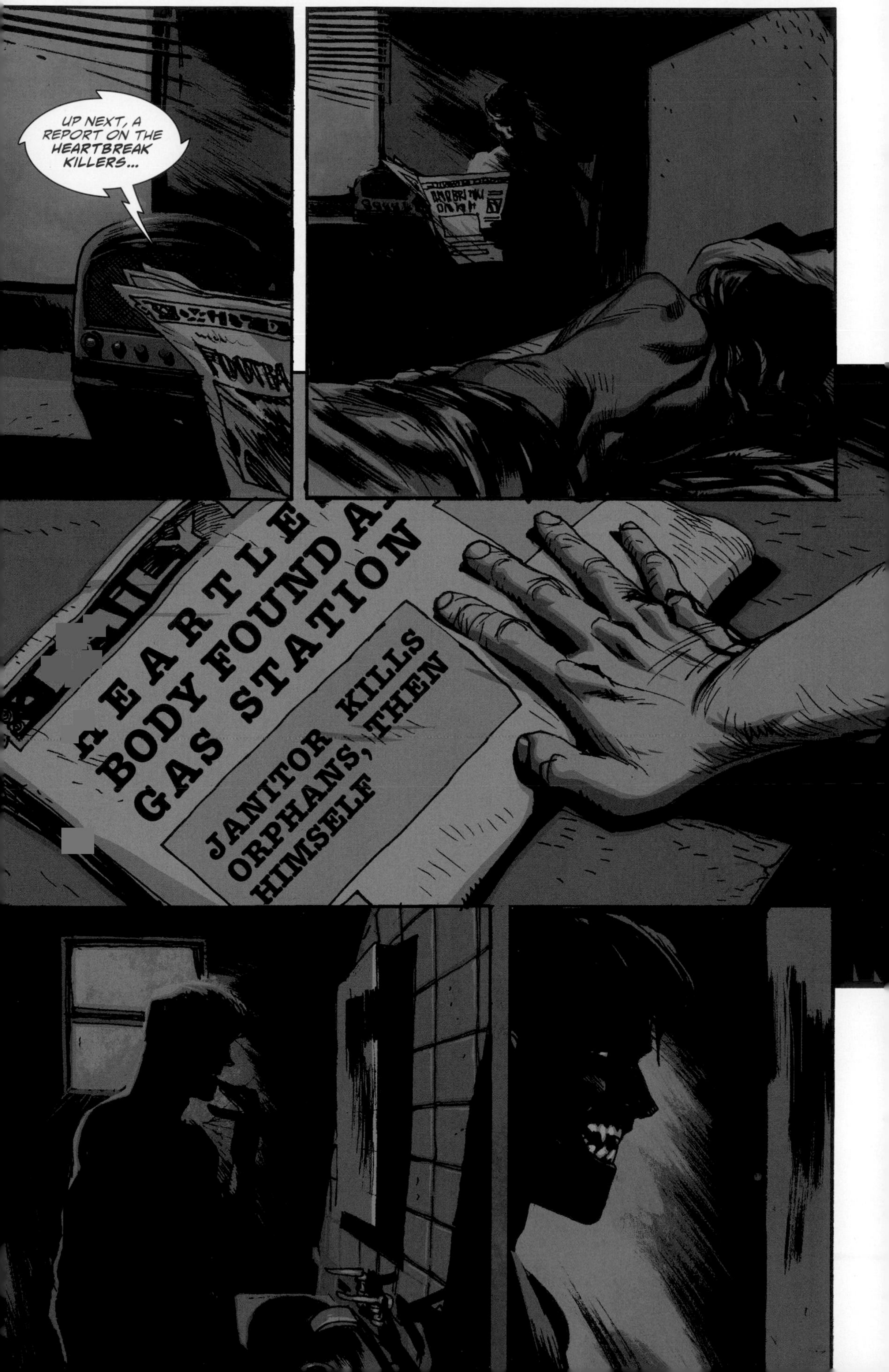
UP NEXT, A REPORT ON THE HEARTBREAK KILLERS...
BODY FOUND
GAS STATION
JANITOR KILLS ORPHANS, THEN HIMSELF

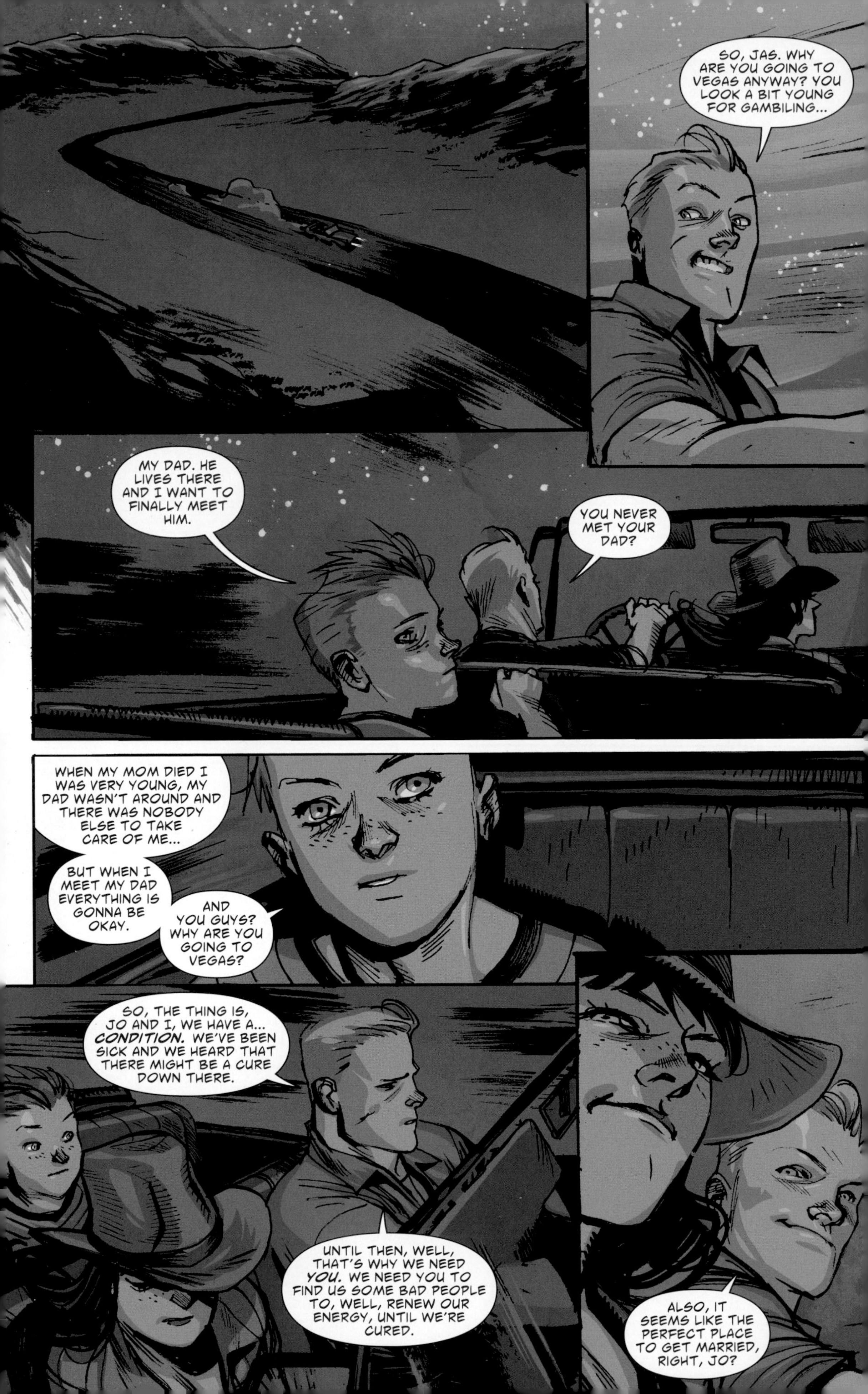
SO, JAS. WHY ARE YOU GOING TO VEGAS ANYWAY? YOU LOOK A BIT YOUNG FOR GAMBILING...
MY DAD. HE LIVES THERE AND I WANT TO FINALLY MEET HIM.
YOU NEVER MET YOUR DAD?
WHEN MY MOM DIED I WAS VERY YOUNG, MY DAD WASN'T AROUND AND THERE WAS NOBODY ELSE TO TAKE CARE OF ME...
BUT WHEN I MEET MY DAD EVERYTHING IS GONNA BE OKAY.
AND YOU GUYS? WHY ARE YOU GOING TO VEGAS?
SO, THE THING IS, JO AND I, WE HAVE A... CONDITION. WE'VE BEEN SICK AND WE HEARD THAT THERE MIGHT BE A CURE DOWN THERE.
UNTIL THEN, WELL, THAT'S WHY WE NEED YOU. WE NEED YOU TO FIND US SOME BAD PEOPLE TO, WELL, RENEW OUR ENERGY, UNTIL WE'RE CURED.
ALSO, IT SEEMS LIKE THE PERFECT PLACE TO GET MARRIED, RIGHT, JO?

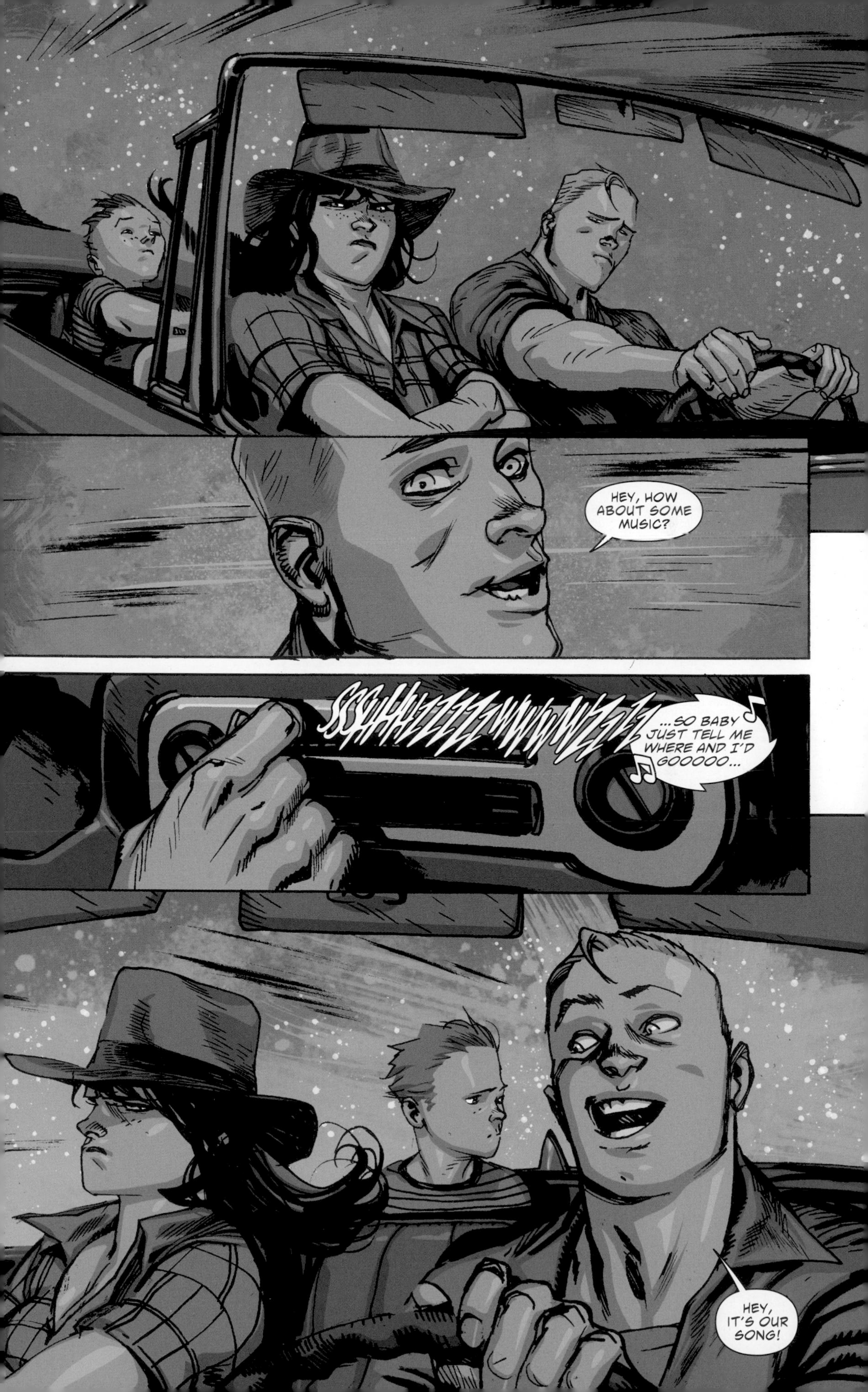
HEY, HOW ABOUT SOME MUSIC?
SSSHHHZZZZZWWWWWZZZZZ
...SO BABY JUST TELL ME WHERE AND I'D GOOOOO...
HEY, IT'S OUR SONG!

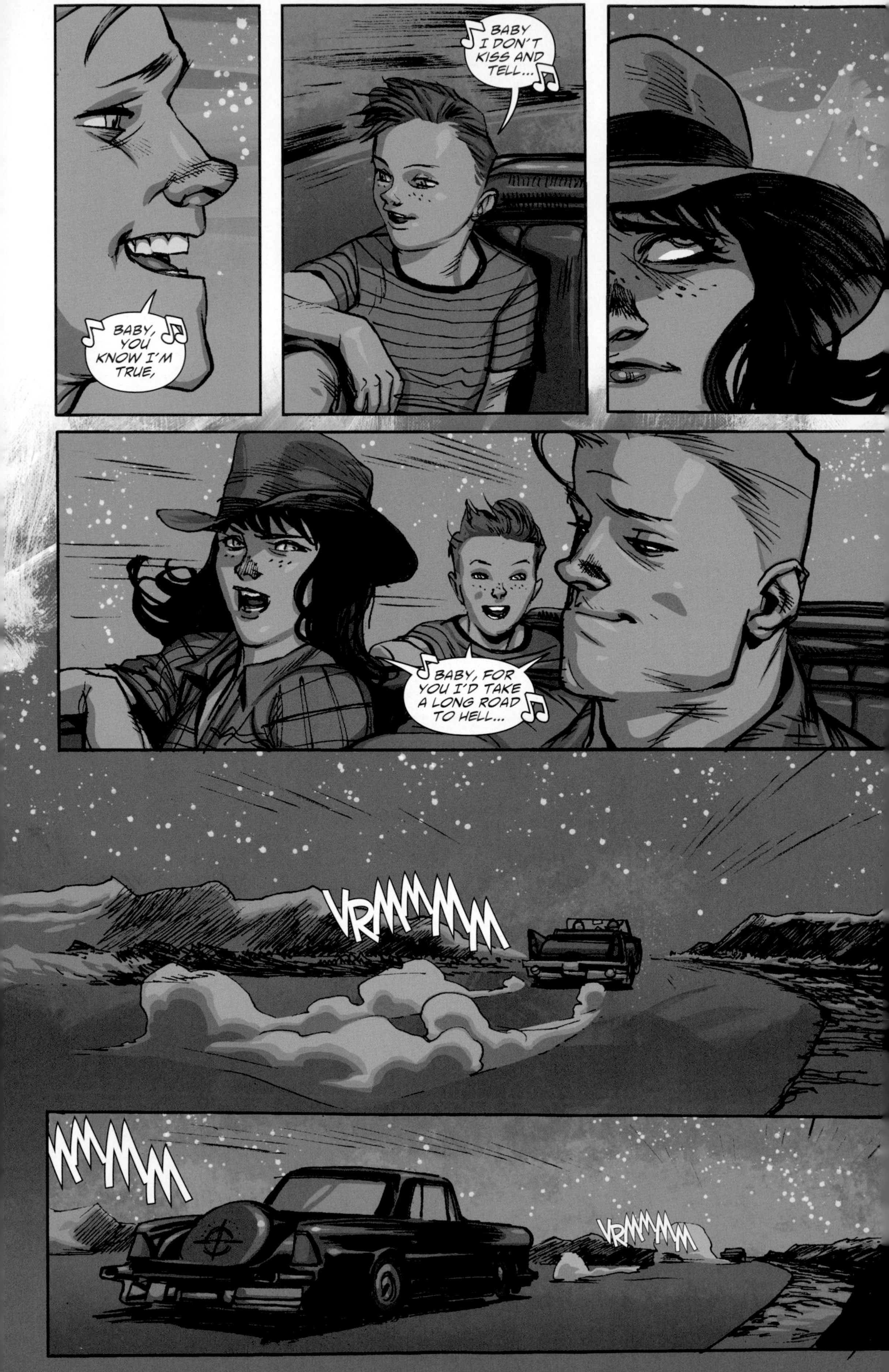
BABY, YOU KNOW I'M TRUE,
BABY I DON'T KISS AND TELL...
BABY, FOR YOU I'D TAKE A LONG ROAD TO HELL...
VRMMMMM
MMMMM
VRMMMMM

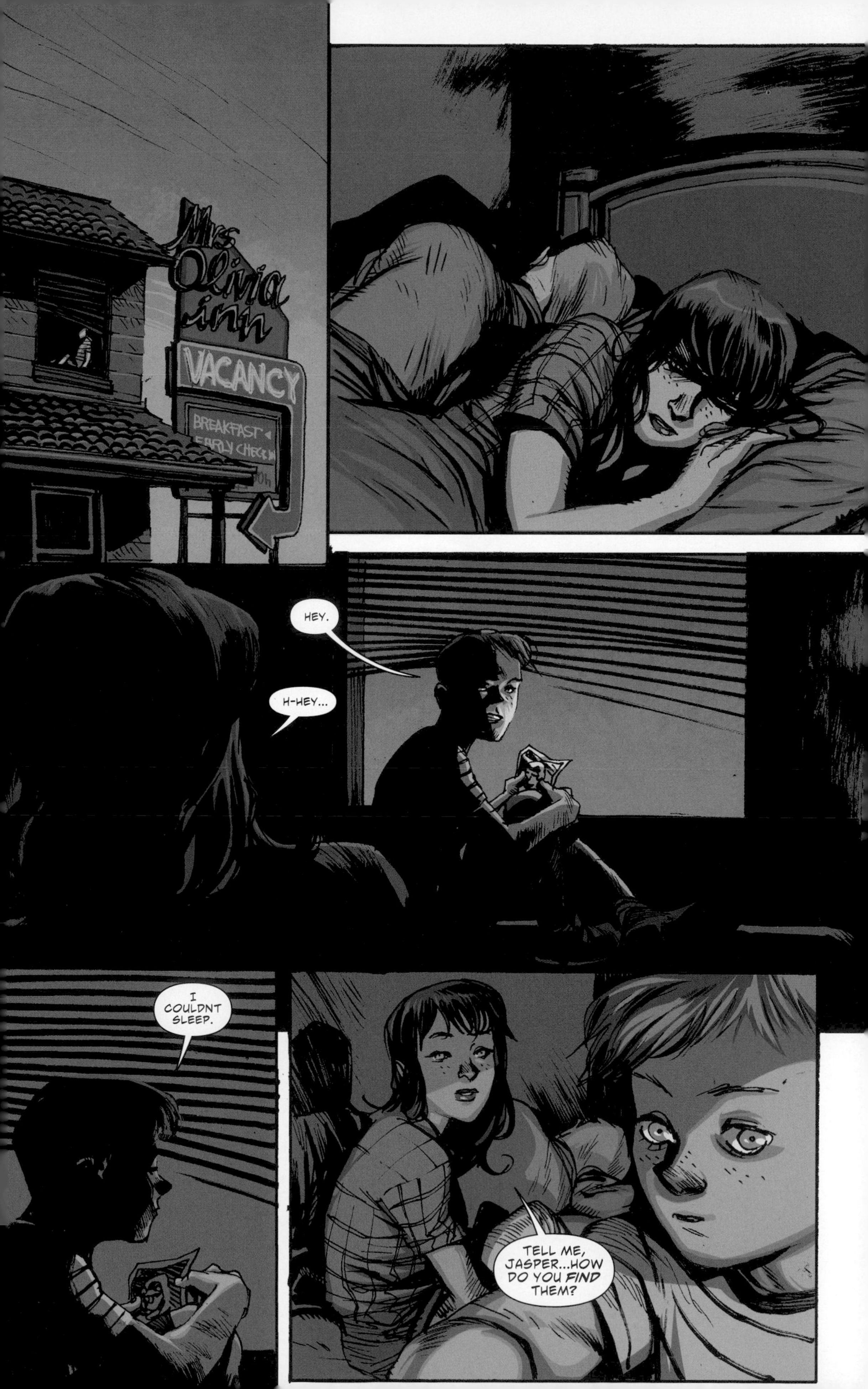
MRS. OLIVIA INN
VACANCY
BREAKFAST
EARLY CHECK
HEY.
H-HEY...
I COULDNT SLEEP.
TELL ME, JASPER...HOW DO YOU *FIND* THEM?

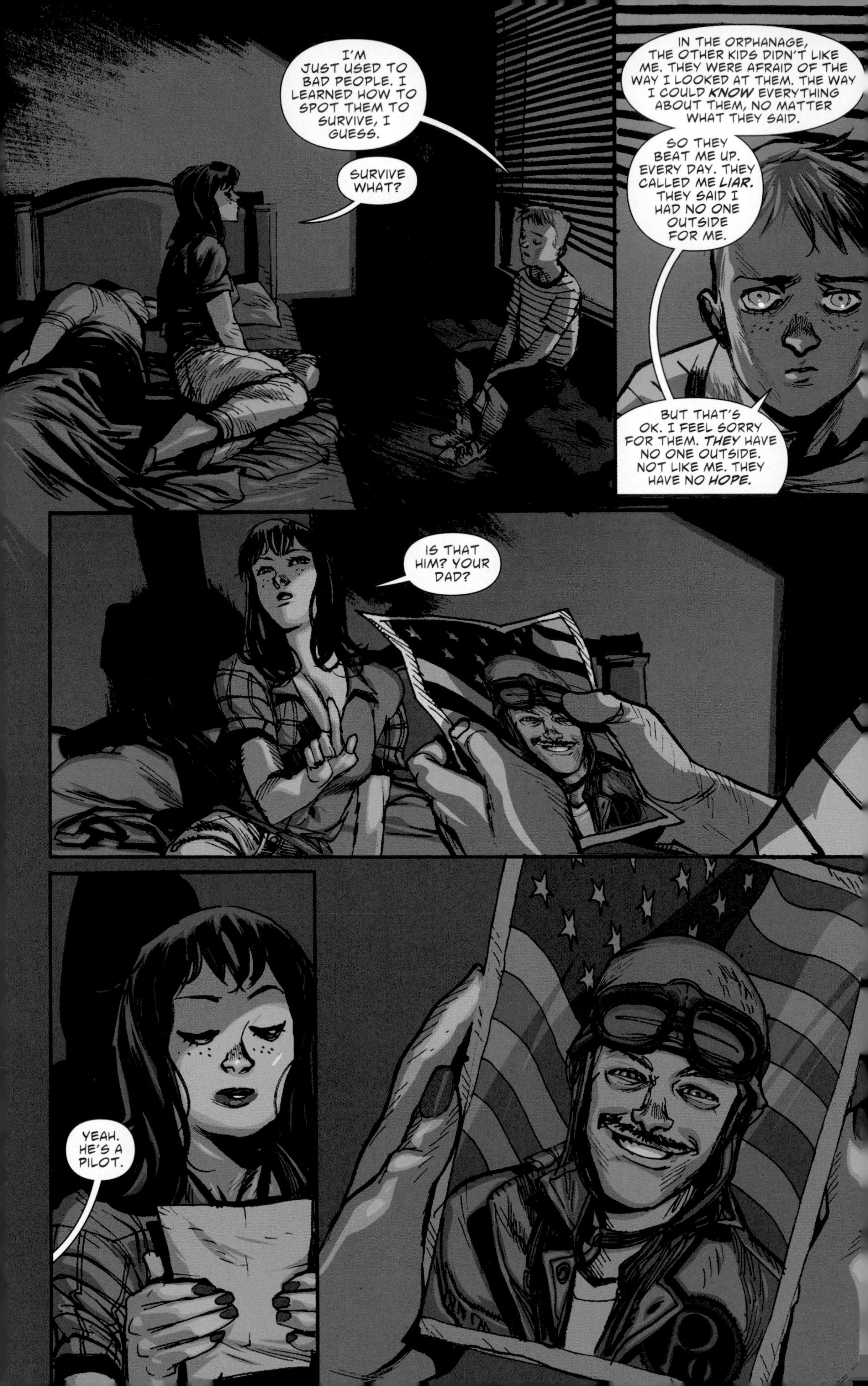
I'M JUST USED TO BAD PEOPLE. I LEARNED HOW TO SPOT THEM TO SURVIVE, I GUESS.
SURVIVE WHAT?
IN THE ORPHANAGE, THE OTHER KIDS DIDN'T LIKE ME. THEY WERE AFRAID OF THE WAY I LOOKED AT THEM. THE WAY I COULD KNOW EVERYTHING ABOUT THEM, NO MATTER WHAT THEY SAID.
SO THEY BEAT ME UP. EVERY DAY. THEY CALLED ME LIAR. THEY SAID I HAD NO ONE OUTSIDE FOR ME.
BUT THAT'S OK. I FEEL SORRY FOR THEM. THEY HAVE NO ONE OUTSIDE. NOT LIKE ME. THEY HAVE NO HOPE.
IS THAT HIM? YOUR DAD?
YEAH. HE'S A PILOT.

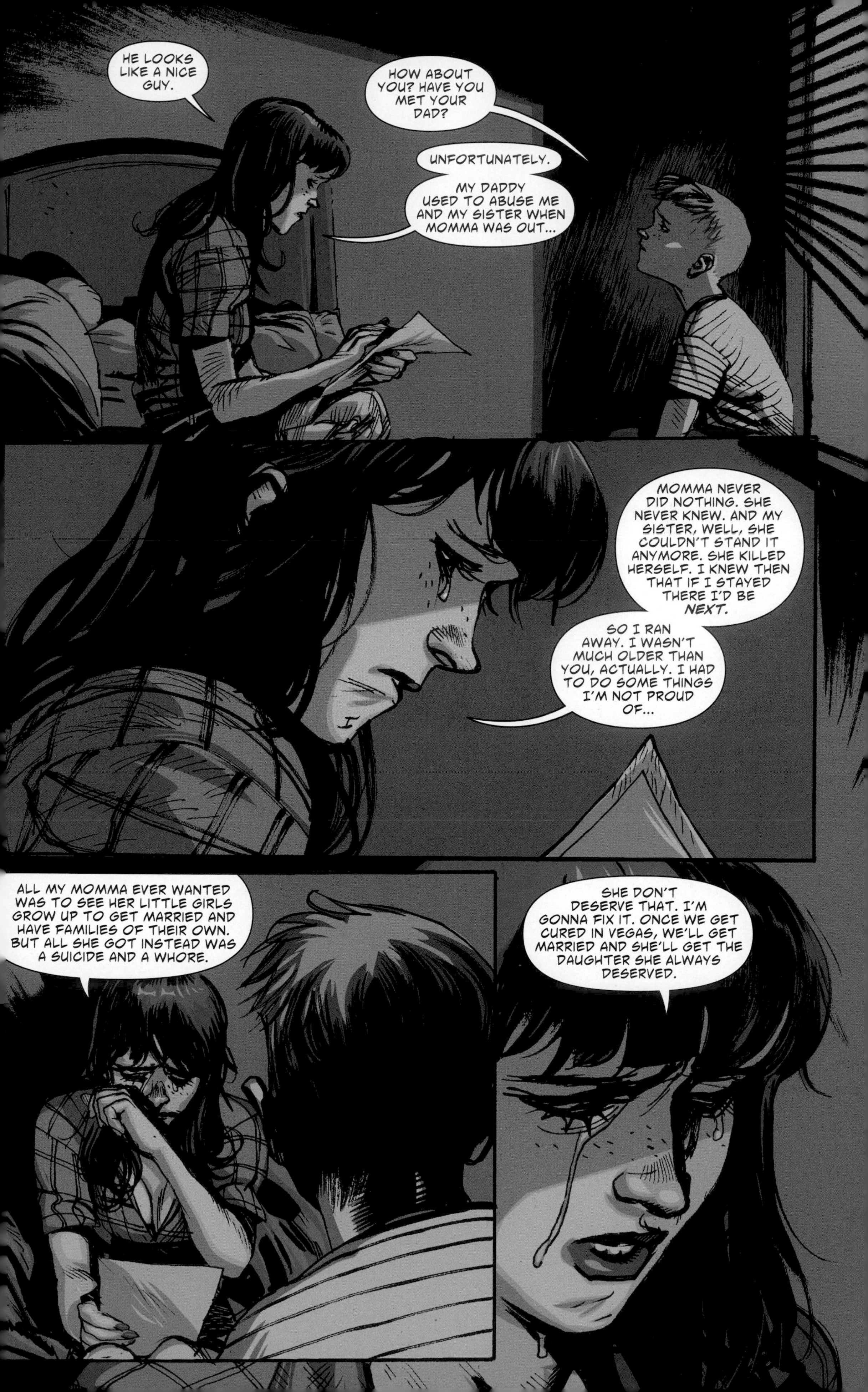
HE LOOKS LIKE A NICE GUY.
HOW ABOUT YOU? HAVE YOU MET YOUR DAD?
UNFORTUNATELY.
MY DADDY USED TO ABUSE ME AND MY SISTER WHEN MOMMA WAS OUT...
MOMMA NEVER DID NOTHING. SHE NEVER KNEW. AND MY SISTER, WELL, SHE COULDN'T STAND IT ANYMORE. SHE KILLED HERSELF. I KNEW THEN THAT IF I STAYED THERE I'D BE *NEXT.*
SO I RAN AWAY. I WASN'T MUCH OLDER THAN YOU, ACTUALLY. I HAD TO DO SOME THINGS I'M NOT PROUD OF...
ALL MY MOMMA EVER WANTED WAS TO SEE HER LITTLE GIRLS GROW UP TO GET MARRIED AND HAVE FAMILIES OF THEIR OWN. BUT ALL SHE GOT INSTEAD WAS A SUICIDE AND A WHORE.
SHE DON'T DESERVE THAT. I'M GONNA FIX IT. ONCE WE GET CURED IN VEGAS, WE'LL GET MARRIED AND SHE'LL GET THE DAUGHTER SHE ALWAYS DESERVED.

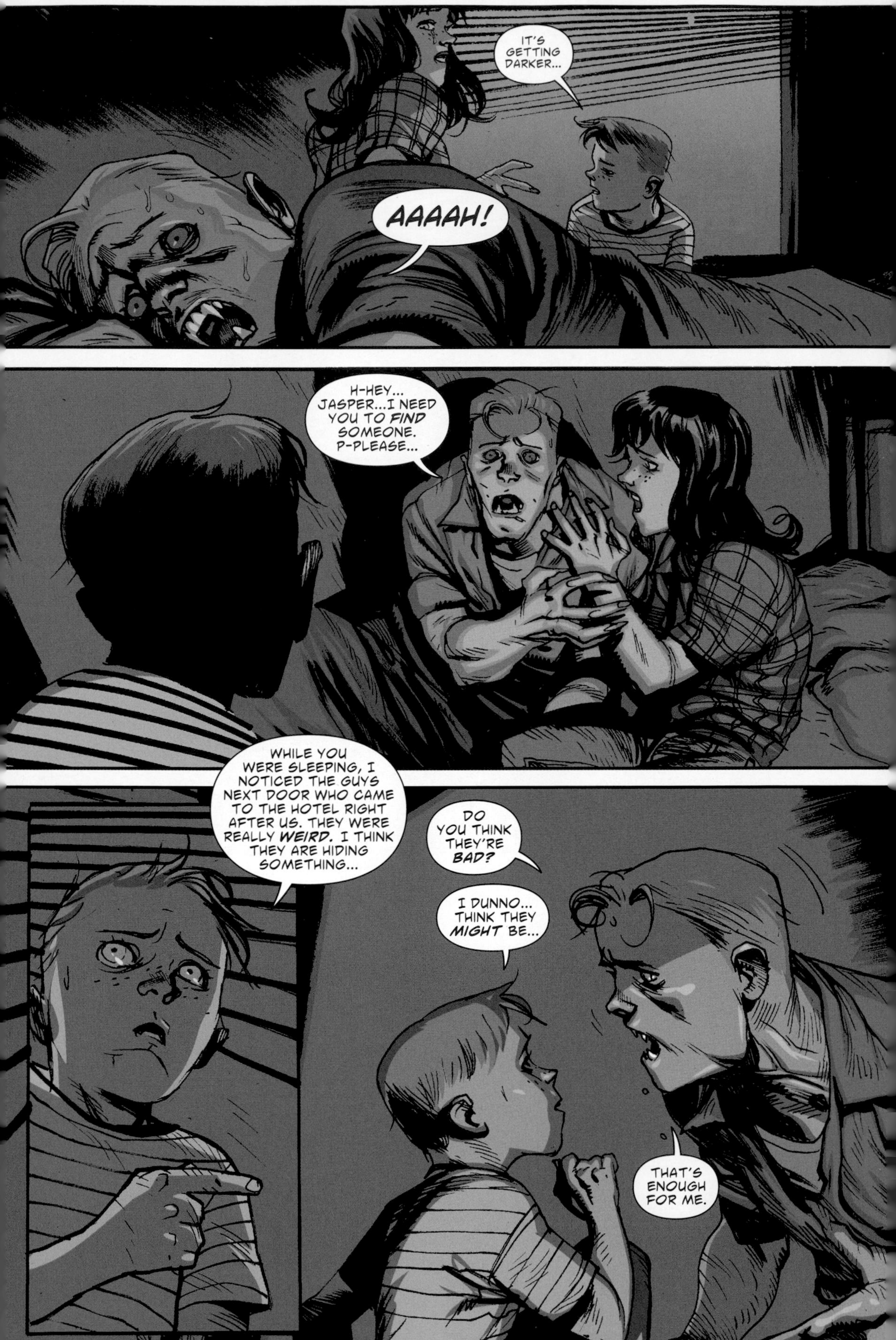
IT'S GETTING DARKER...
AAAAH!
H-HEY... JASPER...I NEED YOU TO FIND SOMEONE. P-PLEASE...
WHILE YOU WERE SLEEPING, I NOTICED THE GUYS NEXT DOOR WHO CAME TO THE HOTEL RIGHT AFTER US. THEY WERE REALLY WEIRD. I THINK THEY ARE HIDING SOMETHING...
DO YOU THINK THEY'RE BAD?
I DUNNO... THINK THEY MIGHT BE...
THAT'S ENOUGH FOR ME.

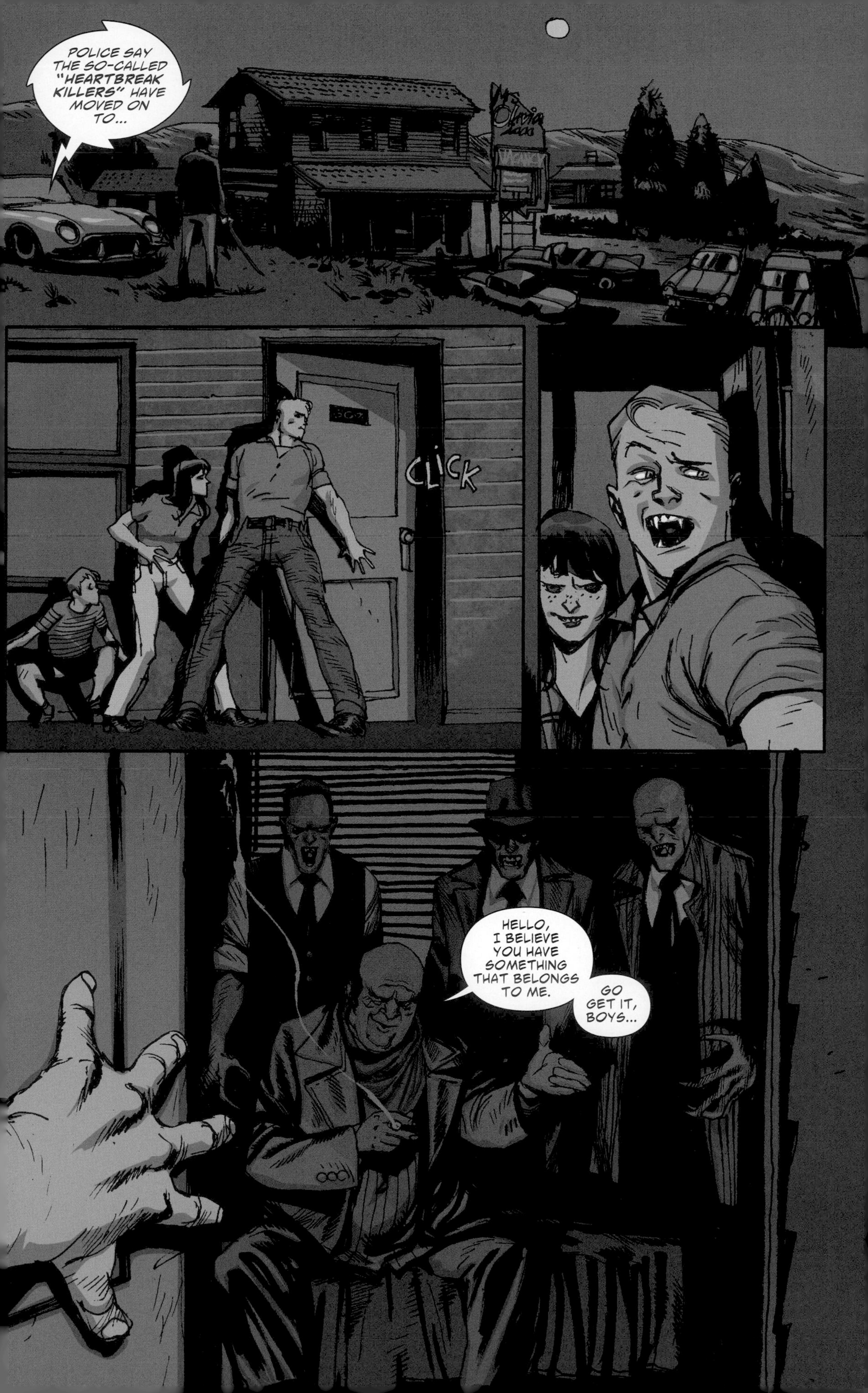
POLICE SAY THE SO-CALLED "HEARTBREAK KILLERS" HAVE MOVED ON TO...
CLICK
HELLO, I BELIEVE YOU HAVE SOMETHING THAT BELONGS TO ME.
GO GET IT, BOYS...

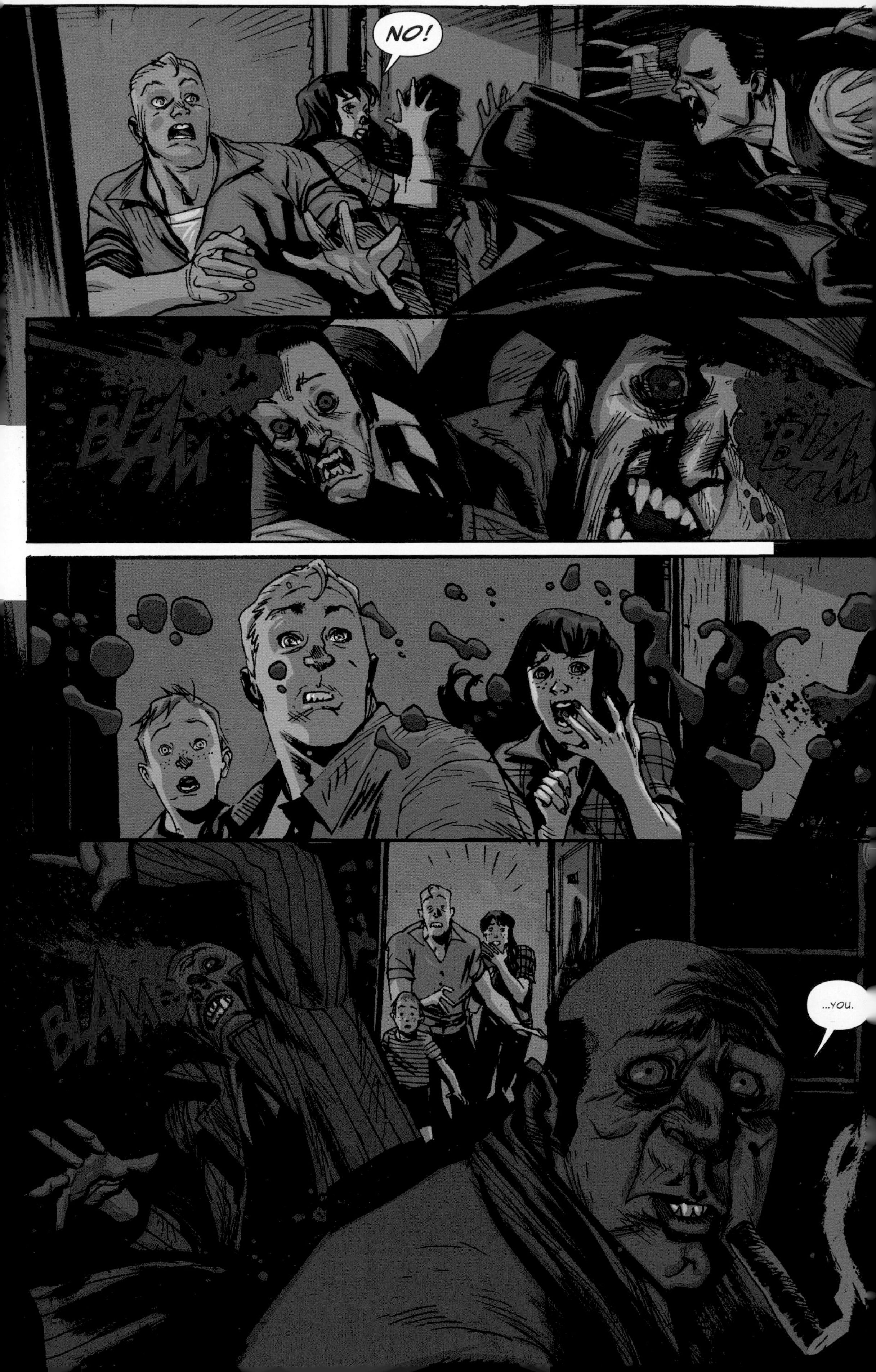
NO!
BLAM
BLAM
BLAM
...YOU.

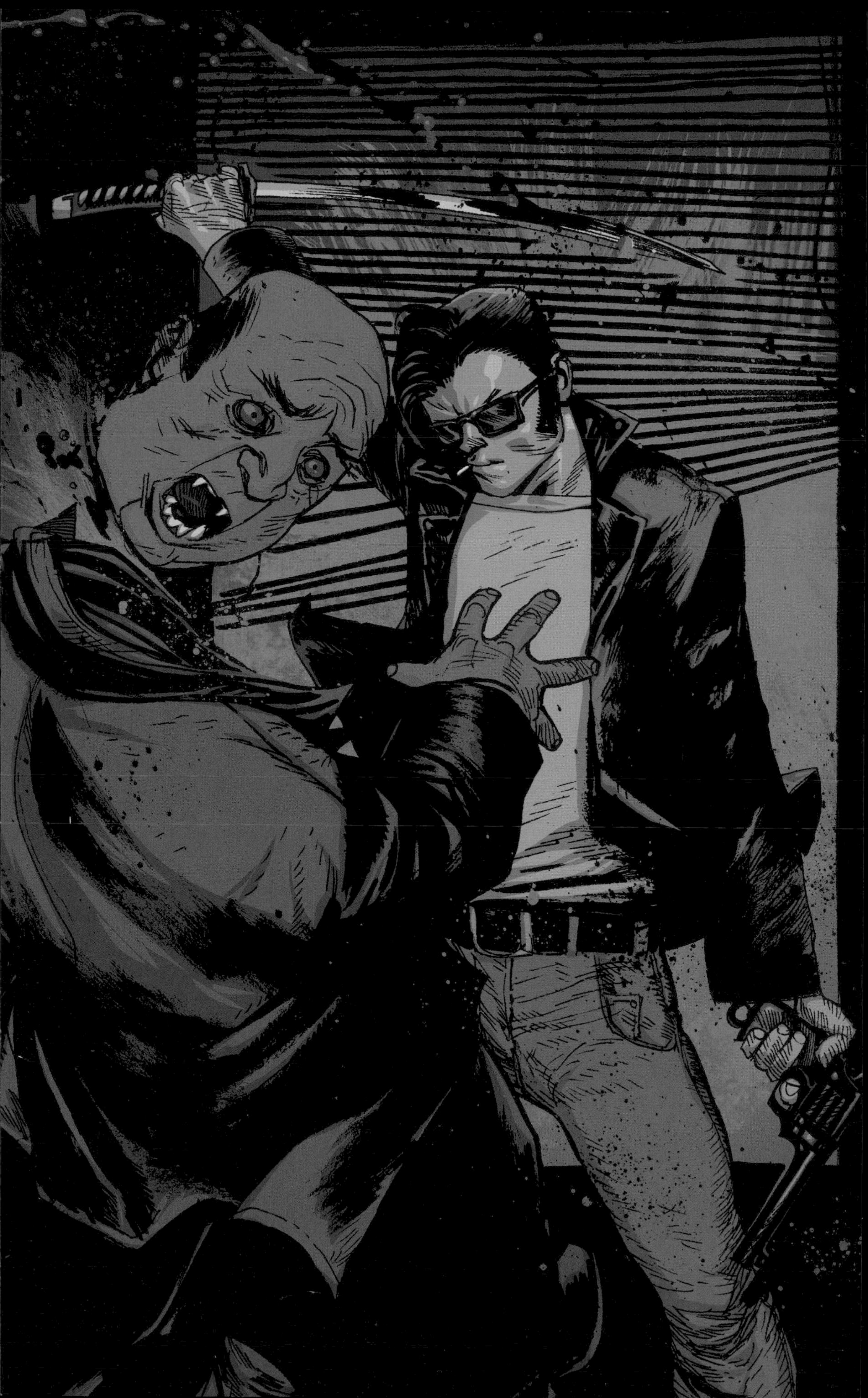

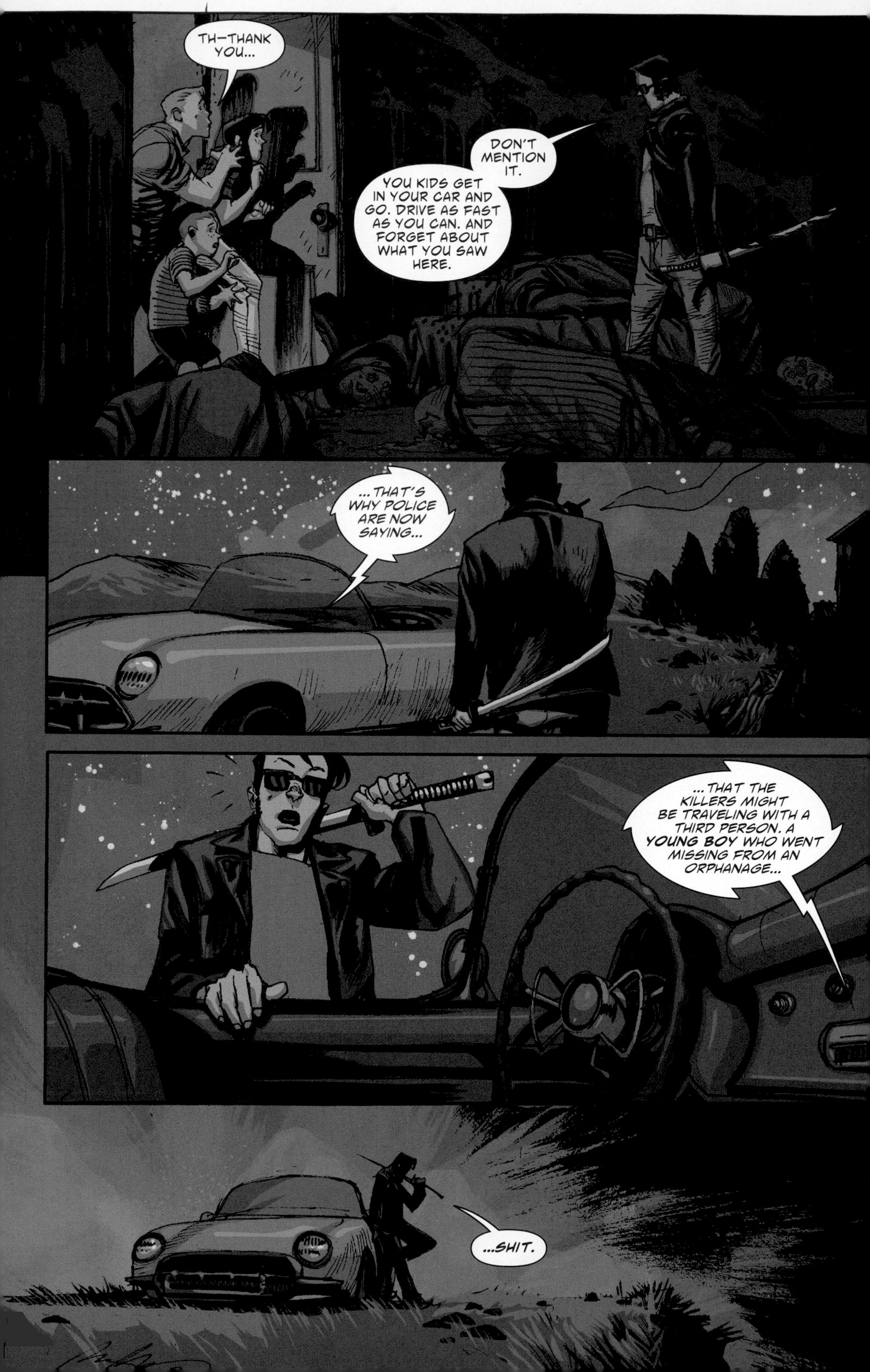
TH—THANK YOU...
DON'T MENTION IT.
YOU KIDS GET IN YOUR CAR AND GO. DRIVE AS FAST AS YOU CAN. AND FORGET ABOUT WHAT YOU SAW HERE.
...THAT'S WHY POLICE ARE NOW SAYING...
...THAT THE KILLERS MIGHT BE TRAVELING WITH A THIRD PERSON. A **YOUNG BOY** WHO WENT MISSING FROM AN ORPHANAGE...
...SHIT.

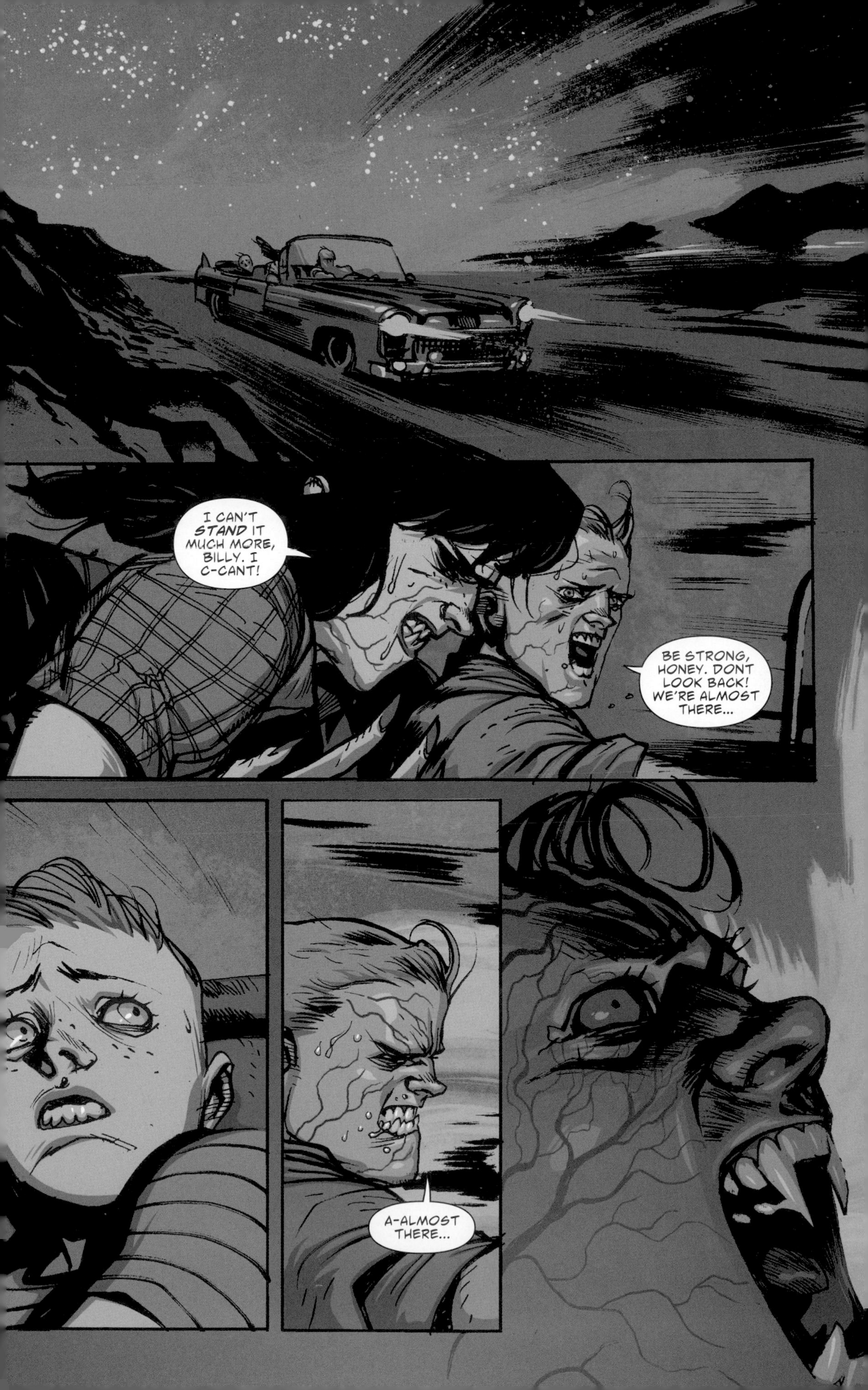
I CAN'T STAND IT MUCH MORE, BILLY. I C-CANT!
BE STRONG, HONEY. DONT LOOK BACK! WE'RE ALMOST THERE...
A-ALMOST THERE...

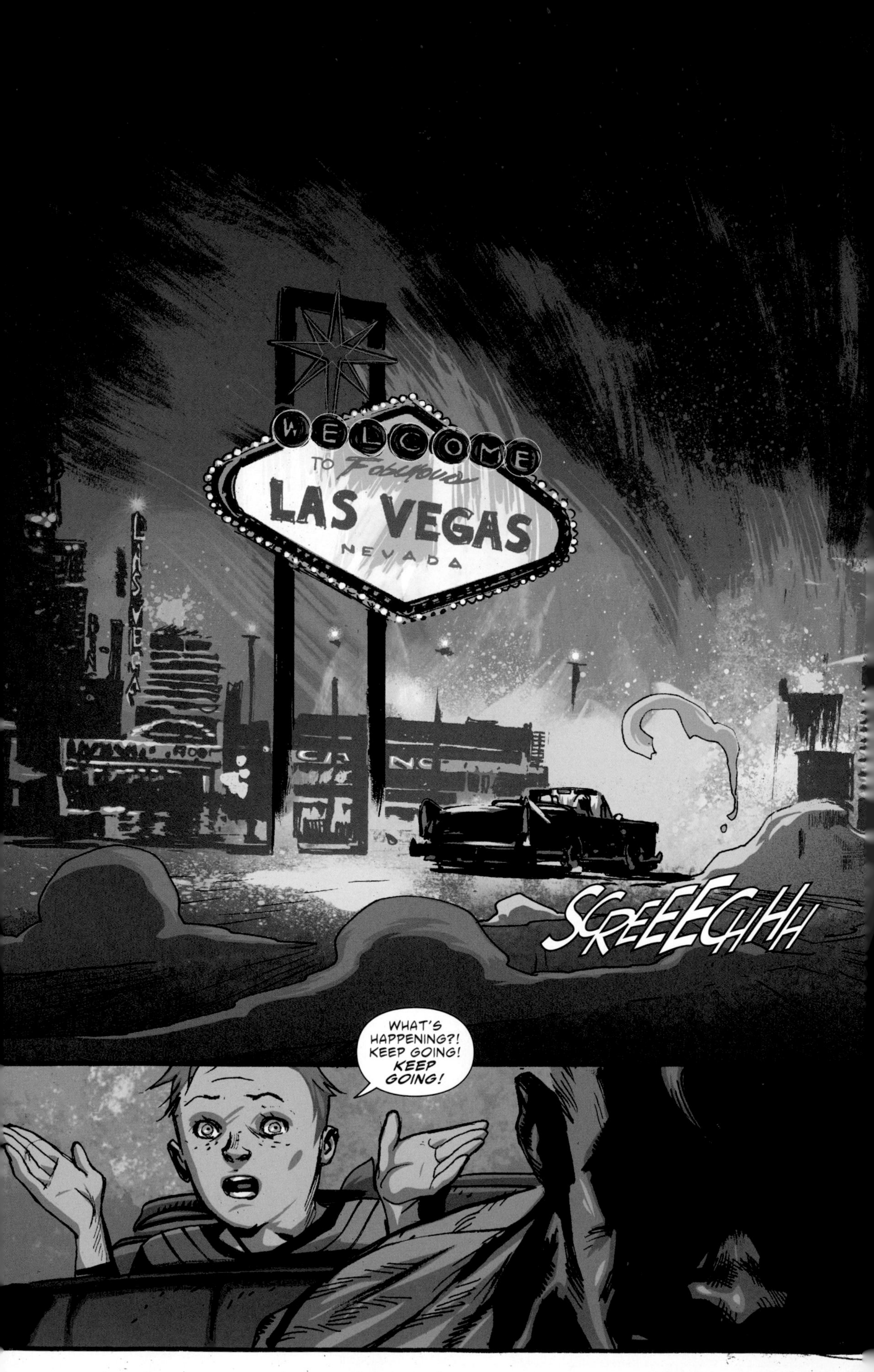
WELCOME
TO Fabulous
LAS VEGAS
NEVADA
SCREEEGHHH
WHAT'S HAPPENING?! KEEP GOING! KEEP GOING!

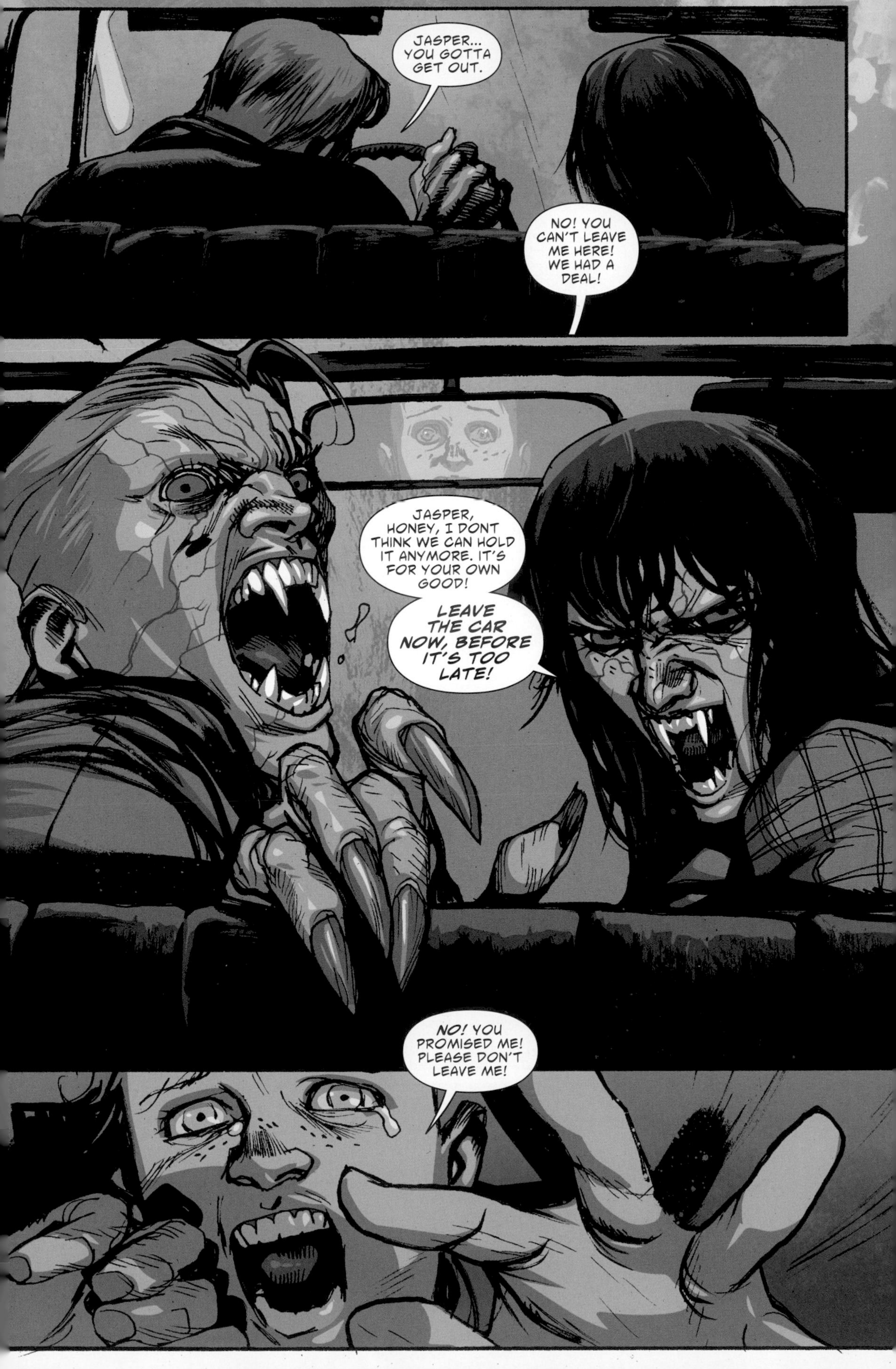

JASPER... YOU GOTTA GET OUT.
NO! YOU CAN'T LEAVE ME HERE! WE HAD A DEAL!
JASPER, HONEY, I DONT THINK WE CAN HOLD IT ANYMORE. IT'S FOR YOUR OWN GOOD!
LEAVE THE CAR NOW, BEFORE IT'S TOO LATE!
NO! YOU PROMISED ME! PLEASE DON'T LEAVE ME!

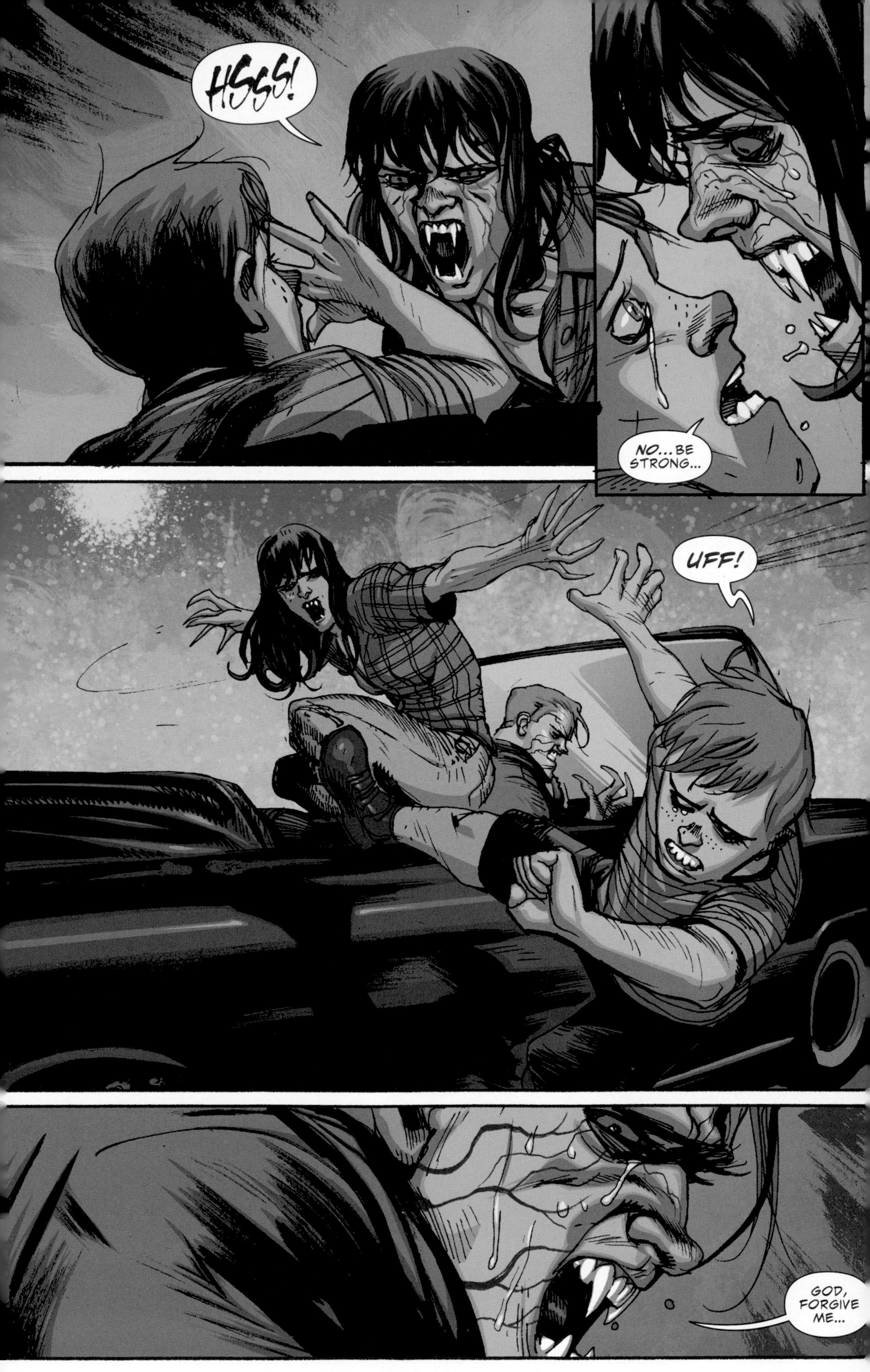
HSSS!
NO...BE STRONG...
UFF!
GOD, FORGIVE ME...

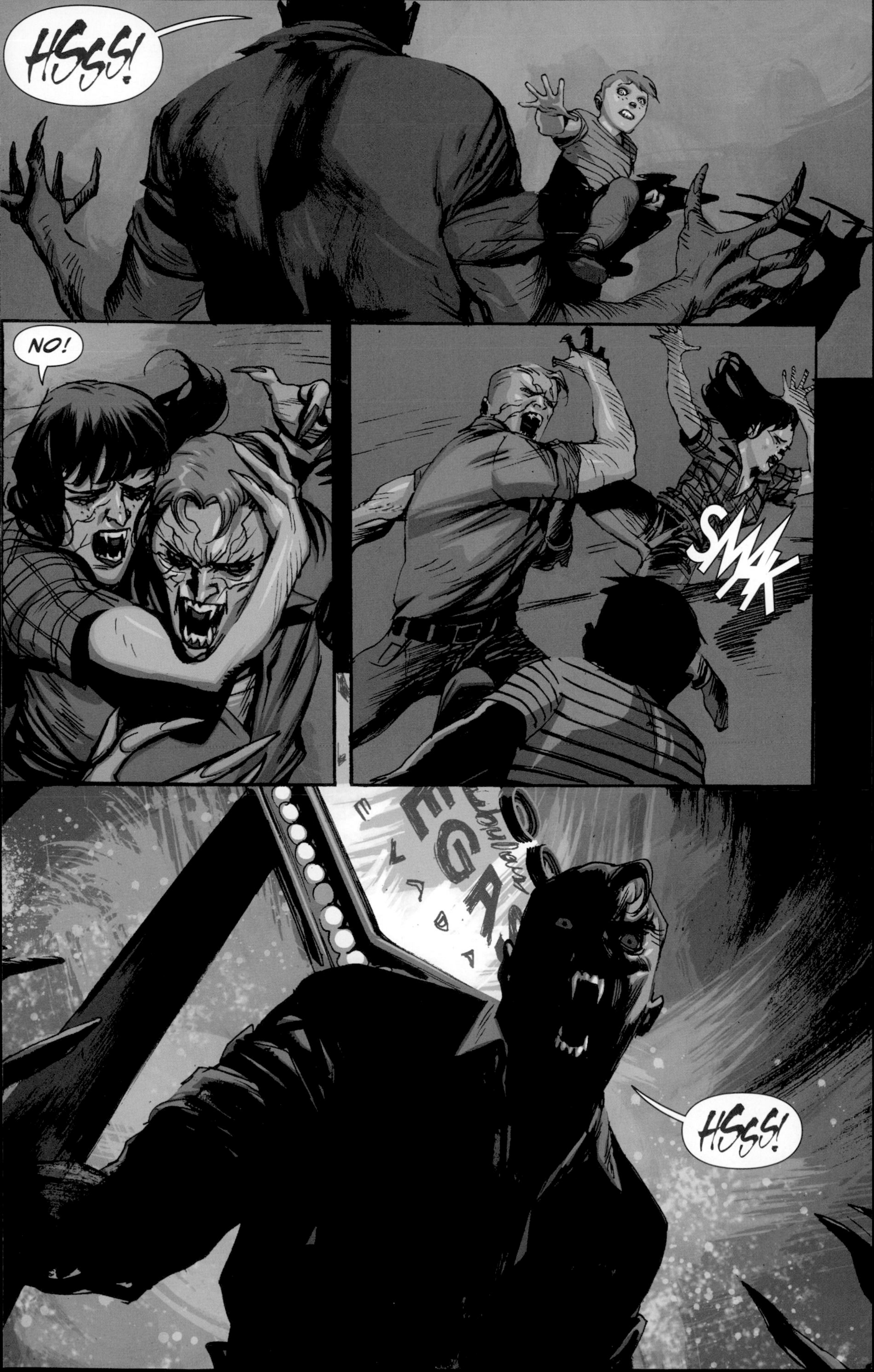
HSSS!
NO!
SMAK
HSSS!

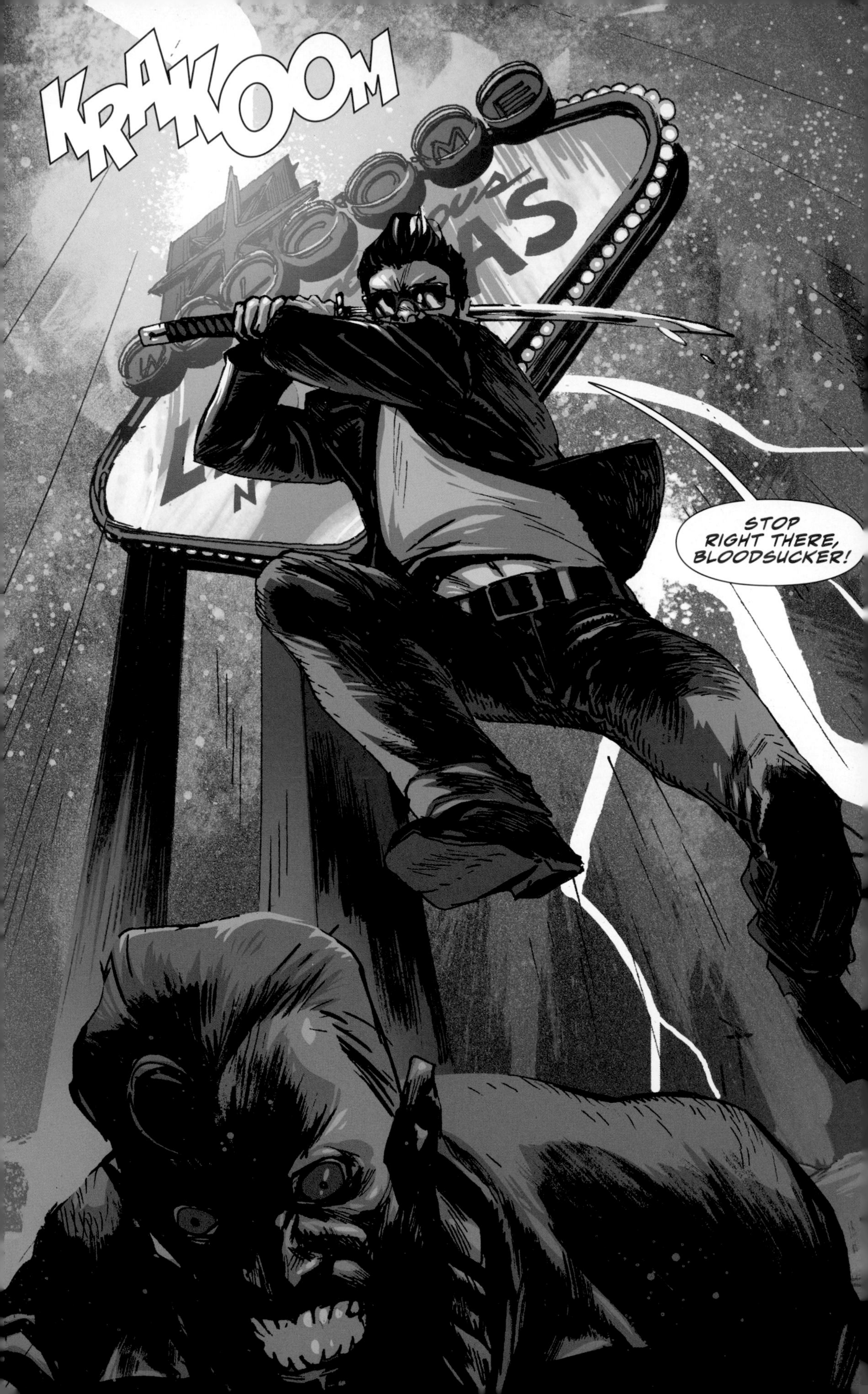
KRAKOOM
STOP RIGHT THERE, BLOODSUCKER!

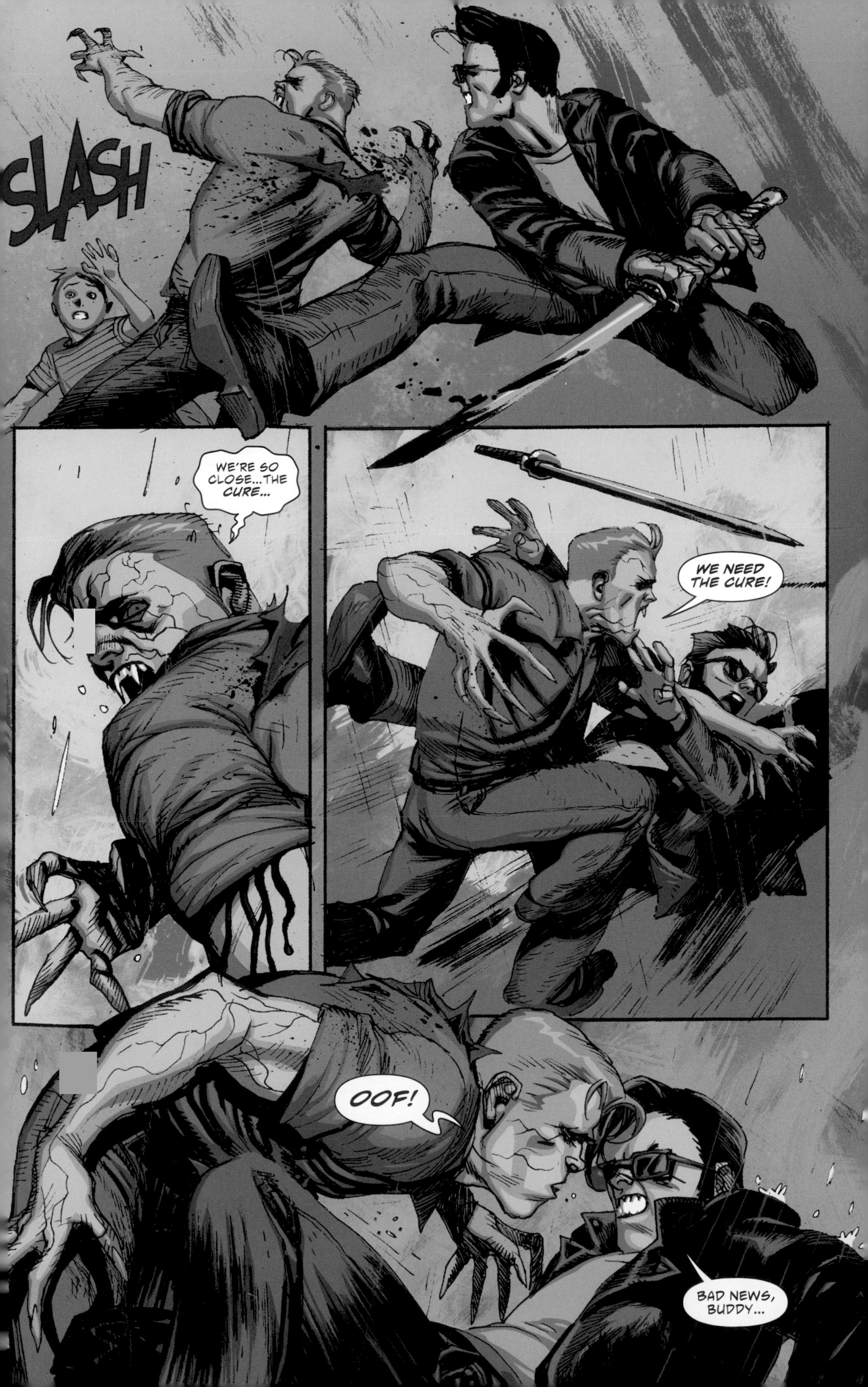
SLASH
WE'RE SO CLOSE...THE CURE...
WE NEED THE CURE!
OOF!
BAD NEWS, BUDDY...

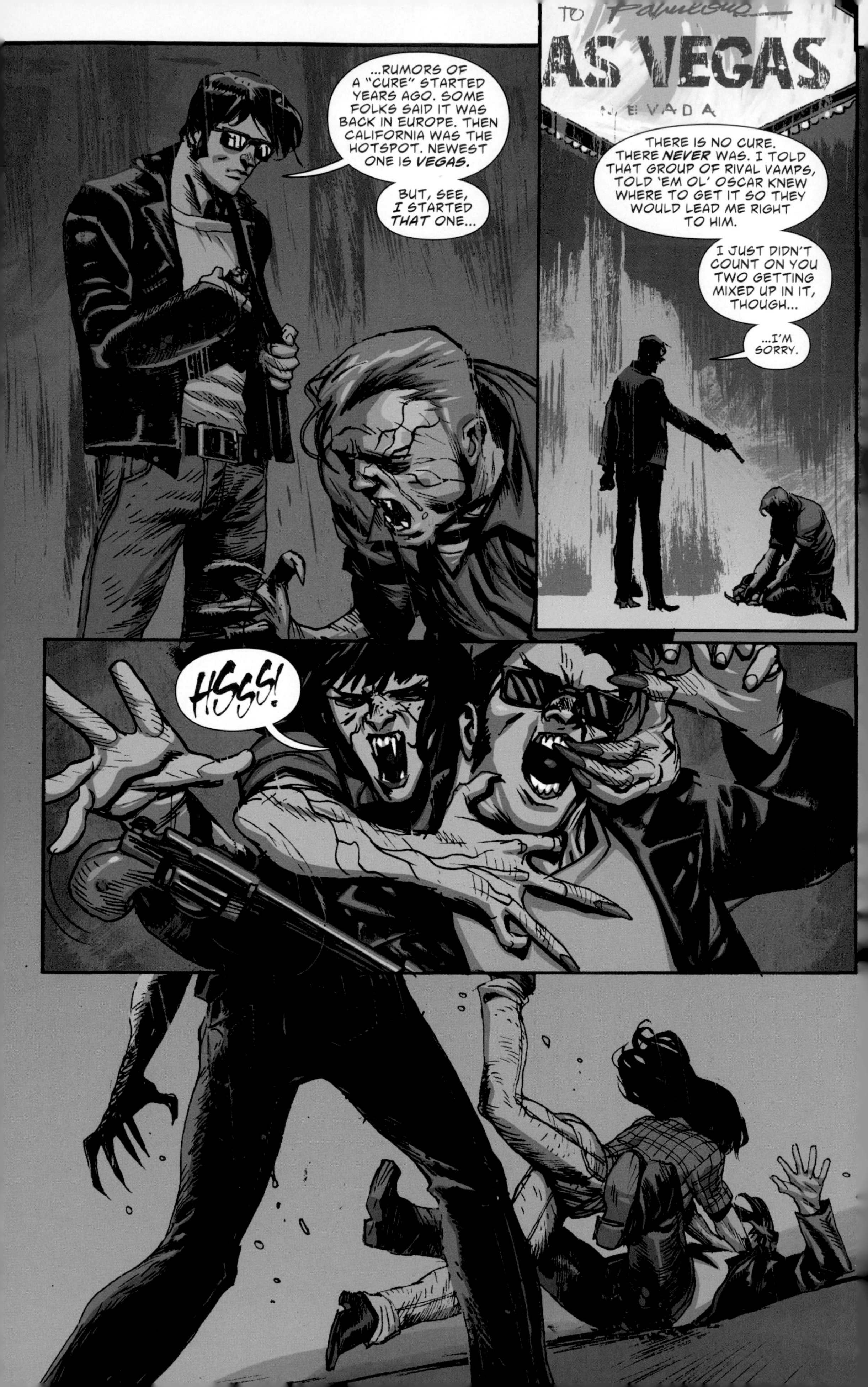

...RUMORS OF A "CURE" STARTED YEARS AGO. SOME FOLKS SAID IT WAS BACK IN EUROPE. THEN CALIFORNIA WAS THE HOTSPOT. NEWEST ONE IS VEGAS.
BUT, SEE, I STARTED THAT ONE...
LAS VEGAS
NEVADA
THERE IS NO CURE. THERE NEVER WAS. I TOLD THAT GROUP OF RIVAL VAMPS, TOLD 'EM OL' OSCAR KNEW WHERE TO GET IT SO THEY WOULD LEAD ME RIGHT TO HIM.
I JUST DIDN'T COUNT ON YOU TWO GETTING MIXED UP IN IT, THOUGH...
...I'M SORRY.
HSSS!

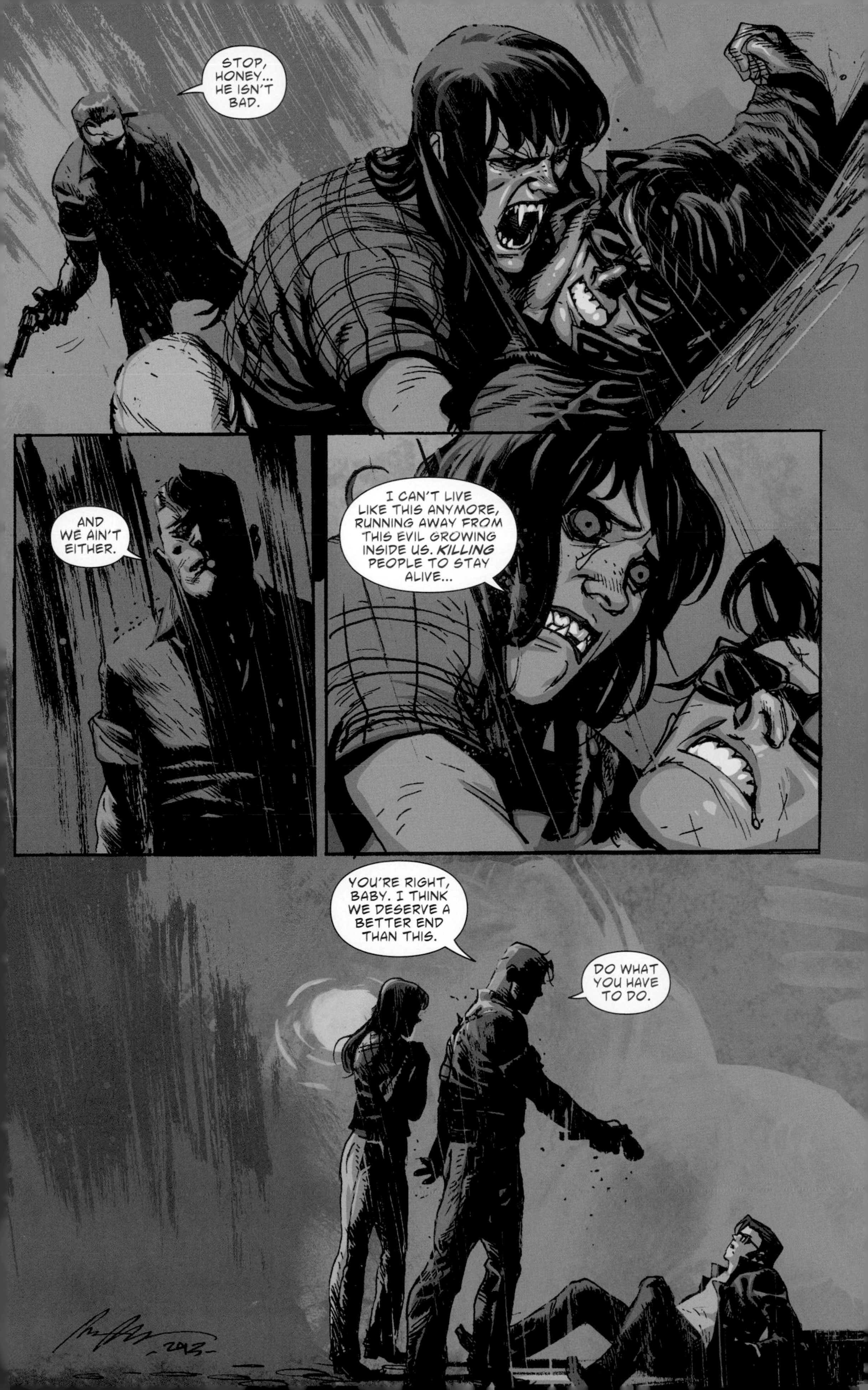
STOP, HONEY... HE ISN'T BAD.
AND WE AIN'T EITHER.
I CAN'T LIVE LIKE THIS ANYMORE, RUNNING AWAY FROM THIS EVIL GROWING INSIDE US. KILLING PEOPLE TO STAY ALIVE...
YOU'RE RIGHT, BABY. I THINK WE DESERVE A BETTER END THAN THIS.
DO WHAT YOU HAVE TO DO.

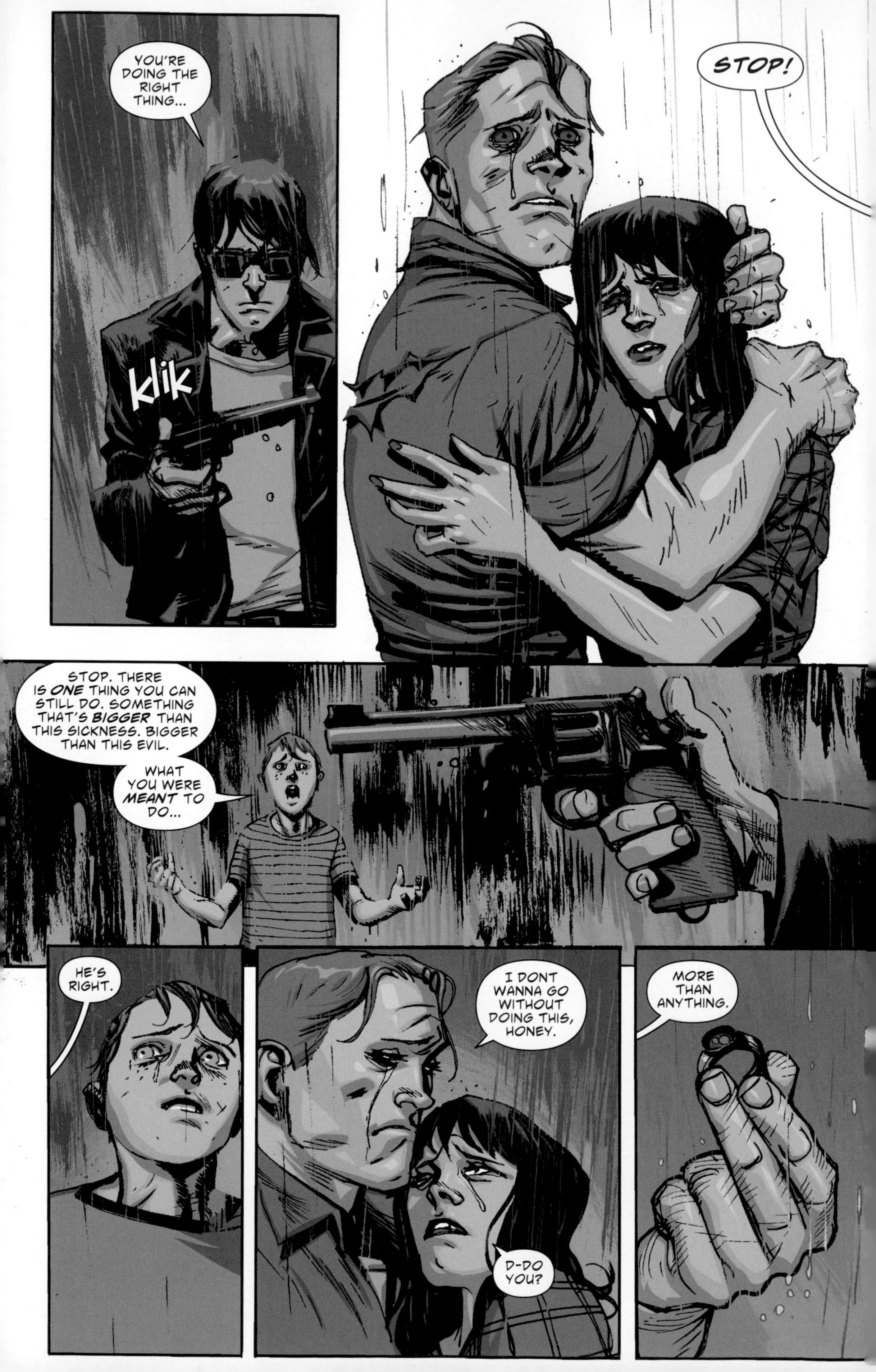
YOU'RE DOING THE RIGHT THING...
klik
STOP!
STOP. THERE IS ONE THING YOU CAN STILL DO. SOMETHING THAT'S BIGGER THAN THIS SICKNESS. BIGGER THAN THIS EVIL.
WHAT YOU WERE MEANT TO DO...
HE'S RIGHT.
I DONT WANNA GO WITHOUT DOING THIS, HONEY.
D-DO YOU?
MORE THAN ANYTHING.

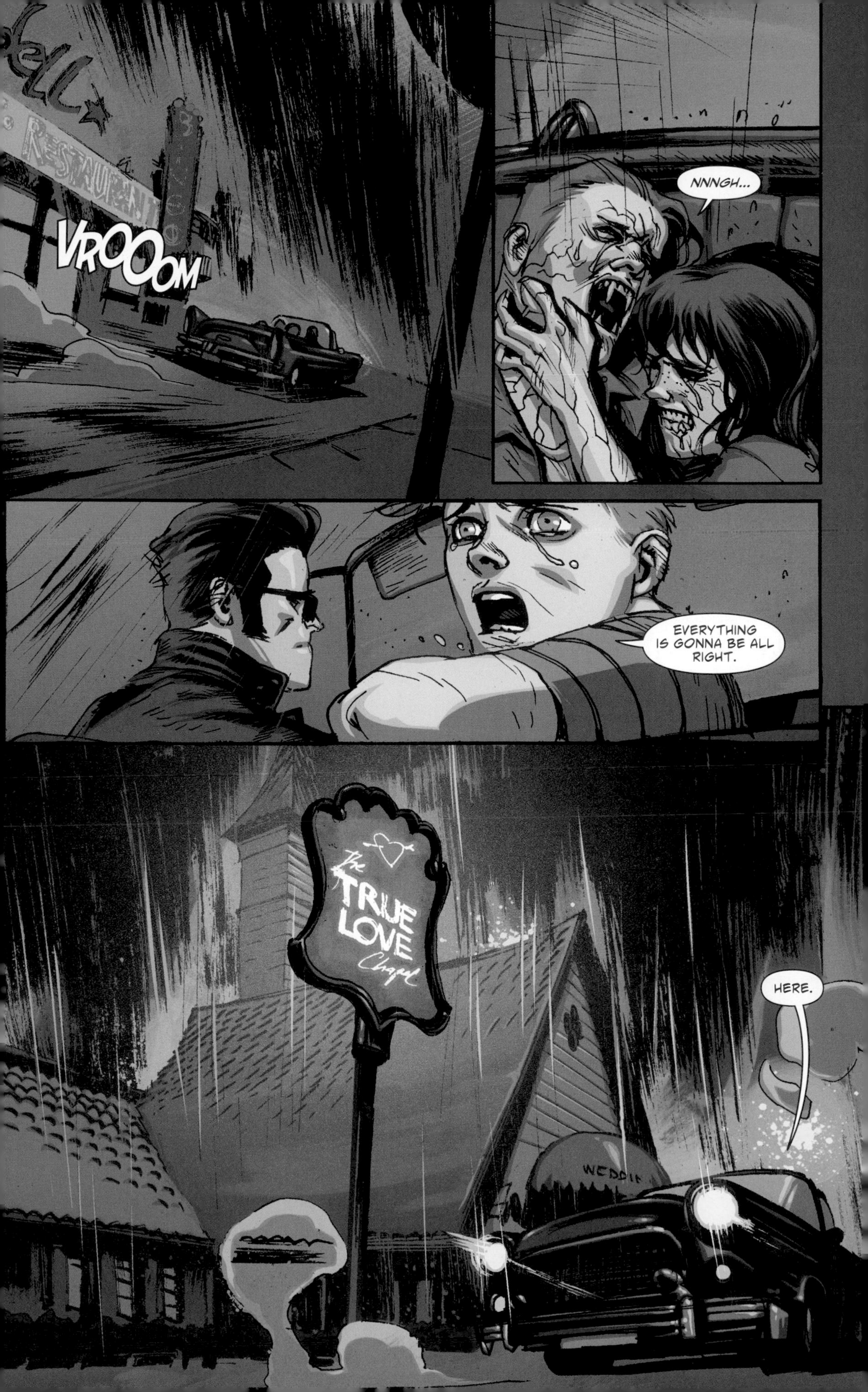

RESTAURANT
VROOOOM
NNNGH...
EVERYTHING IS GONNA BE ALL RIGHT.
The TRUE LOVE Chapel
HERE.

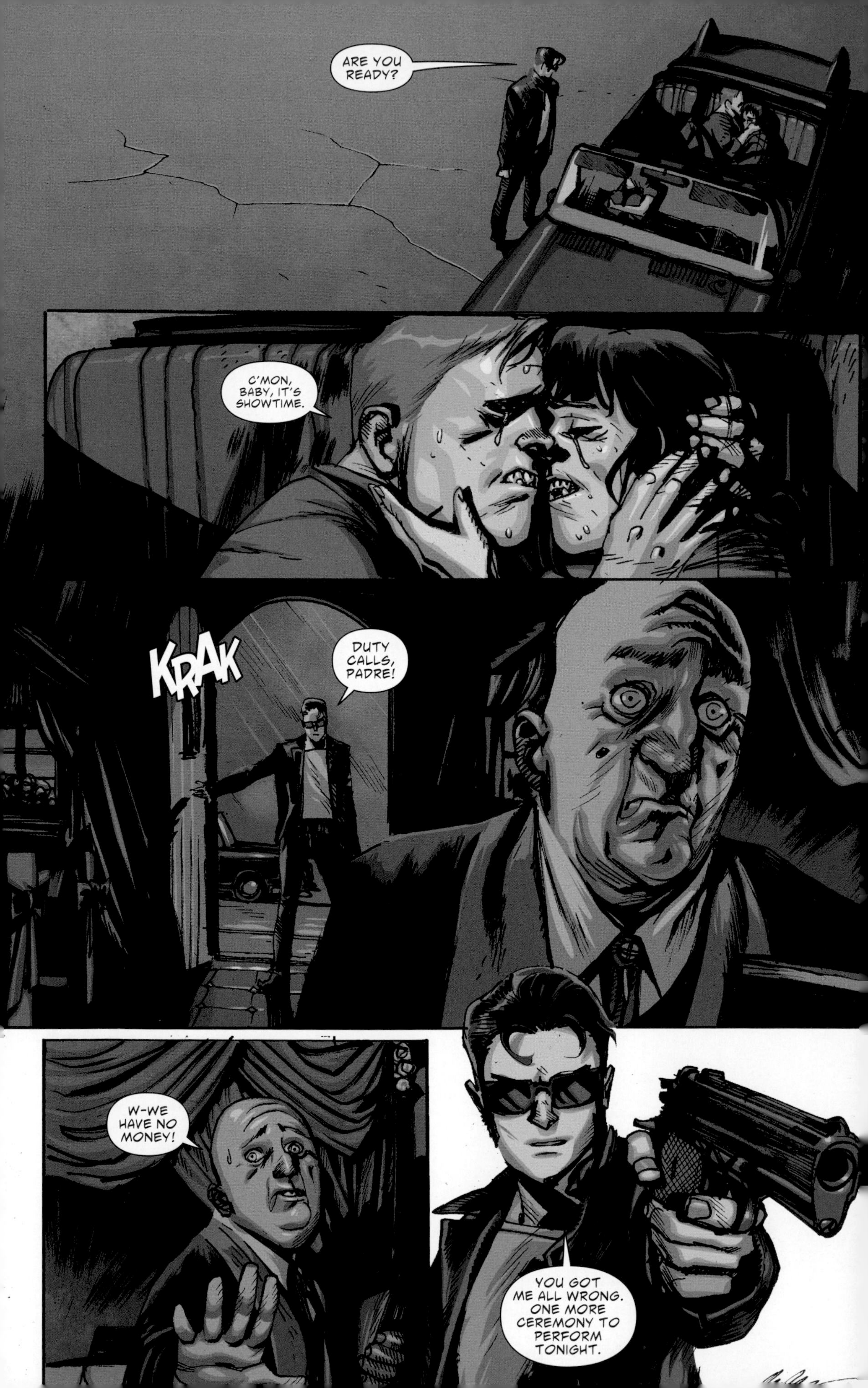
ARE YOU READY?
C'MON, BABY, IT'S SHOWTIME.
KRAK
DUTY CALLS, PADRE!
W-WE HAVE NO MONEY!
YOU GOT ME ALL WRONG. ONE MORE CEREMONY TO PERFORM TONIGHT.

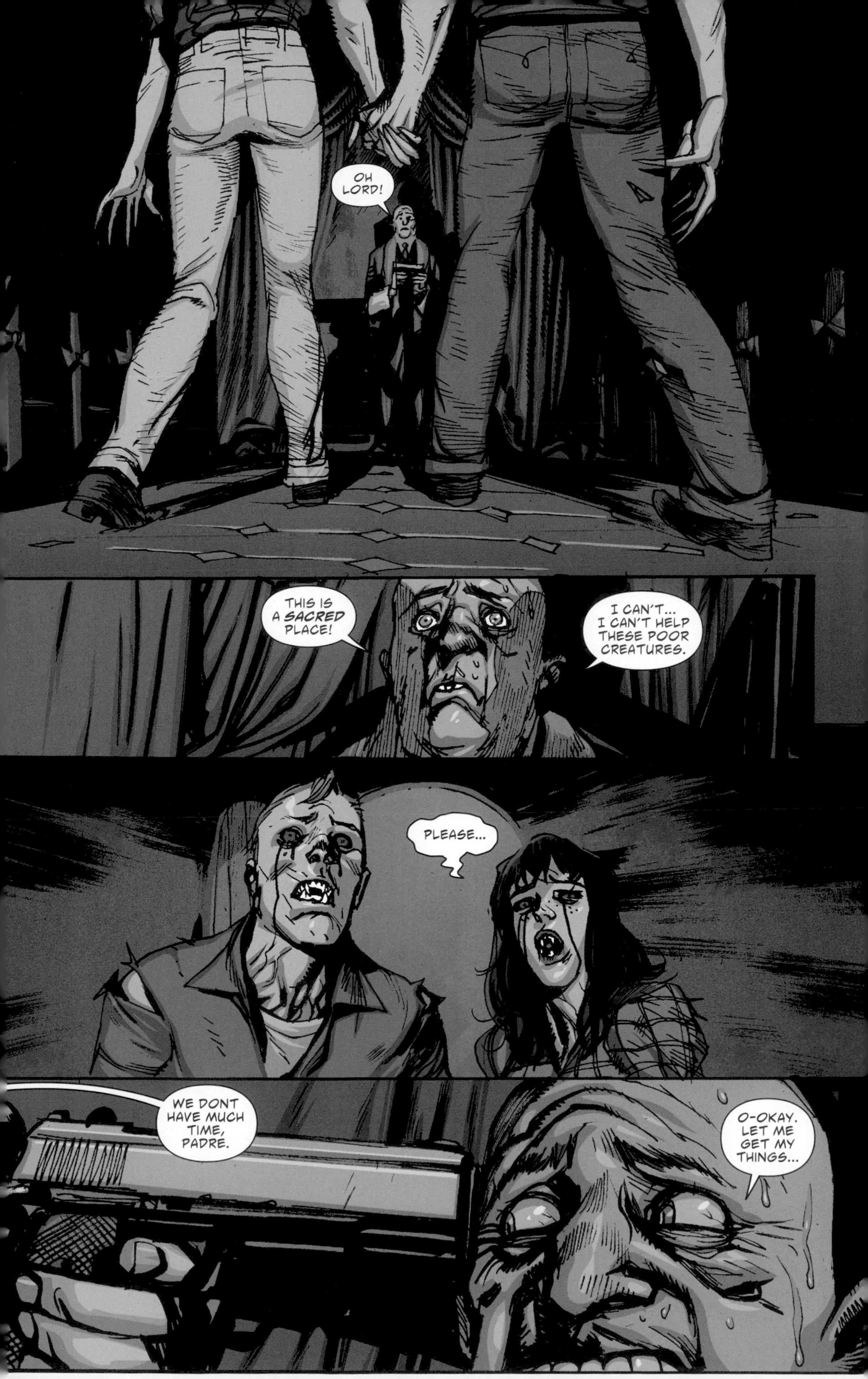
OH LORD!
THIS IS A SACRED PLACE!
I CAN'T... I CAN'T HELP THESE POOR CREATURES.
PLEASE...
WE DONT HAVE MUCH TIME, PADRE.
O-OKAY. LET ME GET MY THINGS...

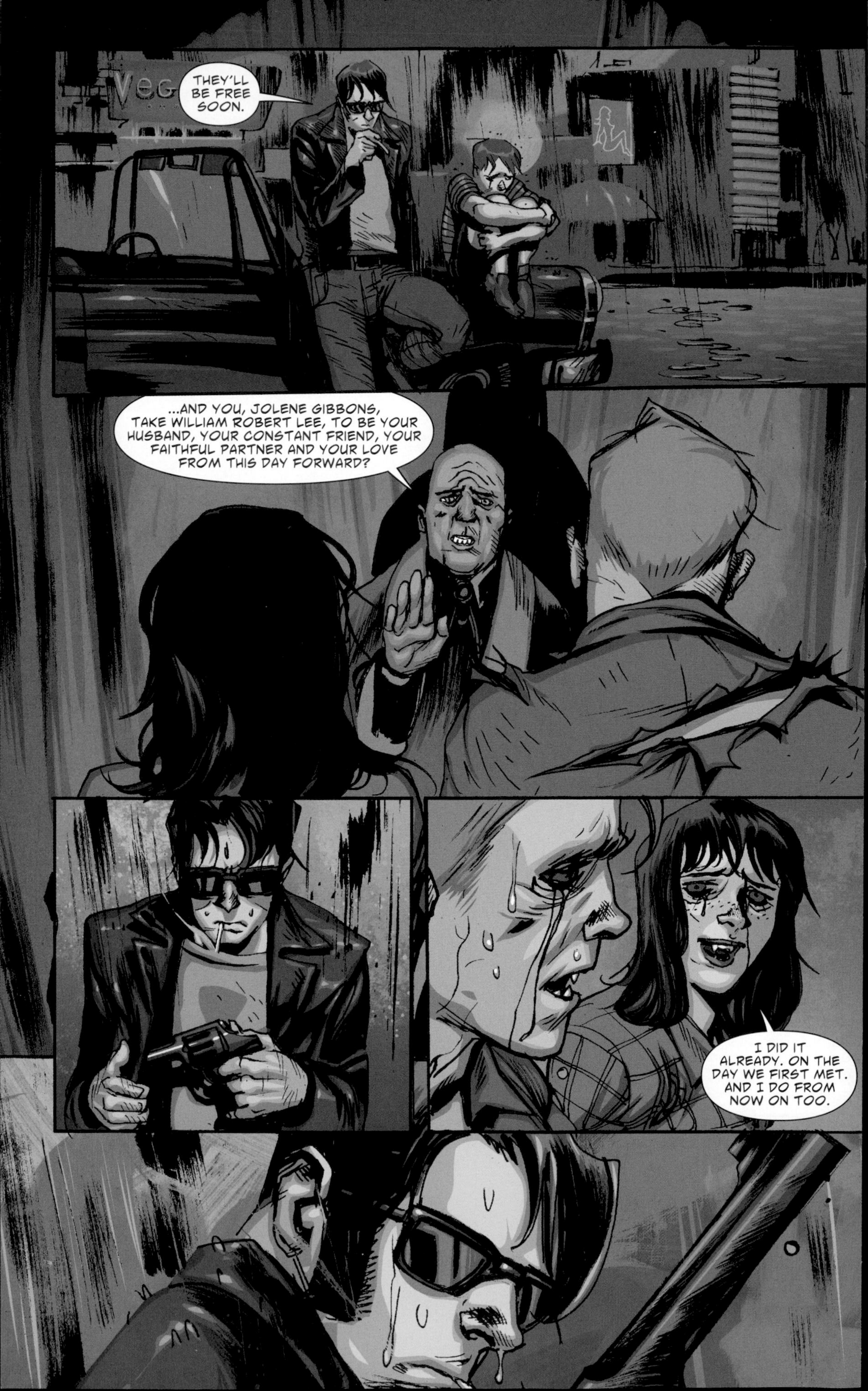
THEY'LL BE FREE SOON.
...AND YOU, JOLENE GIBBONS, TAKE WILLIAM ROBERT LEE, TO BE YOUR HUSBAND, YOUR CONSTANT FRIEND, YOUR FAITHFUL PARTNER AND YOUR LOVE FROM THIS DAY FORWARD?
I DID IT ALREADY. ON THE DAY WE FIRST MET. AND I DO FROM NOW ON TOO.

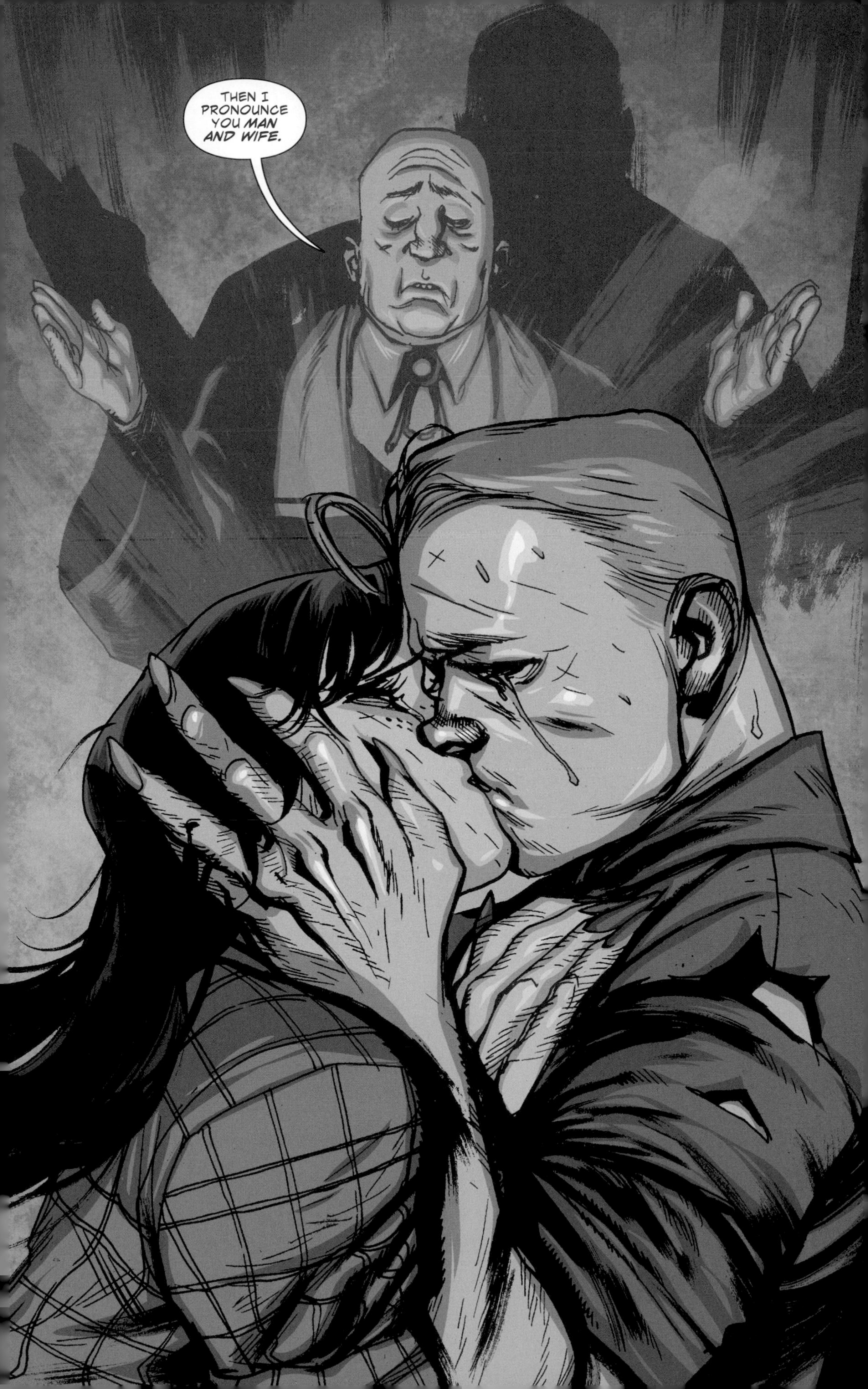
THEN I PRONOUNCE YOU *MAN AND WIFE.*

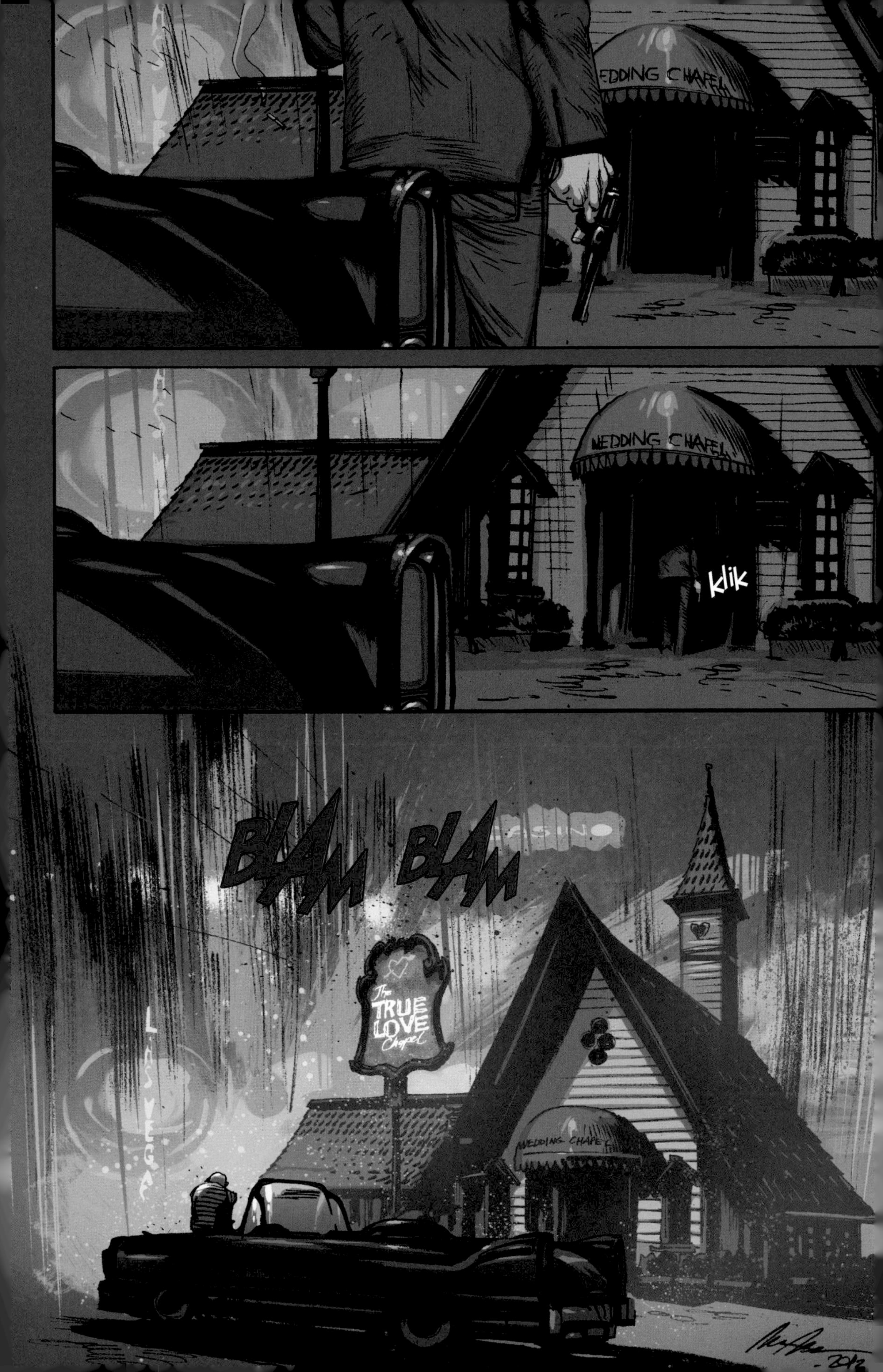
EDDING CHAPEL
klik
BLAM BLAM
The TRUE LOVE Chapel
WEDDING CHAPEL

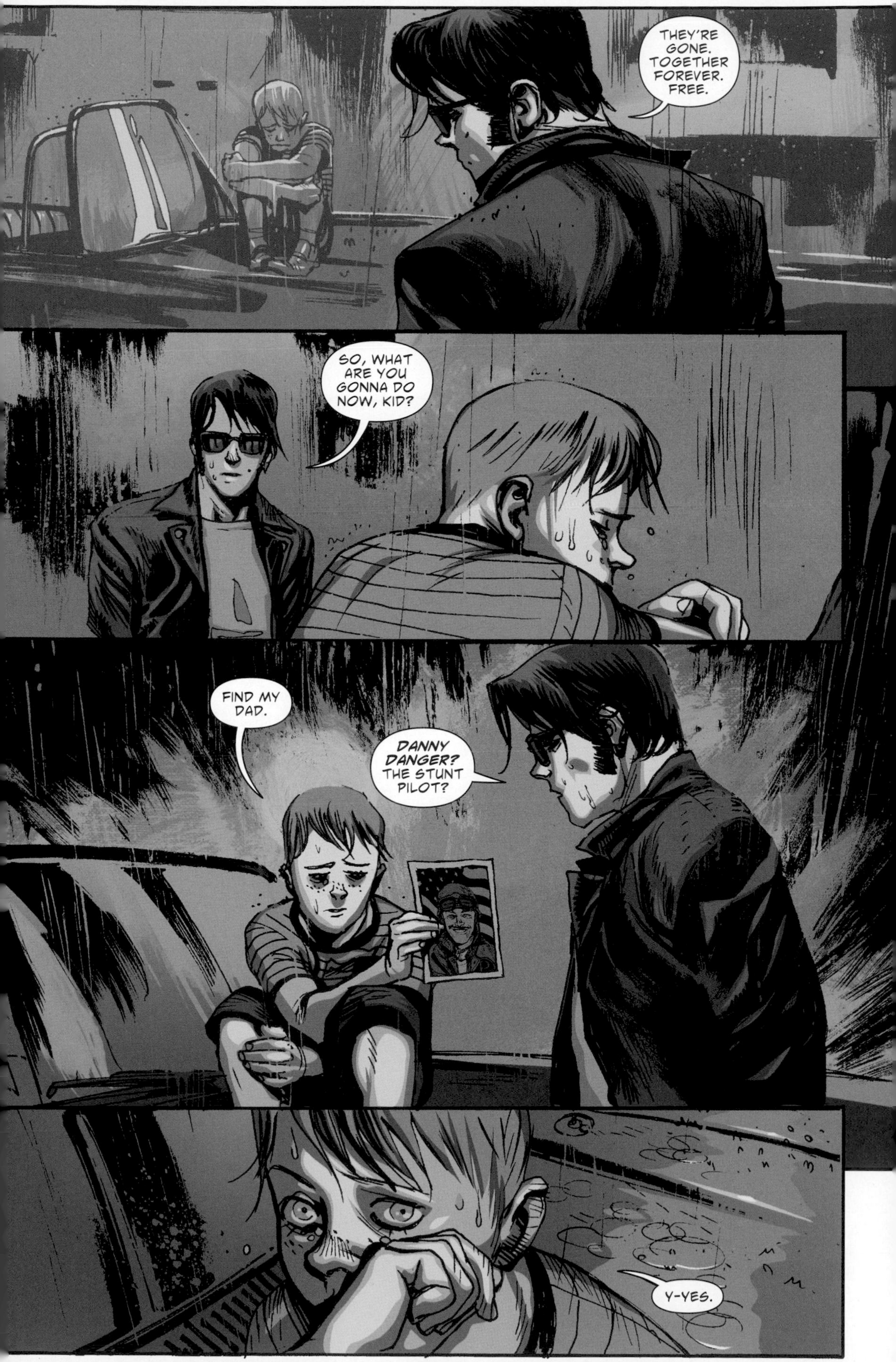
THEY'RE GONE. TOGETHER FOREVER. FREE.
SO, WHAT ARE YOU GONNA DO NOW, KID?
FIND MY DAD.
DANNY DANGER? THE STUNT PILOT?
Y-YES.

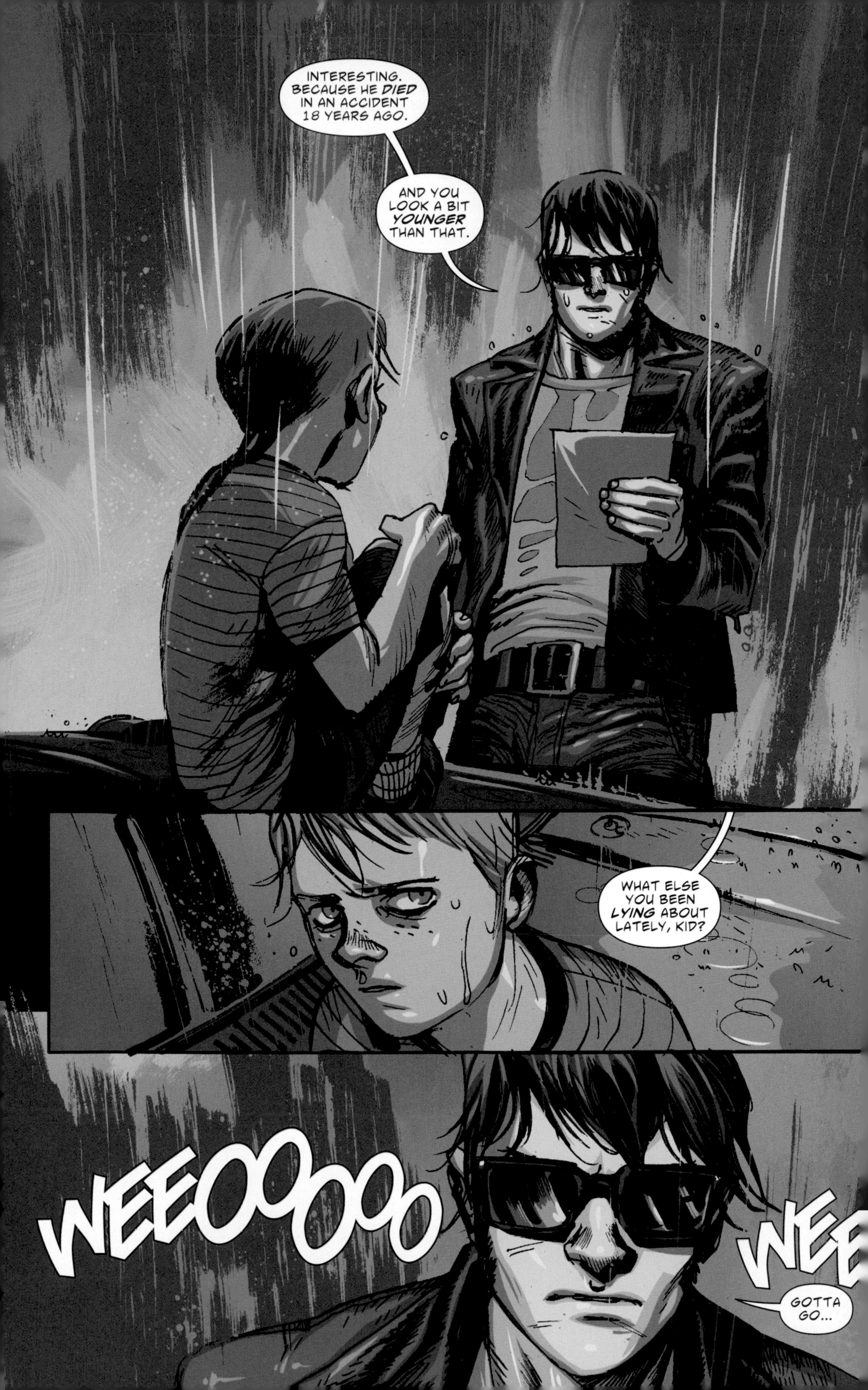
INTERESTING. BECAUSE HE DIED IN AN ACCIDENT 18 YEARS AGO.
AND YOU LOOK A BIT YOUNGER THAN THAT.
WHAT ELSE YOU BEEN LYING ABOUT LATELY, KID?
WEEOOOOO
WEE
GOTTA GO...

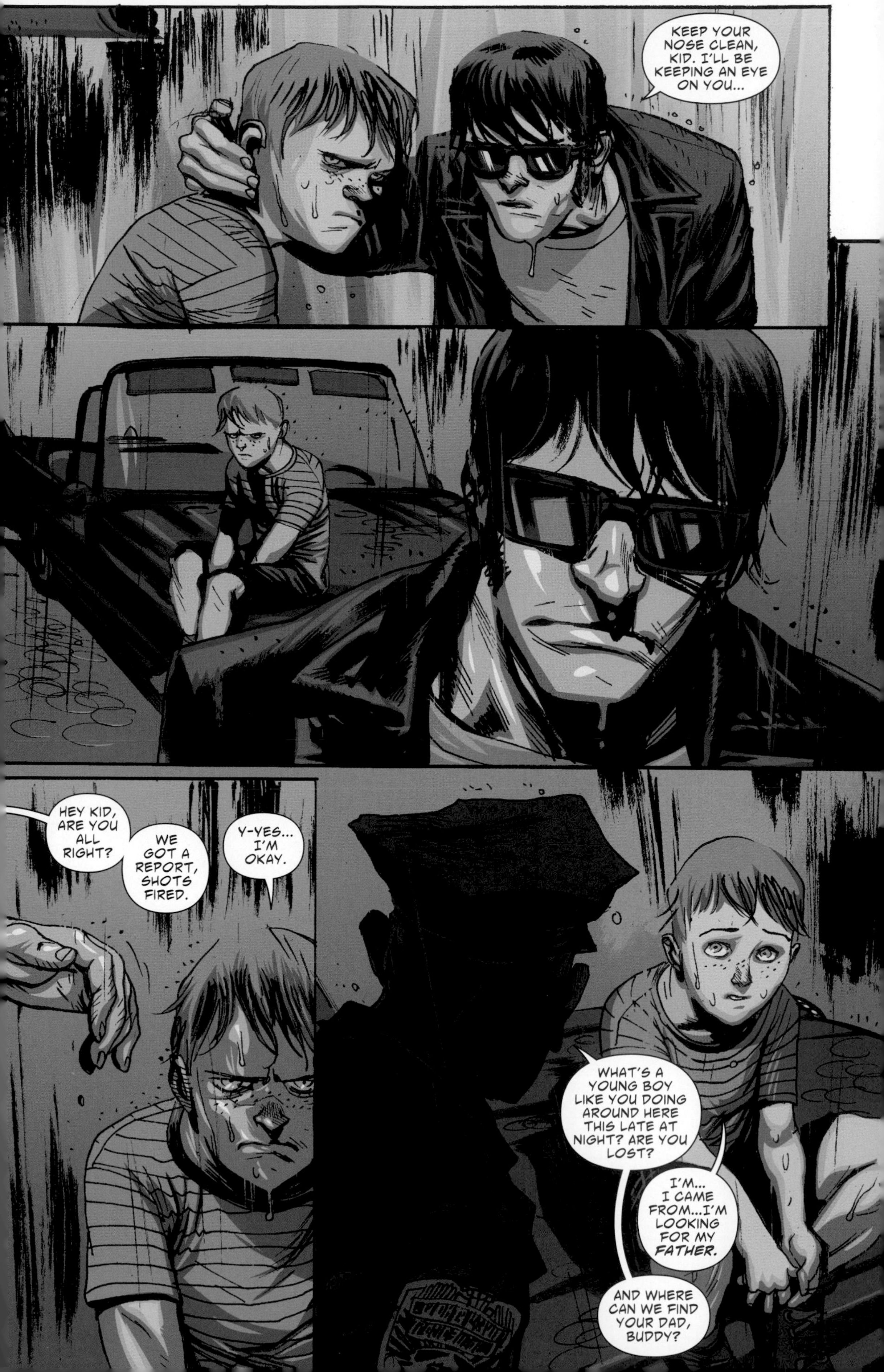
KEEP YOUR NOSE CLEAN, KID. I'LL BE KEEPING AN EYE ON YOU...
HEY KID, ARE YOU ALL RIGHT?
WE GOT A REPORT, SHOTS FIRED.
Y-YES... I'M OKAY.
WHAT'S A YOUNG BOY LIKE YOU DOING AROUND HERE THIS LATE AT NIGHT? ARE YOU LOST?
I'M... I CAME FROM...I'M LOOKING FOR MY *FATHER.*
AND WHERE CAN WE FIND YOUR DAD, BUDDY?

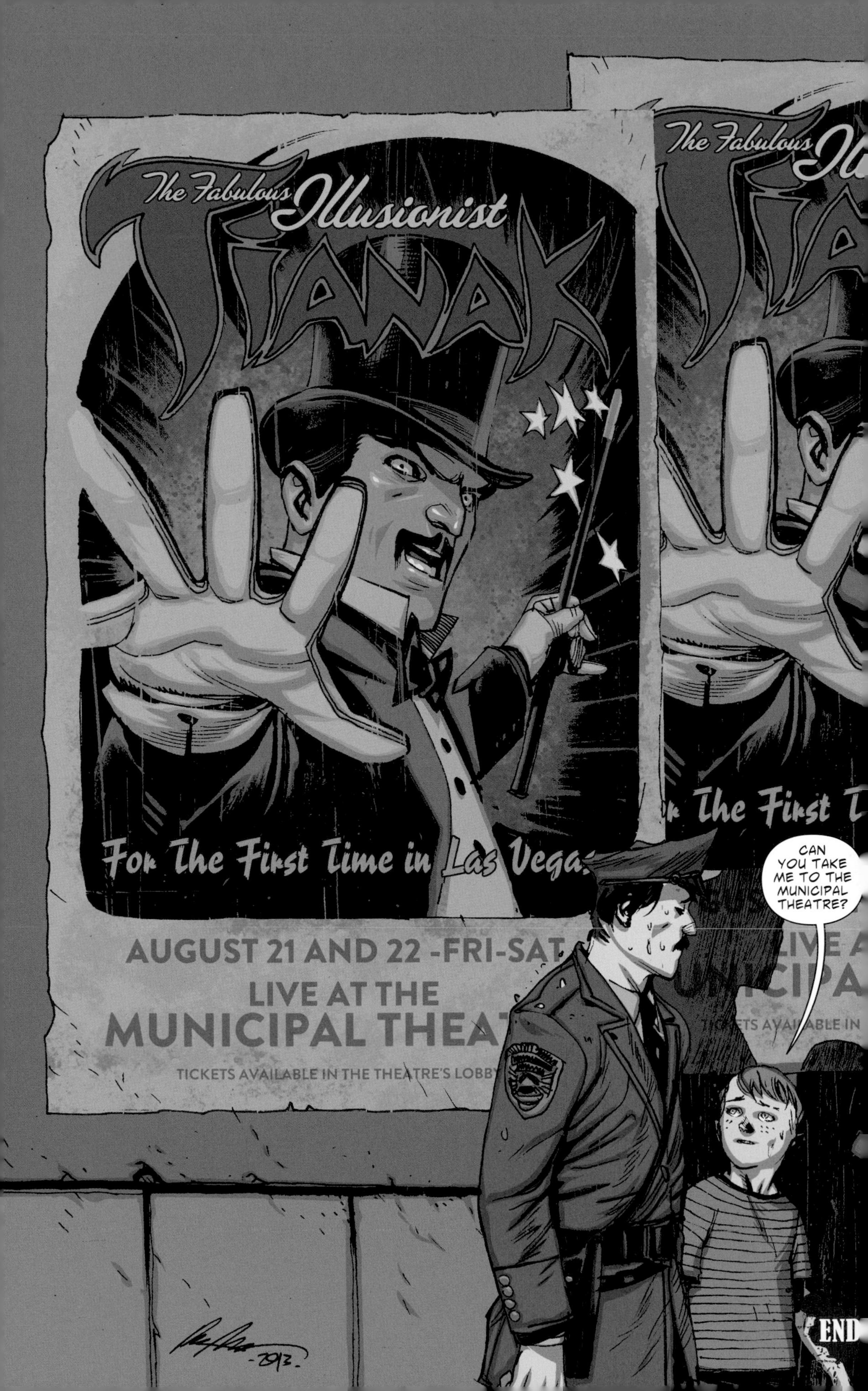
The Fabulous Illusionist
ZANAX
For The First Time in Las Vegas
AUGUST 21 AND 22 -FRI-SAT
LIVE AT THE
MUNICIPAL THEAT
TICKETS AVAILABLE IN THE THEATRE'S LOBBY
CAN YOU TAKE ME TO THE MUNICIPAL THEATRE?
END

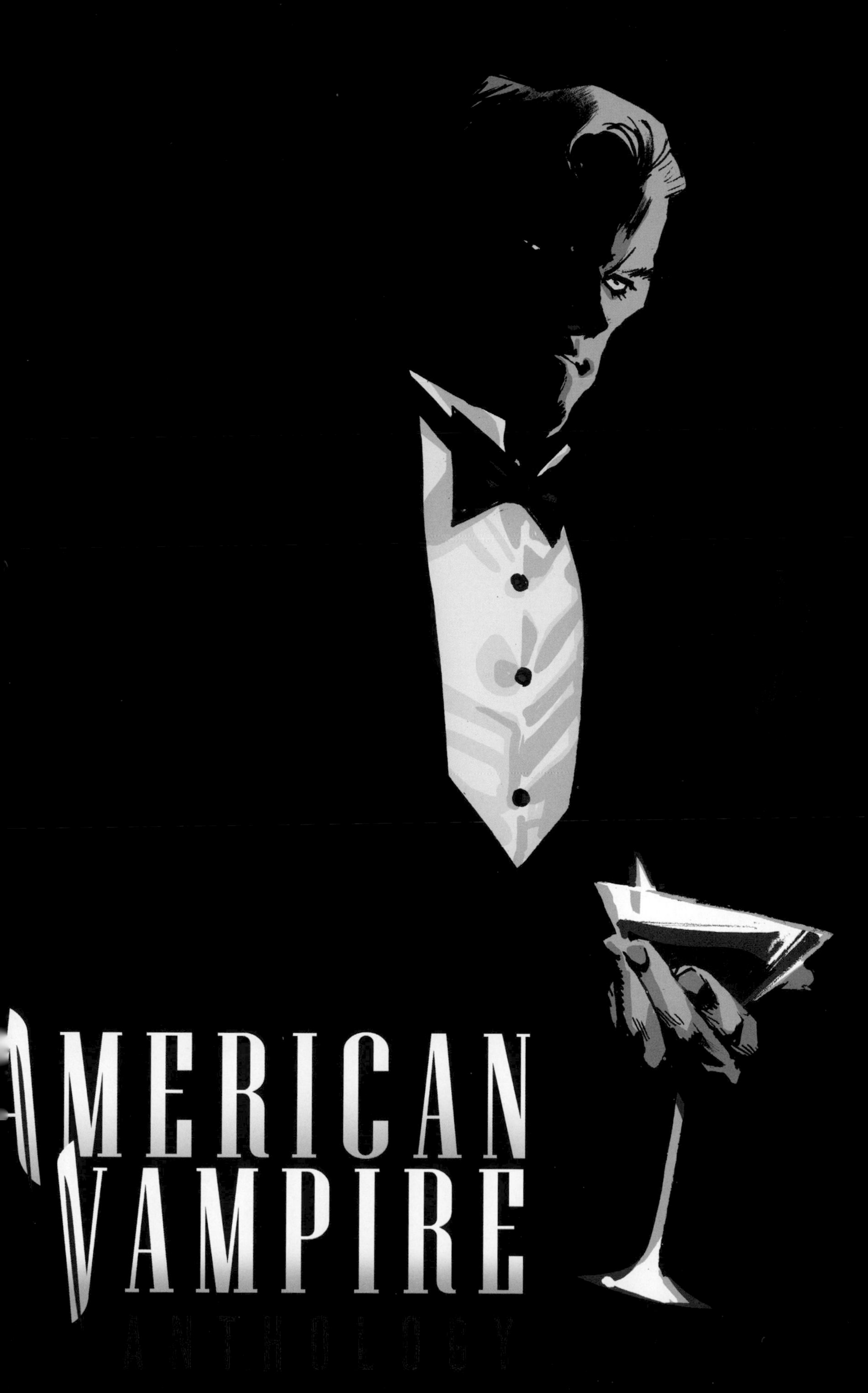
AMERICAN
VAMPIRE
ANTHOLOGY

AMERICAN VAMPIRE ANTHOLOGY

THE MAN COMES AROUND PART 1

Scott Snyder
Writer

Rafael Albuquerque
Artist

LOST COLONY

Jason Aaron
Writer

Declan Shalvey
Artist

BLEEDING KANSAS

Rafael Albuquerque
Writer

Ivo Milazzo
Artist

CANADIAN VAMPIRE

Jeff Lemire
Writer

Ray Fawkes
Artist

GREED

Becky Cloonan
Writer & Artist

THE PRODUCERS

Francesco Francavilla
Writer & Artist

ESSENCE OF LIFE

Gail Simone
Writer

Tula Lotay
Artist

LAST NIGHT

Gabriel Bá & Fábio Moon
Writers & Artists

PORTLAND, 1940

Greg Rucka
Writer

JP Leon
Artist

THE MAN COMES AROUND PART 2

Scott Snyder
Writer

Rafael Albuquerque
Artist

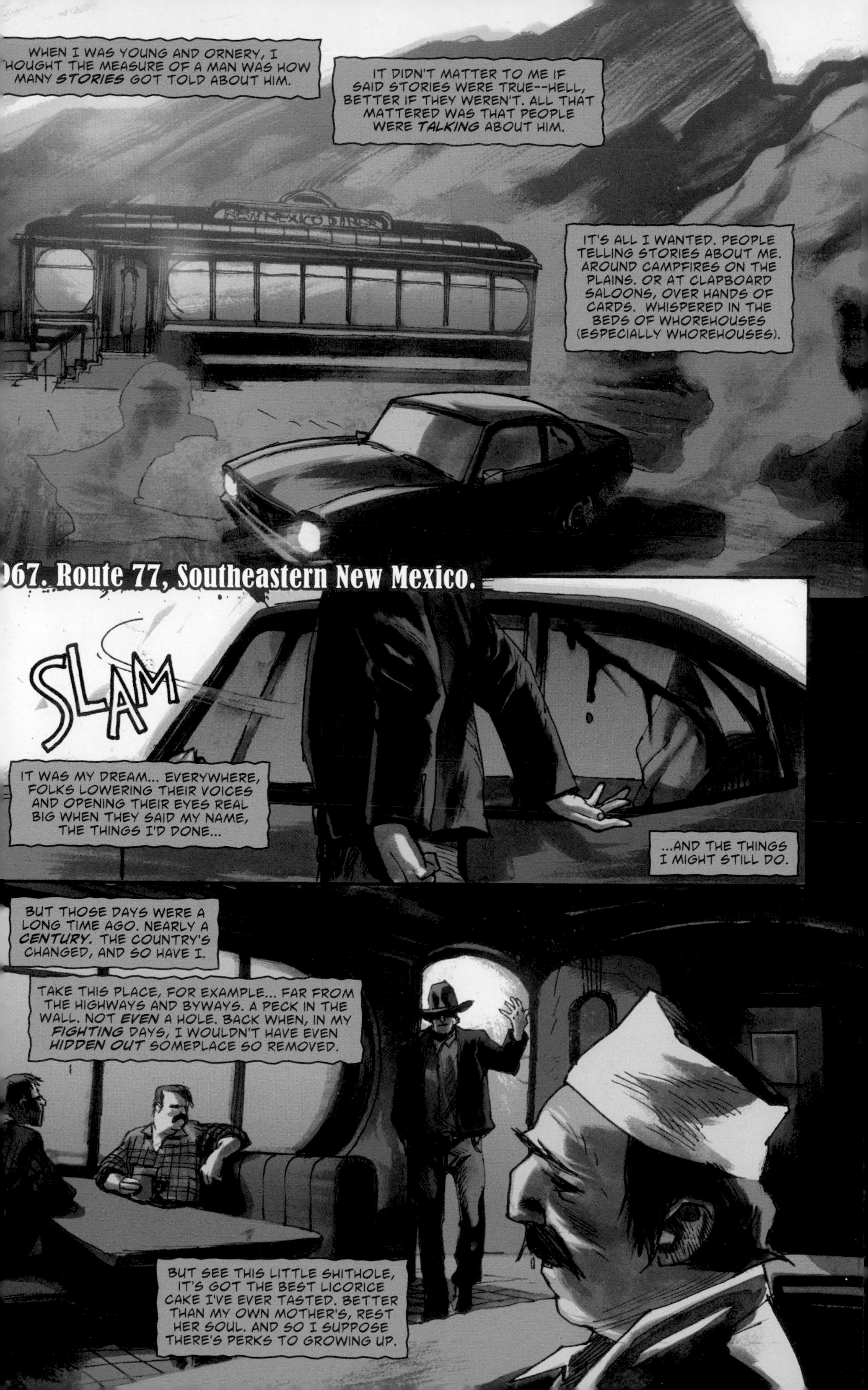
WHEN I WAS YOUNG AND ORNERY, I THOUGHT THE MEASURE OF A MAN WAS HOW MANY STORIES GOT TOLD ABOUT HIM.
IT DIDN'T MATTER TO ME IF SAID STORIES WERE TRUE--HELL, BETTER IF THEY WEREN'T. ALL THAT MATTERED WAS THAT PEOPLE WERE TALKING ABOUT HIM.
IT'S ALL I WANTED. PEOPLE TELLING STORIES ABOUT ME. AROUND CAMPFIRES ON THE PLAINS. OR AT CLAPBOARD SALOONS, OVER HANDS OF CARDS. WHISPERED IN THE BEDS OF WHOREHOUSES (ESPECIALLY WHOREHOUSES).
967. Route 77, Southeastern New Mexico.
SLAM
IT WAS MY DREAM... EVERYWHERE, FOLKS LOWERING THEIR VOICES AND OPENING THEIR EYES REAL BIG WHEN THEY SAID MY NAME, THE THINGS I'D DONE...
...AND THE THINGS I MIGHT STILL DO.
BUT THOSE DAYS WERE A LONG TIME AGO. NEARLY A CENTURY. THE COUNTRY'S CHANGED, AND SO HAVE I.
TAKE THIS PLACE, FOR EXAMPLE... FAR FROM THE HIGHWAYS AND BYWAYS. A PECK IN THE WALL. NOT EVEN A HOLE. BACK WHEN, IN MY FIGHTING DAYS, I WOULDN'T HAVE EVEN HIDDEN OUT SOMEPLACE SO REMOVED.
BUT SEE THIS LITTLE SHITHOLE, IT'S GOT THE BEST LICORICE CAKE I'VE EVER TASTED. BETTER THAN MY OWN MOTHER'S, REST HER SOUL. AND SO I SUPPOSE THERE'S PERKS TO GROWING UP.

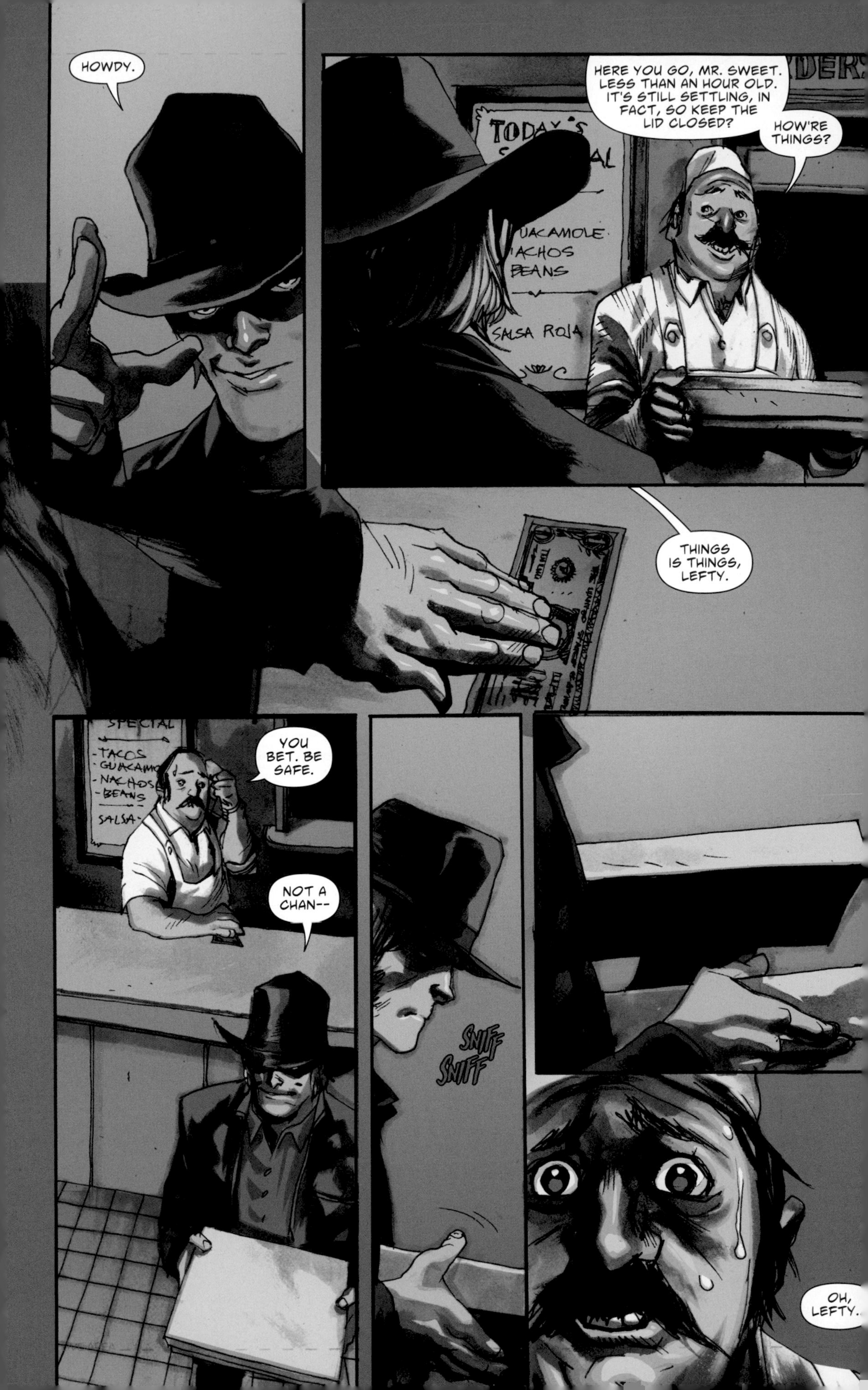
HOWDY.
HERE YOU GO, MR. SWEET. LESS THAN AN HOUR OLD. IT'S STILL SETTLING, IN FACT, SO KEEP THE LID CLOSED?
HOW'RE THINGS?
THINGS IS THINGS, LEFTY.
YOU BET. BE SAFE.
NOT A CHAN--
SNIFF SNIFF
OH, LEFTY.

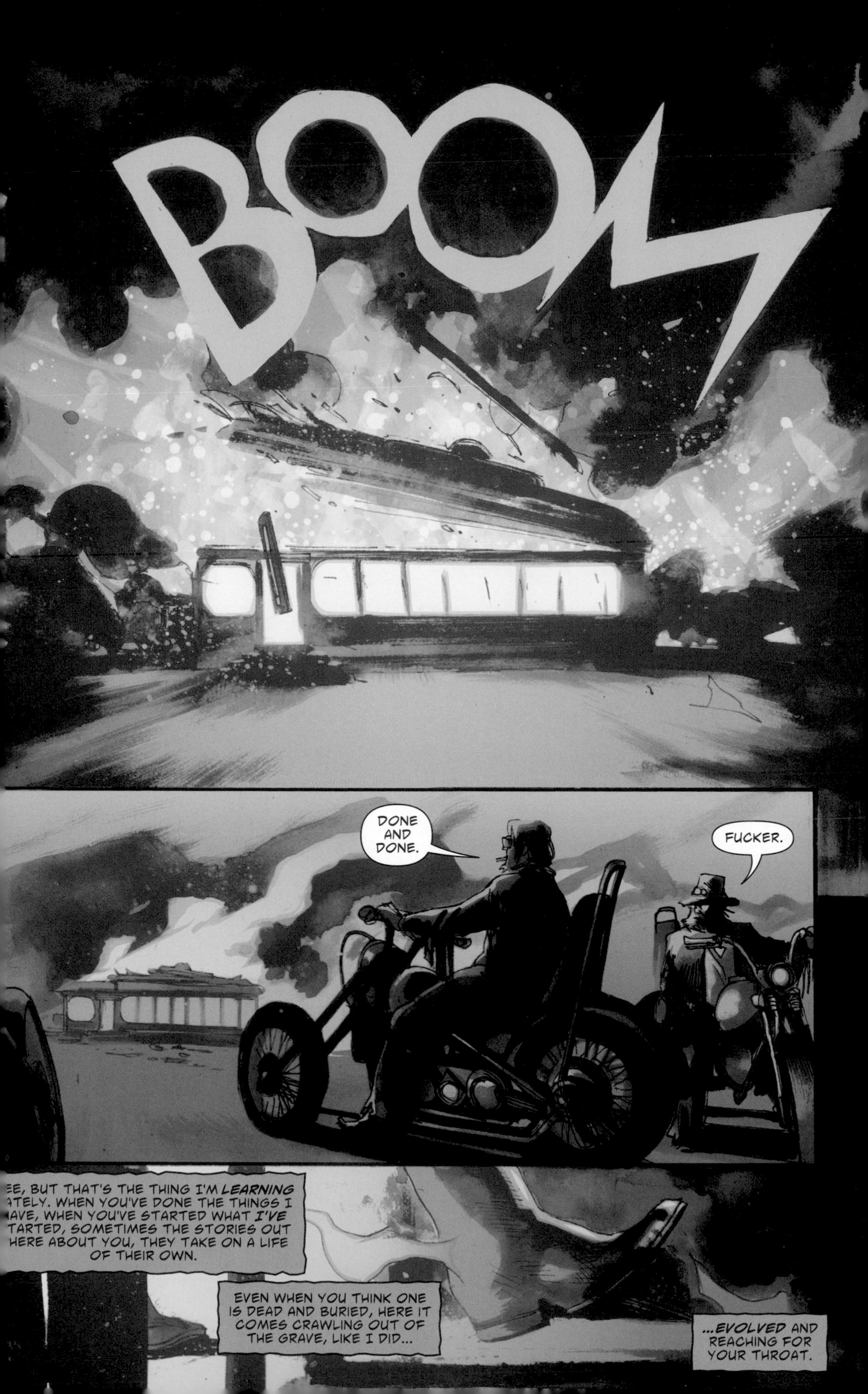
BOOM
DONE AND DONE.
FUCKER.
EE, BUT THAT'S THE THING I'M LEARNING ATELY. WHEN YOU'VE DONE THE THINGS I AVE, WHEN YOU'VE STARTED WHAT I'VE TARTED, SOMETIMES THE STORIES OUT HERE ABOUT YOU, THEY TAKE ON A LIFE OF THEIR OWN.
EVEN WHEN YOU THINK ONE IS DEAD AND BURIED, HERE IT COMES CRAWLING OUT OF THE GRAVE, LIKE I DID...
...EVOLVED AND REACHING FOR YOUR THROAT.

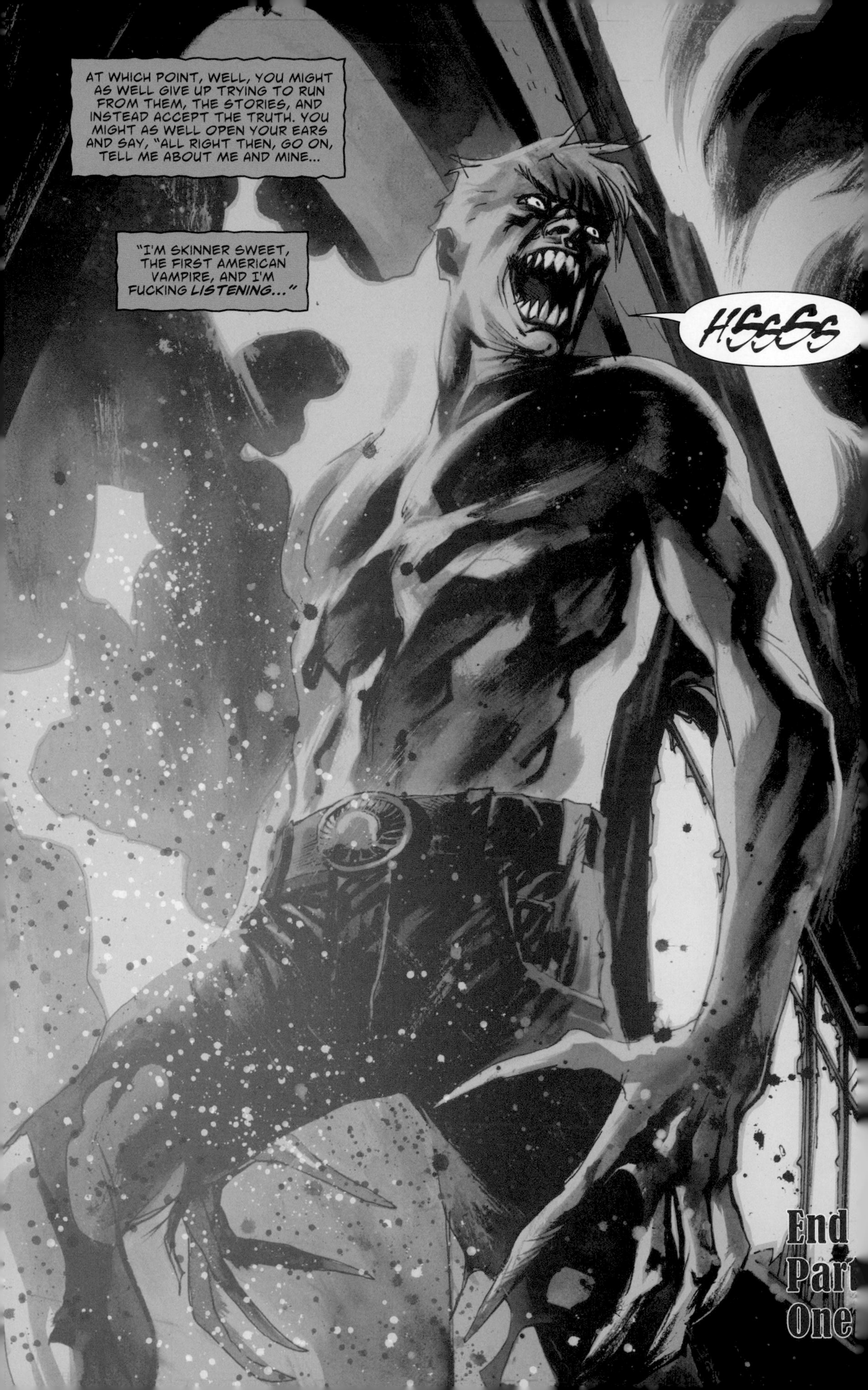
AT WHICH POINT, WELL, YOU MIGHT AS WELL GIVE UP TRYING TO RUN FROM THEM, THE STORIES, AND INSTEAD ACCEPT THE TRUTH. YOU MIGHT AS WELL OPEN YOUR EARS AND SAY, "ALL RIGHT THEN, GO ON, TELL ME ABOUT ME AND MINE...
"I'M SKINNER SWEET, THE FIRST AMERICAN VAMPIRE, AND I'M FUCKING *LISTENING...*"
HSSSS
End Part One

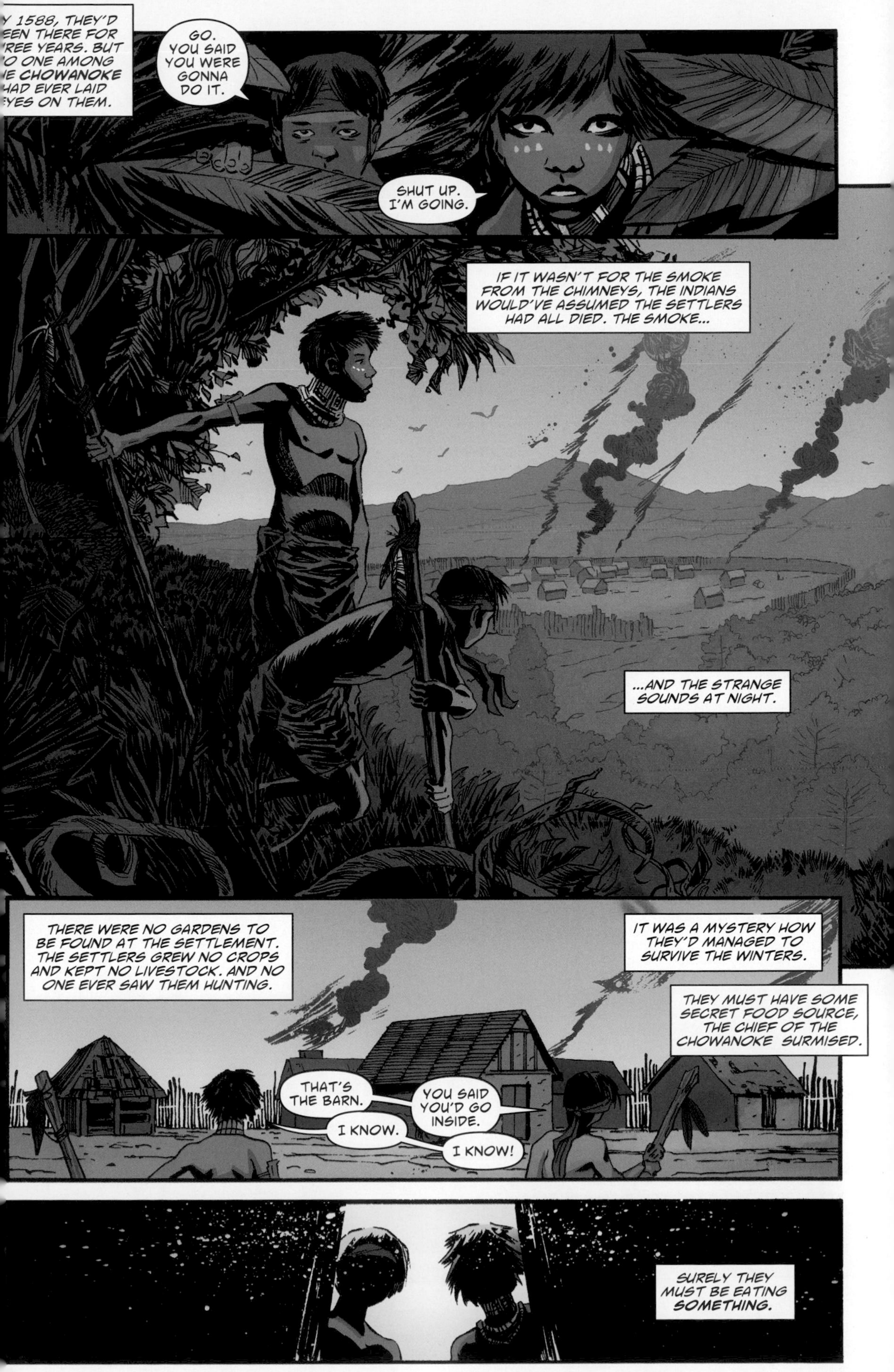
Y 1588, THEY'D
EEEN THERE FOR
HREE YEARS. BUT
O ONE AMONG
HE CHOWANOKE
HAD EVER LAID
EYES ON THEM.
GO. YOU SAID YOU WERE GONNA DO IT.
SHUT UP. I'M GOING.
IF IT WASN'T FOR THE SMOKE FROM THE CHIMNEYS, THE INDIANS WOULD'VE ASSUMED THE SETTLERS HAD ALL DIED. THE SMOKE...
...AND THE STRANGE SOUNDS AT NIGHT.
THERE WERE NO GARDENS TO BE FOUND AT THE SETTLEMENT. THE SETTLERS GREW NO CROPS AND KEPT NO LIVESTOCK. AND NO ONE EVER SAW THEM HUNTING.
IT WAS A MYSTERY HOW THEY'D MANAGED TO SURVIVE THE WINTERS.
THEY MUST HAVE SOME SECRET FOOD SOURCE, THE CHIEF OF THE CHOWANOKE SURMISED.
THAT'S THE BARN.
YOU SAID YOU'D GO INSIDE.
I KNOW.
I KNOW!
SURELY THEY MUST BE EATING SOMETHING.

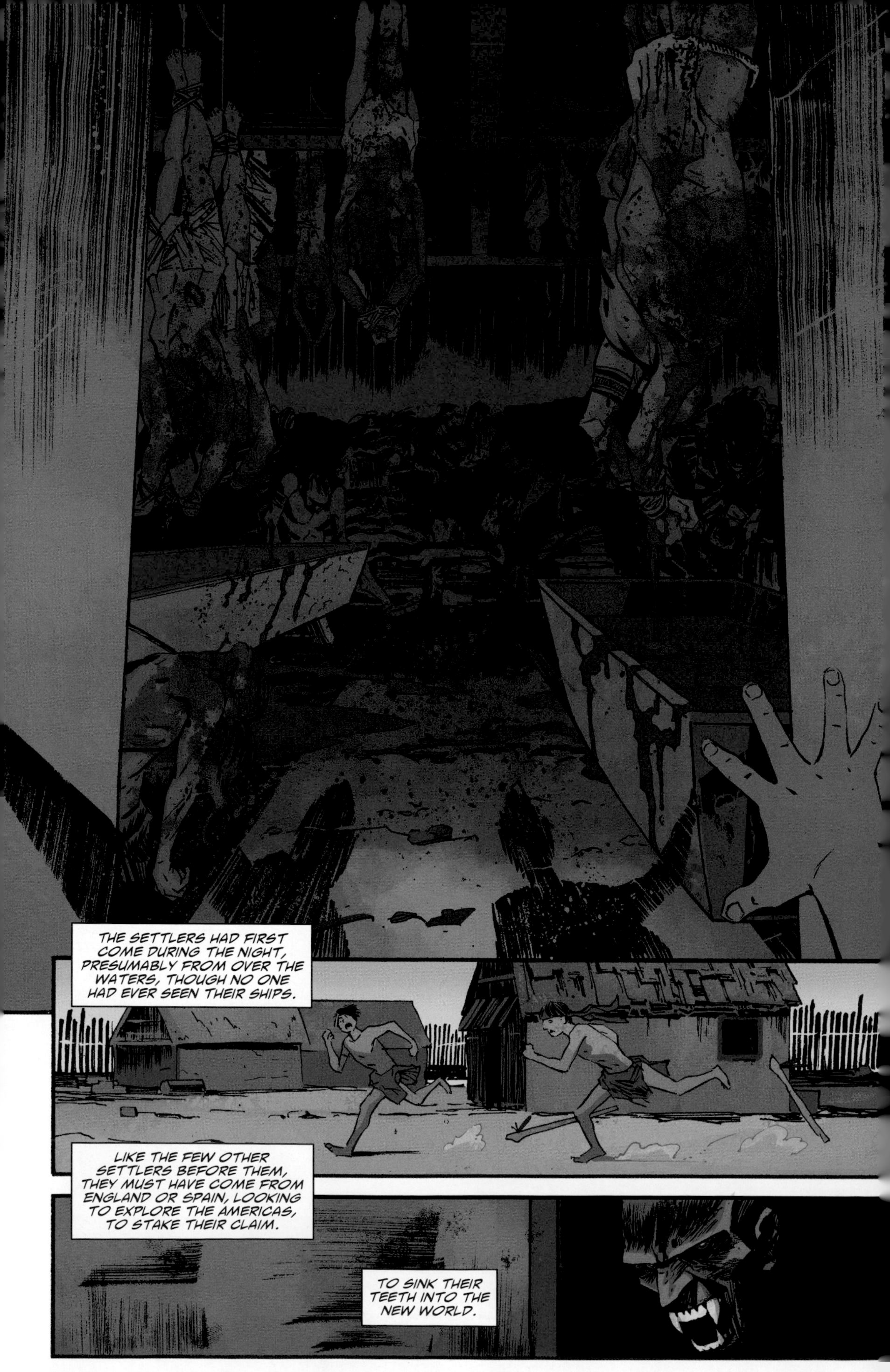
THE SETTLERS HAD FIRST COME DURING THE NIGHT, PRESUMABLY FROM OVER THE WATERS, THOUGH NO ONE HAD EVER SEEN THEIR SHIPS.
LIKE THE FEW OTHER SETTLERS BEFORE THEM, THEY MUST HAVE COME FROM ENGLAND OR SPAIN, LOOKING TO EXPLORE THE AMERICAS, TO STAKE THEIR CLAIM.
TO SINK THEIR TEETH INTO THE NEW WORLD.

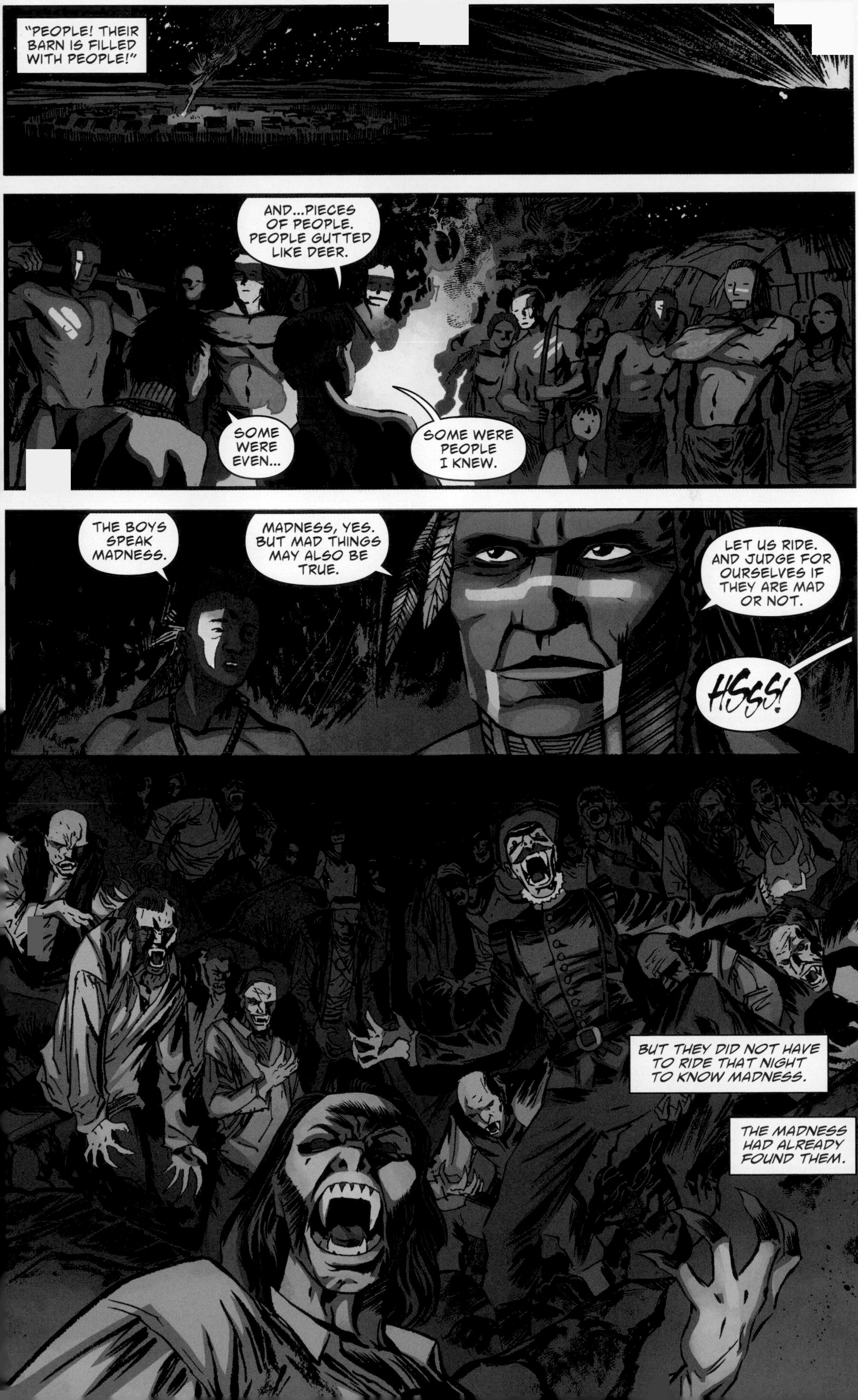
"PEOPLE! THEIR BARN IS FILLED WITH PEOPLE!"
AND...PIECES OF PEOPLE. PEOPLE GUTTED LIKE DEER.
SOME WERE EVEN...
SOME WERE PEOPLE I KNEW.
THE BOYS SPEAK MADNESS.
MADNESS, YES. BUT MAD THINGS MAY ALSO BE TRUE.
LET US RIDE. AND JUDGE FOR OURSELVES IF THEY ARE MAD OR NOT.
HSSS!
BUT THEY DID NOT HAVE TO RIDE THAT NIGHT TO KNOW MADNESS.
THE MADNESS HAD ALREADY FOUND THEM.

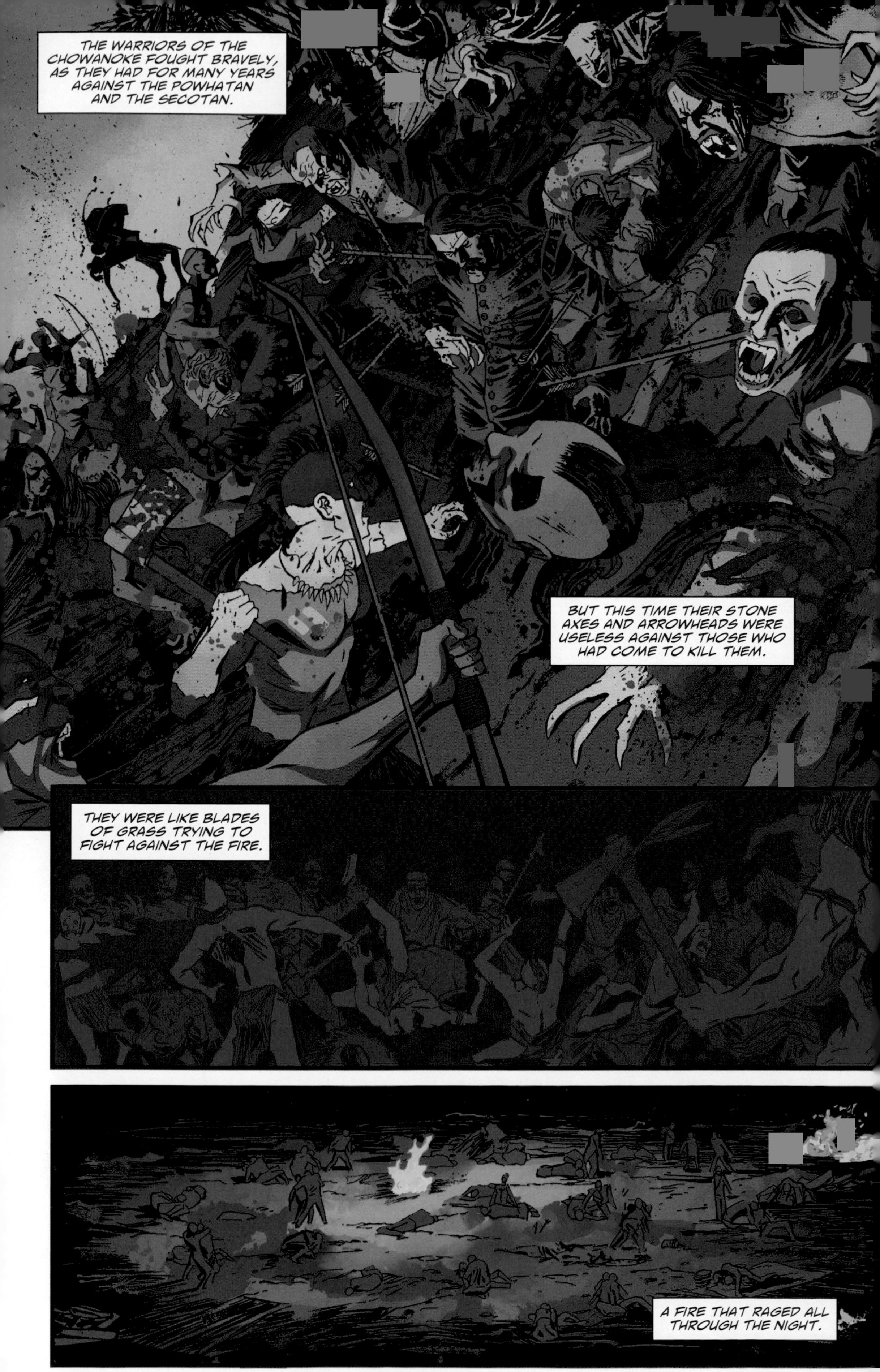
THE WARRIORS OF THE CHOWANOKE FOUGHT BRAVELY, AS THEY HAD FOR MANY YEARS AGAINST THE POWHATAN AND THE SECOTAN.
BUT THIS TIME THEIR STONE AXES AND ARROWHEADS WERE USELESS AGAINST THOSE WHO HAD COME TO KILL THEM.
THEY WERE LIKE BLADES OF GRASS TRYING TO FIGHT AGAINST THE FIRE.
A FIRE THAT RAGED ALL THROUGH THE NIGHT.

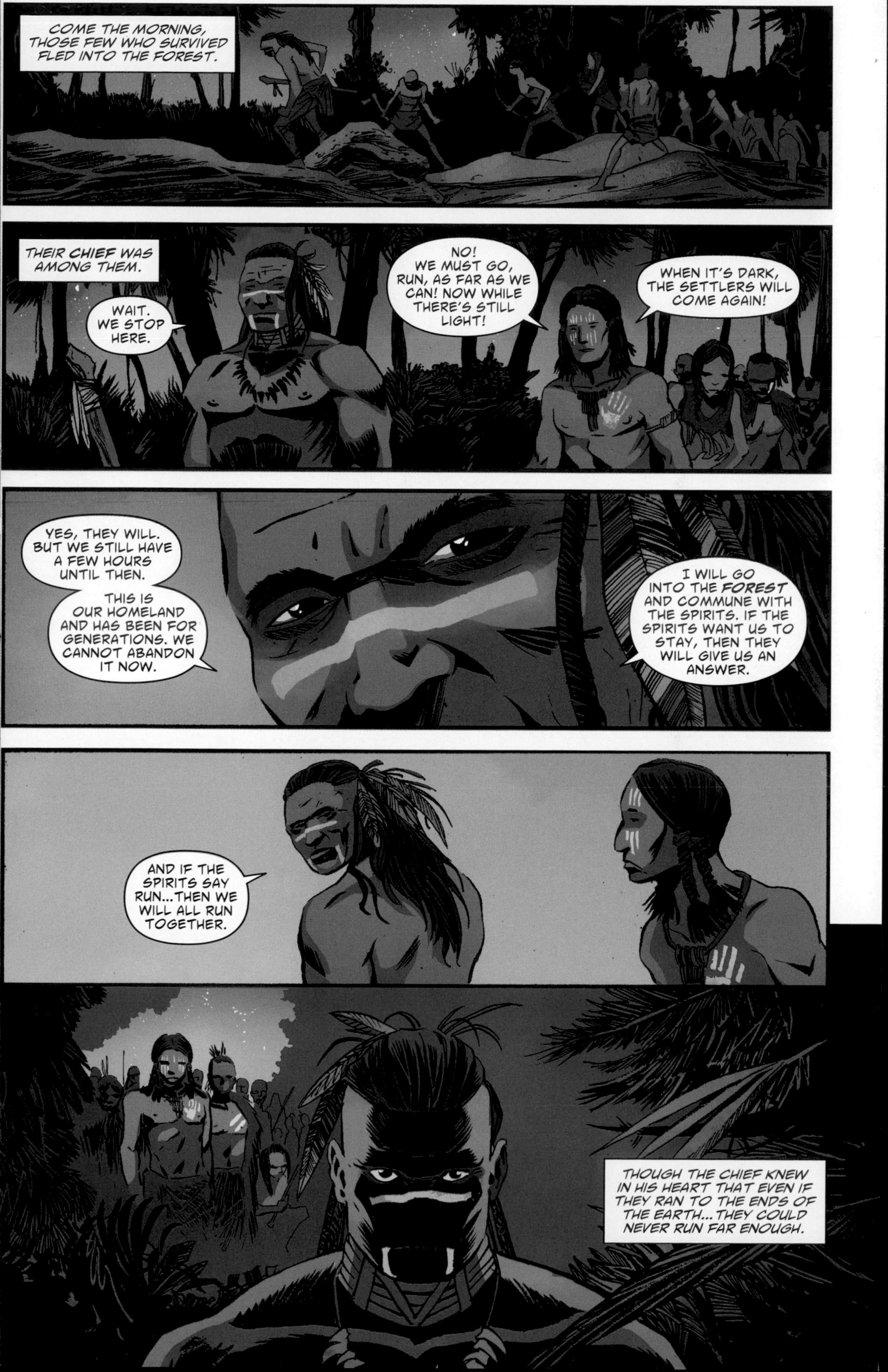
COME THE MORNING, THOSE FEW WHO SURVIVED FLED INTO THE FOREST.
THEIR CHIEF WAS AMONG THEM.
WAIT. WE STOP HERE.
NO! WE MUST GO, RUN, AS FAR AS WE CAN! NOW WHILE THERE'S STILL LIGHT!
WHEN IT'S DARK, THE SETTLERS WILL COME AGAIN!
YES, THEY WILL. BUT WE STILL HAVE A FEW HOURS UNTIL THEN.
THIS IS OUR HOMELAND AND HAS BEEN FOR GENERATIONS. WE CANNOT ABANDON IT NOW.
I WILL GO INTO THE FOREST AND COMMUNE WITH THE SPIRITS. IF THE SPIRITS WANT US TO STAY, THEN THEY WILL GIVE US AN ANSWER.
AND IF THE SPIRITS SAY RUN...THEN WE WILL ALL RUN TOGETHER.
THOUGH THE CHIEF KNEW IN HIS HEART THAT EVEN IF THEY RAN TO THE ENDS OF THE EARTH...THEY COULD NEVER RUN FAR ENOUGH.

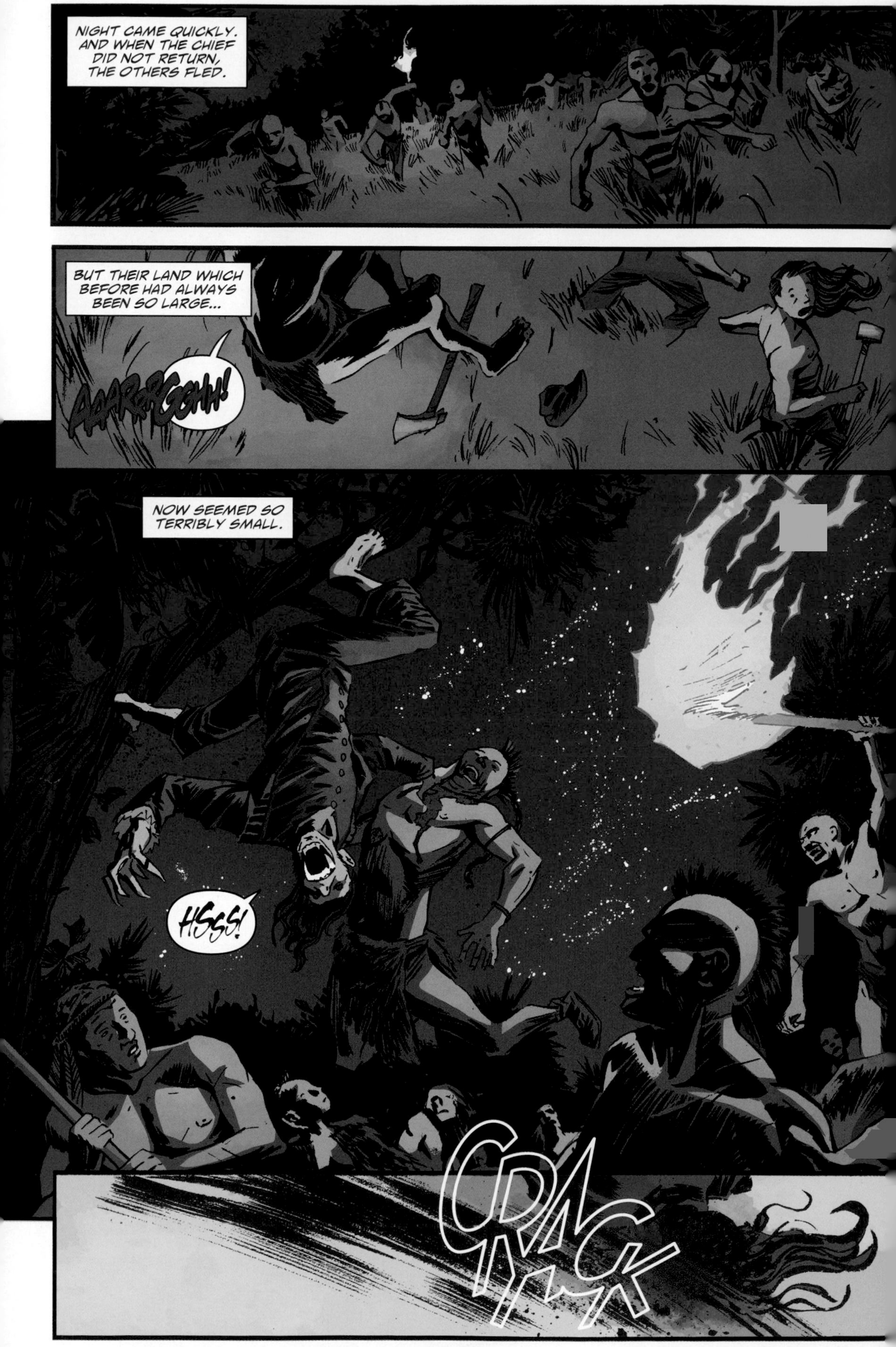
NIGHT CAME QUICKLY. AND WHEN THE CHIEF DID NOT RETURN, THE OTHERS FLED.
BUT THEIR LAND WHICH BEFORE HAD ALWAYS BEEN SO LARGE...
AAARRRGGHH!
NOW SEEMED SO TERRIBLY SMALL.
HSSS!
CRACK

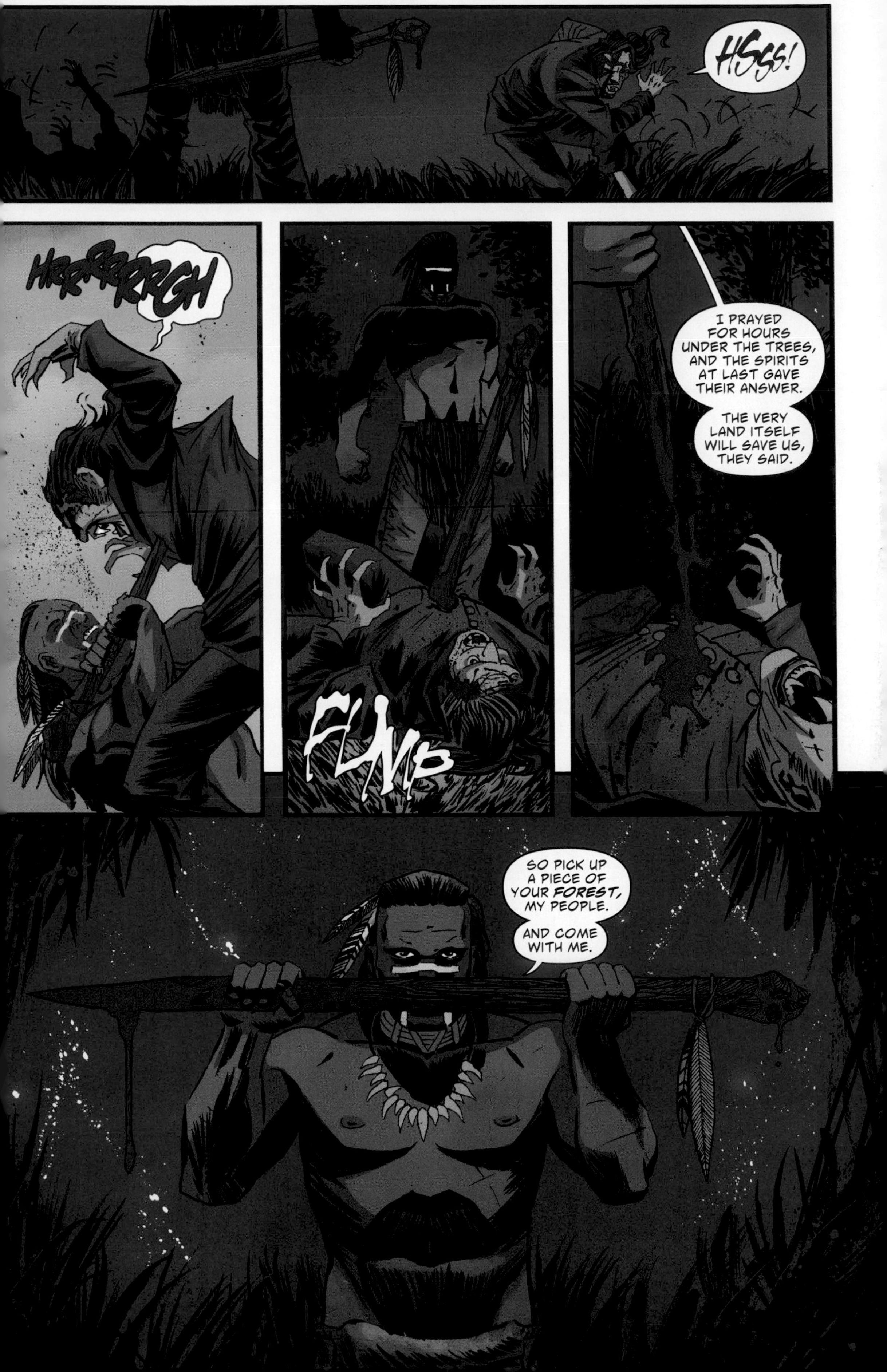
HSSS!
HRRRRRRRGH
FLMP
I PRAYED FOR HOURS UNDER THE TREES, AND THE SPIRITS AT LAST GAVE THEIR ANSWER.
THE VERY LAND ITSELF WILL SAVE US, THEY SAID.
SO PICK UP A PIECE OF YOUR *FOREST*, MY PEOPLE.
AND COME WITH ME.

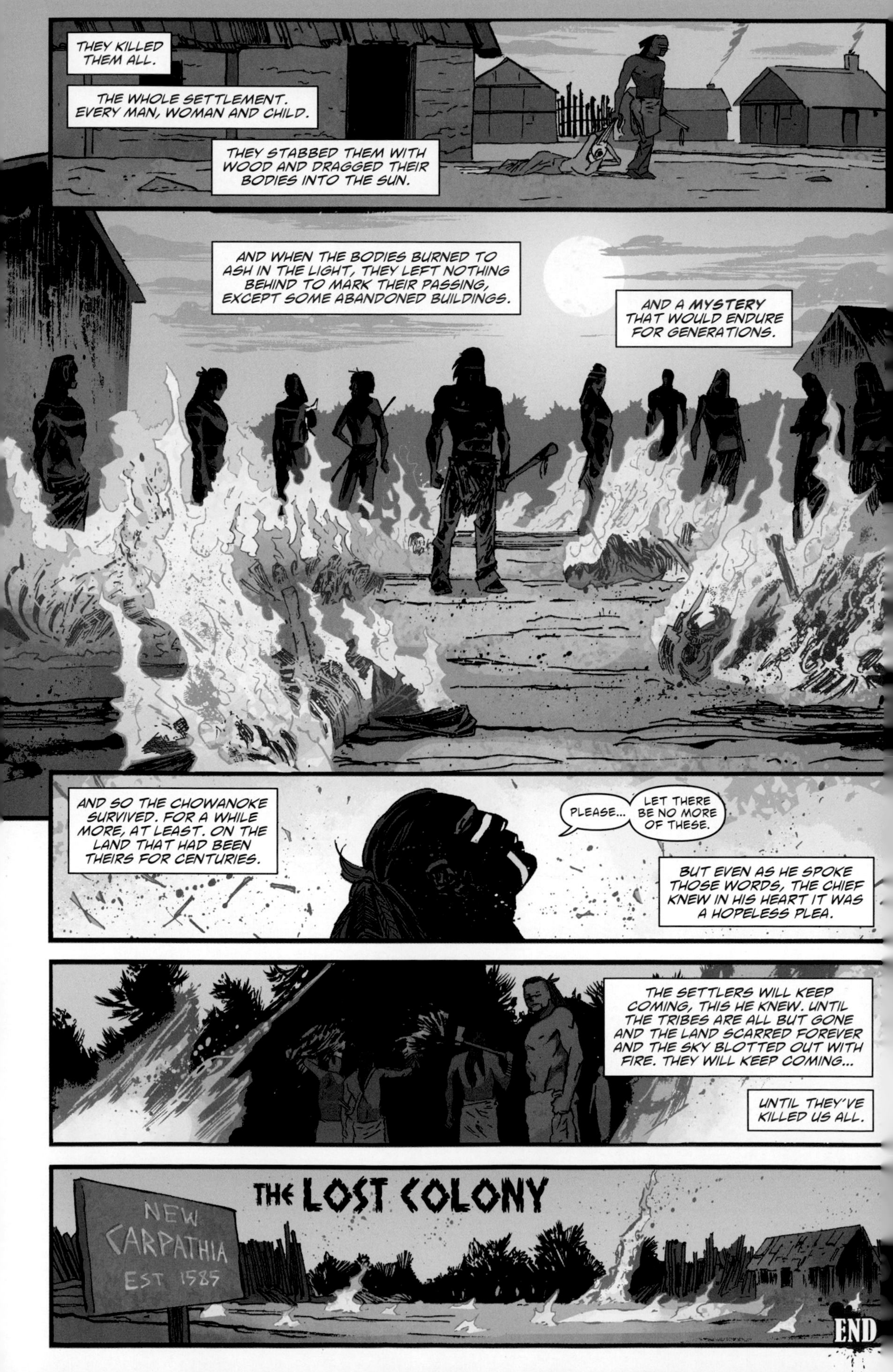
THEY KILLED THEM ALL.
THE WHOLE SETTLEMENT. EVERY MAN, WOMAN AND CHILD.
THEY STABBED THEM WITH WOOD AND DRAGGED THEIR BODIES INTO THE SUN.
AND WHEN THE BODIES BURNED TO ASH IN THE LIGHT, THEY LEFT NOTHING BEHIND TO MARK THEIR PASSING, EXCEPT SOME ABANDONED BUILDINGS.
AND A MYSTERY THAT WOULD ENDURE FOR GENERATIONS.
AND SO THE CHOWANOKE SURVIVED. FOR A WHILE MORE, AT LEAST. ON THE LAND THAT HAD BEEN THEIRS FOR CENTURIES.
PLEASE...
LET THERE BE NO MORE OF THESE.
BUT EVEN AS HE SPOKE THOSE WORDS, THE CHIEF KNEW IN HIS HEART IT WAS A HOPELESS PLEA.
THE SETTLERS WILL KEEP COMING, THIS HE KNEW. UNTIL THE TRIBES ARE ALL BUT GONE AND THE LAND SCARRED FOREVER AND THE SKY BLOTTED OUT WITH FIRE. THEY WILL KEEP COMING...
UNTIL THEY'VE KILLED US ALL.
THE LOST COLONY
NEW CARPATHIA EST 1585
END

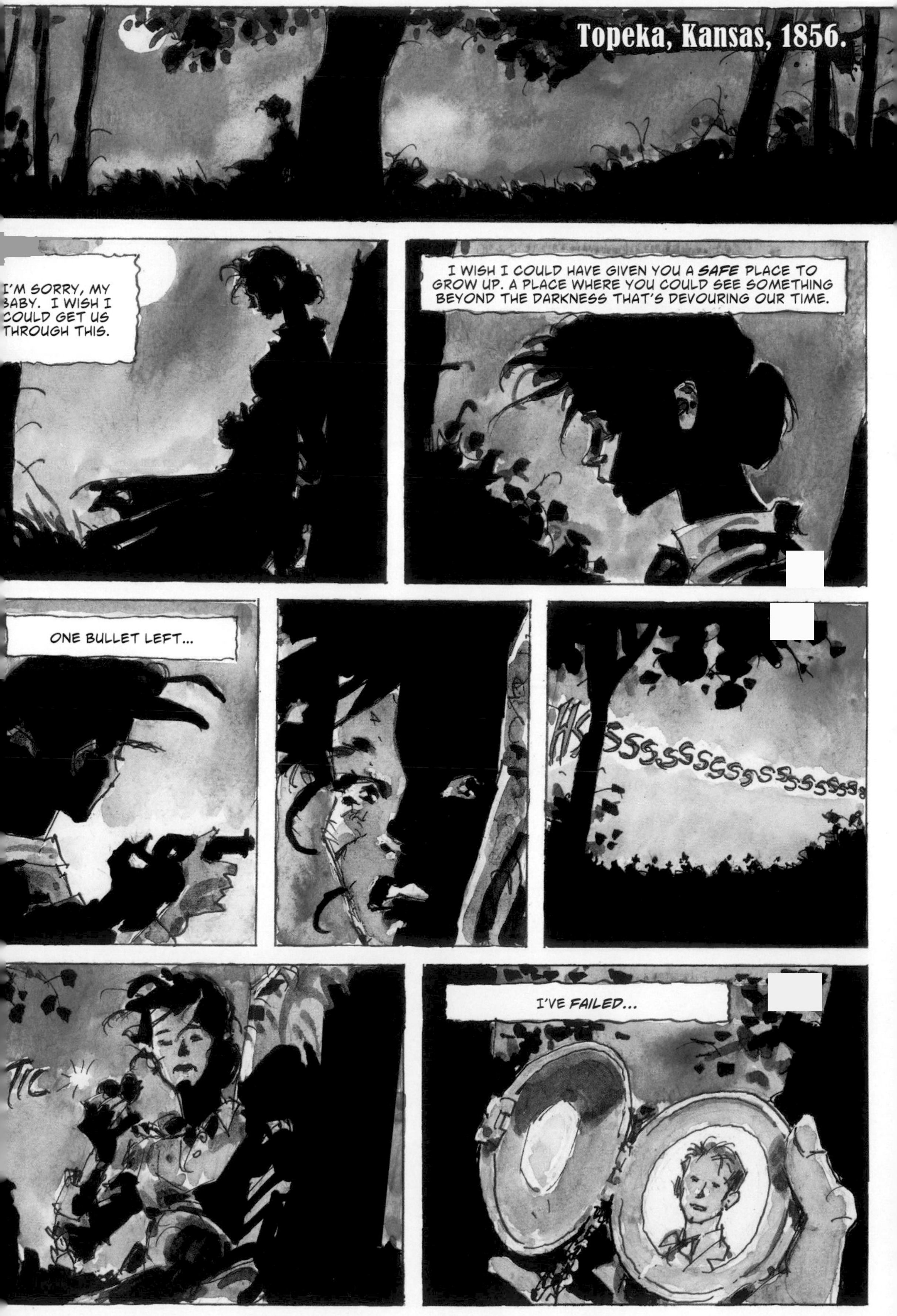
Topeka, Kansas, 1856.
I'M SORRY, MY BABY. I WISH I COULD GET US THROUGH THIS.
I WISH I COULD HAVE GIVEN YOU A SAFE PLACE TO GROW UP. A PLACE WHERE YOU COULD SEE SOMETHING BEYOND THE DARKNESS THAT'S DEVOURING OUR TIME.
ONE BULLET LEFT...
HSSSSSSSSSSSSSSSSSSSS
TIC
I'VE FAILED...

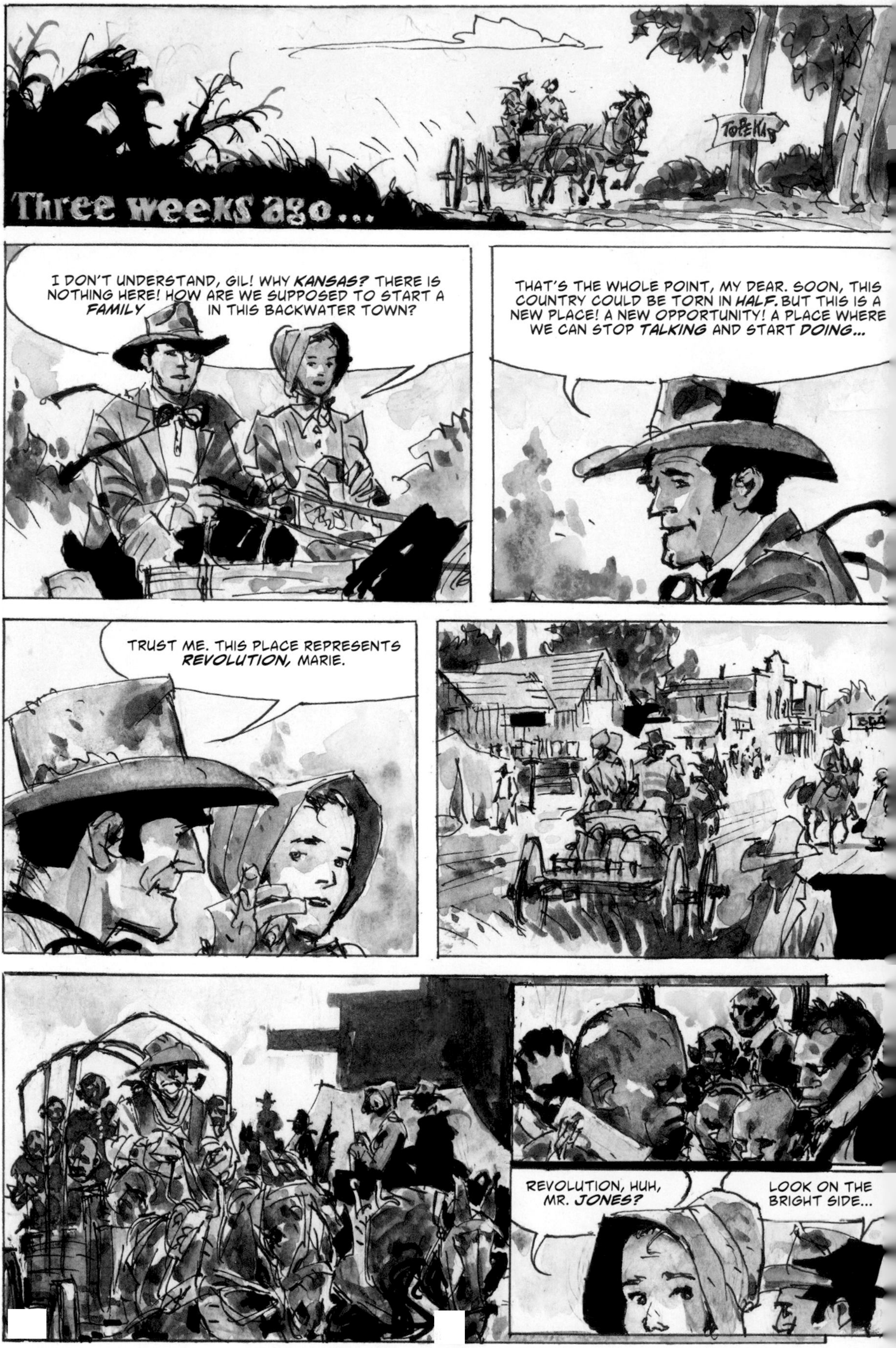
Three weeks ago...
TOPEKA
I DON'T UNDERSTAND, GIL! WHY KANSAS? THERE IS NOTHING HERE! HOW ARE WE SUPPOSED TO START A FAMILY IN THIS BACKWATER TOWN?
THAT'S THE WHOLE POINT, MY DEAR. SOON, THIS COUNTRY COULD BE TORN IN HALF. BUT THIS IS A NEW PLACE! A NEW OPPORTUNITY! A PLACE WHERE WE CAN STOP TALKING AND START DOING...
TRUST ME. THIS PLACE REPRESENTS REVOLUTION, MARIE.
REVOLUTION, HUH, MR. JONES?
LOOK ON THE BRIGHT SIDE...

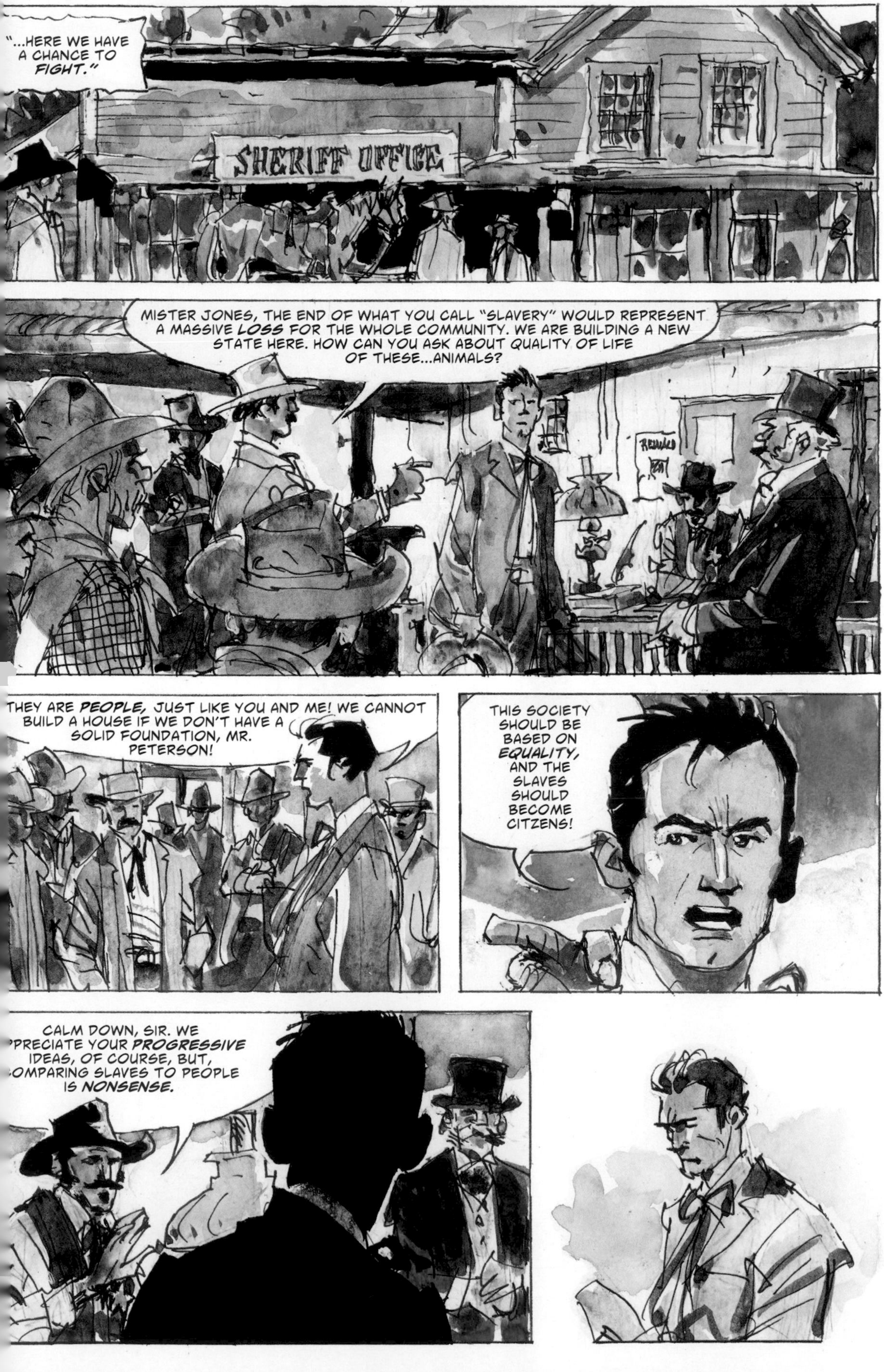
"...HERE WE HAVE A CHANCE TO *FIGHT*."
SHERIFF OFFICE
MISTER JONES, THE END OF WHAT YOU CALL "SLAVERY" WOULD REPRESENT A MASSIVE *LOSS* FOR THE WHOLE COMMUNITY. WE ARE BUILDING A NEW STATE HERE. HOW CAN YOU ASK ABOUT QUALITY OF LIFE OF THESE...ANIMALS?
THEY ARE *PEOPLE,* JUST LIKE YOU AND ME! WE CANNOT BUILD A HOUSE IF WE DON'T HAVE A SOLID FOUNDATION, MR. PETERSON!
THIS SOCIETY SHOULD BE BASED ON *EQUALITY,* AND THE SLAVES SHOULD BECOME CITIZENS!
CALM DOWN, SIR. WE PPRECIATE YOUR *PROGRESSIVE* IDEAS, OF COURSE, BUT, OMPARING SLAVES TO PEOPLE IS *NONSENSE.*

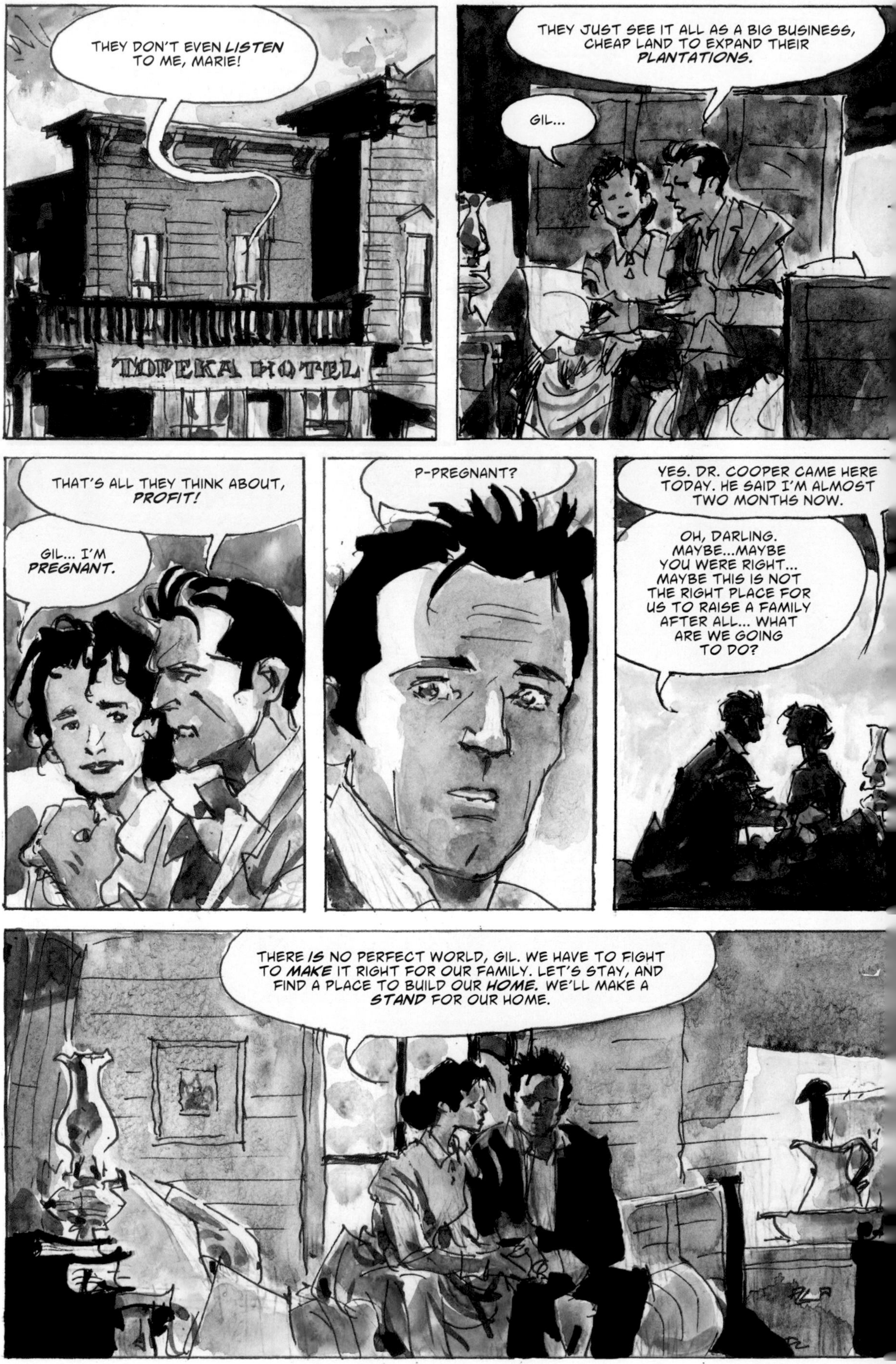
THEY DON'T EVEN LISTEN TO ME, MARIE!
TOPEKA HOTEL
THEY JUST SEE IT ALL AS A BIG BUSINESS, CHEAP LAND TO EXPAND THEIR PLANTATIONS.
GIL...
THAT'S ALL THEY THINK ABOUT, PROFIT!
GIL... I'M PREGNANT.
P-PREGNANT?
YES. DR. COOPER CAME HERE TODAY. HE SAID I'M ALMOST TWO MONTHS NOW.
OH, DARLING. MAYBE...MAYBE YOU WERE RIGHT... MAYBE THIS IS NOT THE RIGHT PLACE FOR US TO RAISE A FAMILY AFTER ALL... WHAT ARE WE GOING TO DO?
THERE IS NO PERFECT WORLD, GIL. WE HAVE TO FIGHT TO MAKE IT RIGHT FOR OUR FAMILY. LET'S STAY, AND FIND A PLACE TO BUILD OUR HOME. WE'LL MAKE A STAND FOR OUR HOME.

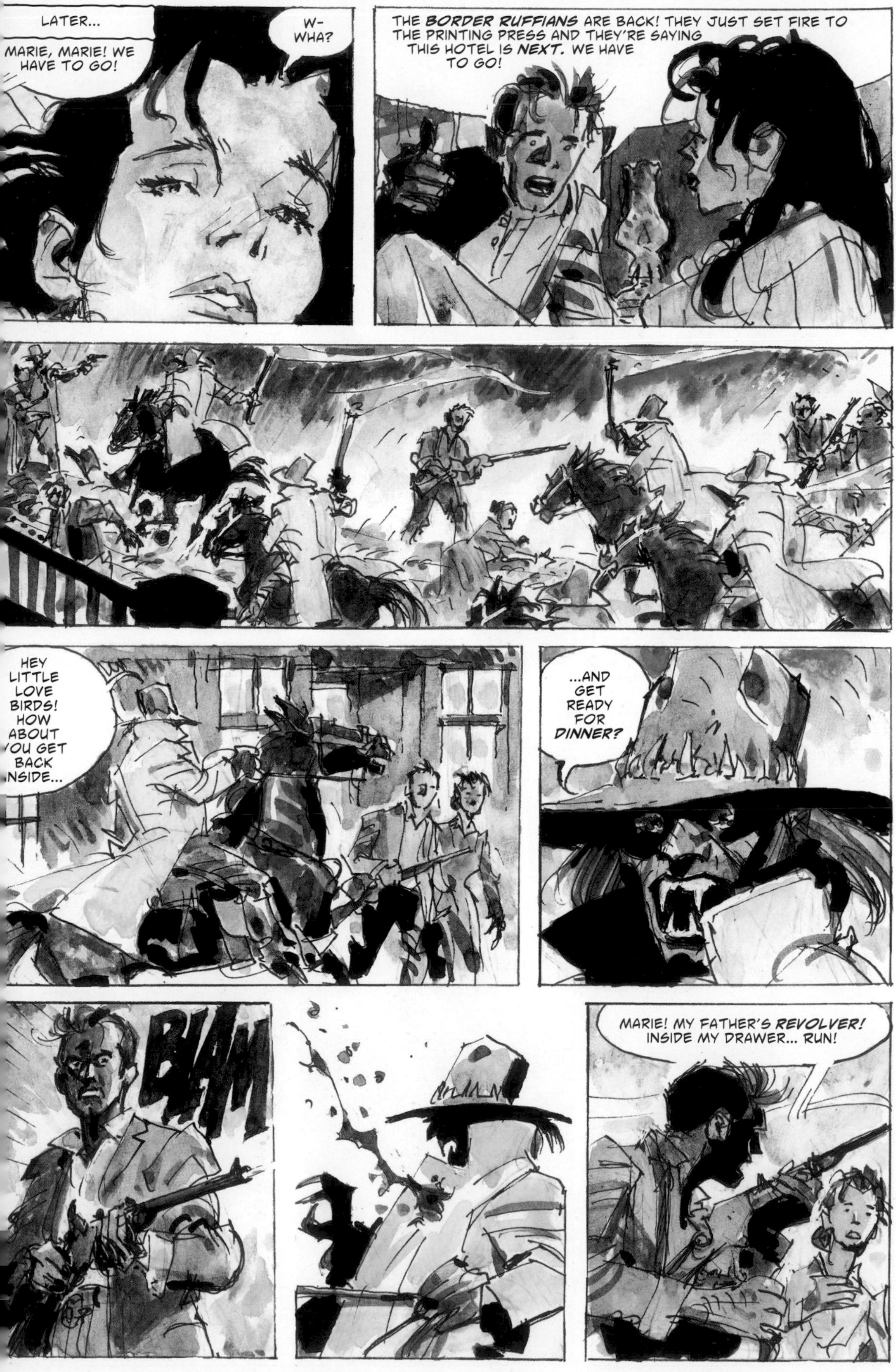
LATER...
MARIE, MARIE! WE HAVE TO GO!
W-WHA?
THE BORDER RUFFIANS ARE BACK! THEY JUST SET FIRE TO THE PRINTING PRESS AND THEY'RE SAYING THIS HOTEL IS NEXT. WE HAVE TO GO!
HEY LITTLE LOVE BIRDS! HOW ABOUT YOU GET BACK INSIDE...
...AND GET READY FOR DINNER?
BLAM
MARIE! MY FATHER'S REVOLVER! INSIDE MY DRAWER... RUN!

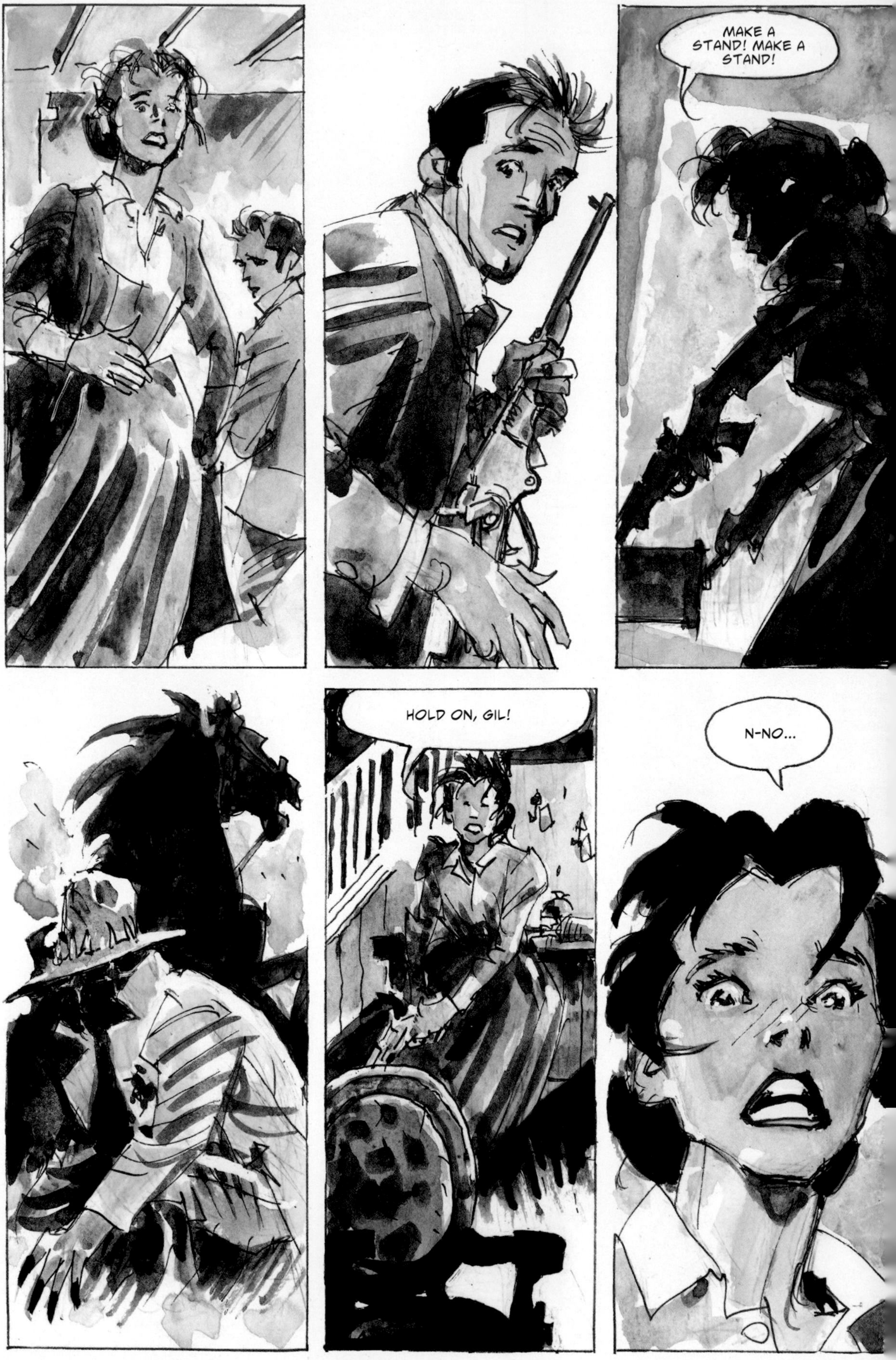
MAKE A STAND! MAKE A STAND!
HOLD ON, GIL!
N-NO...

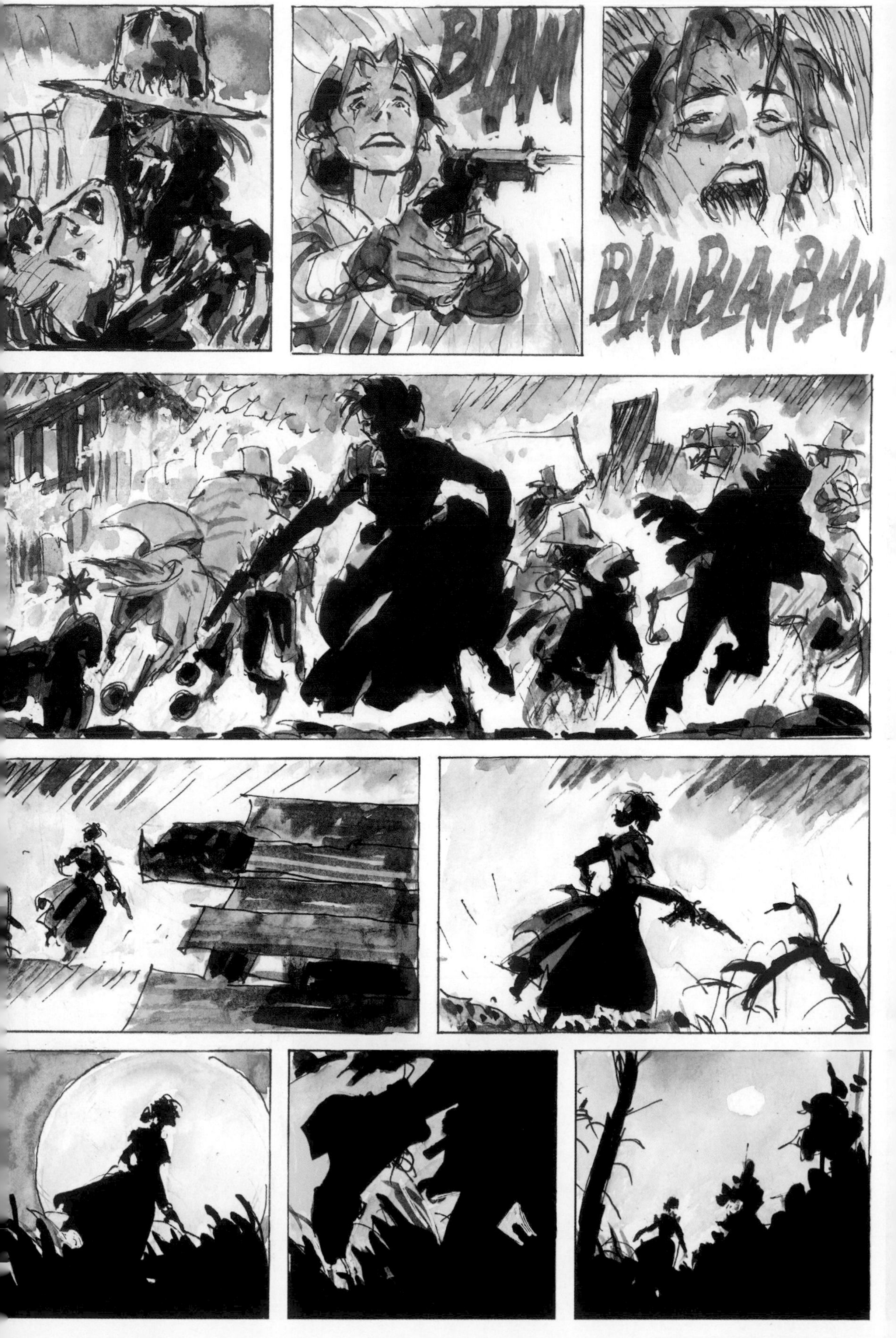
BLAM
BLAMBLAMBLAM

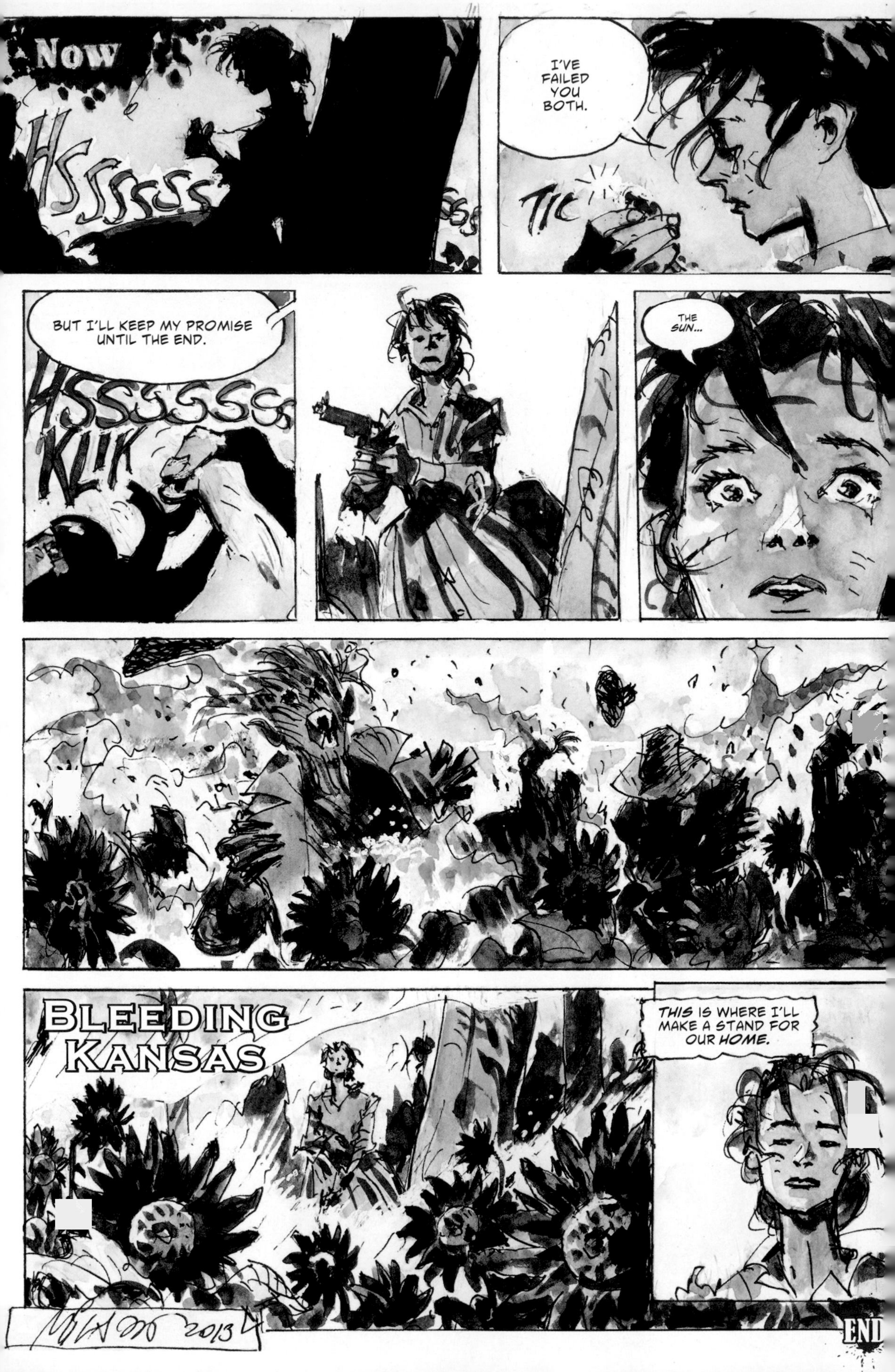
NOW
HSSSSSS
I'VE FAILED YOU BOTH.
TIC
BUT I'LL KEEP MY PROMISE UNTIL THE END.
HSSSSSSS
KLIK
THE SUN...
BLEEDING KANSAS
THIS IS WHERE I'LL MAKE A STAND FOR OUR HOME.
END

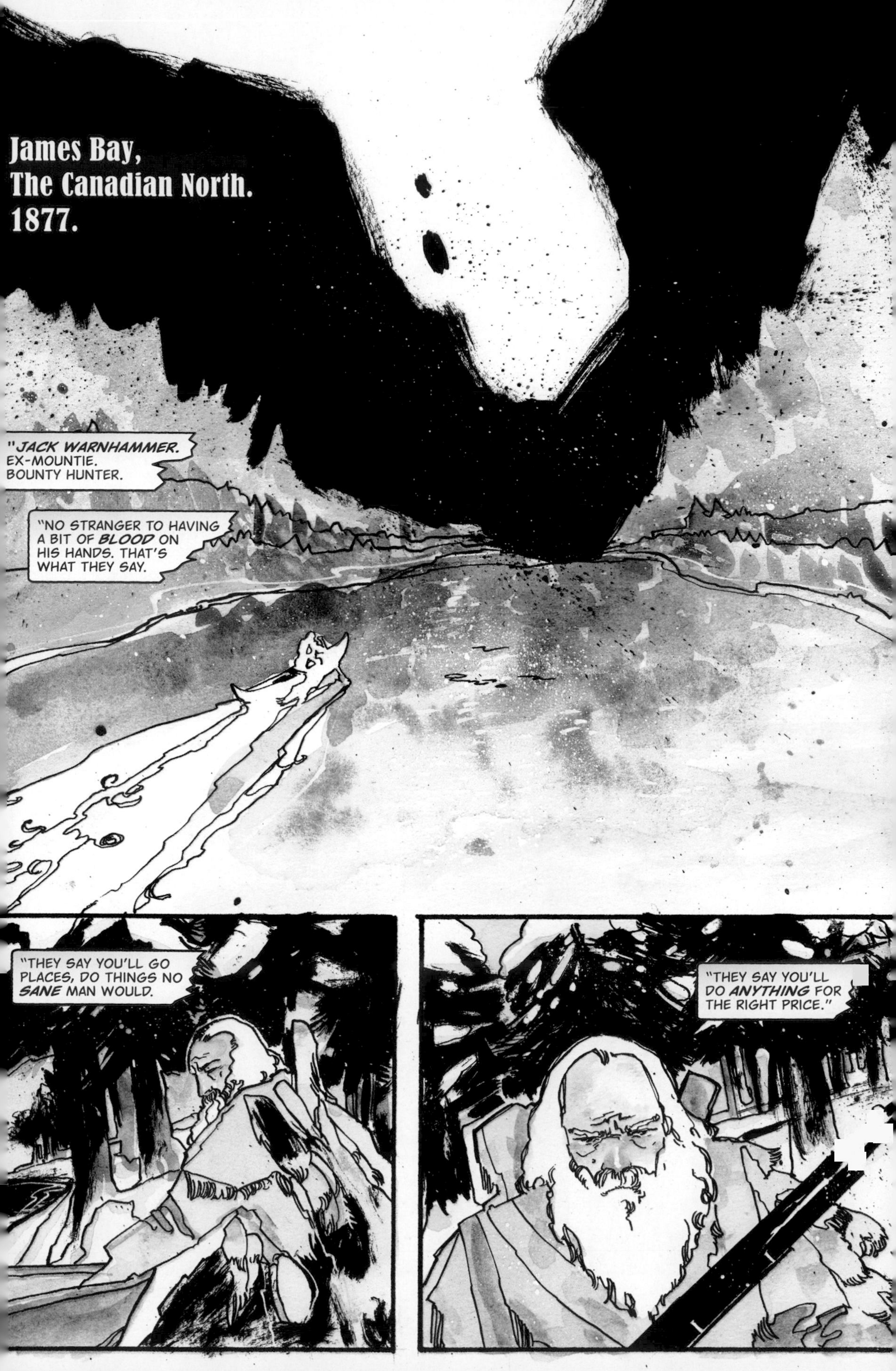
James Bay,
The Canadian North.
1877.
"JACK WARNHAMMER. EX-MOUNTIE. BOUNTY HUNTER.
"NO STRANGER TO HAVING A BIT OF BLOOD ON HIS HANDS. THAT'S WHAT THEY SAY.
"THEY SAY YOU'LL GO PLACES, DO THINGS NO SANE MAN WOULD.
"THEY SAY YOU'LL DO ANYTHING FOR THE RIGHT PRICE."

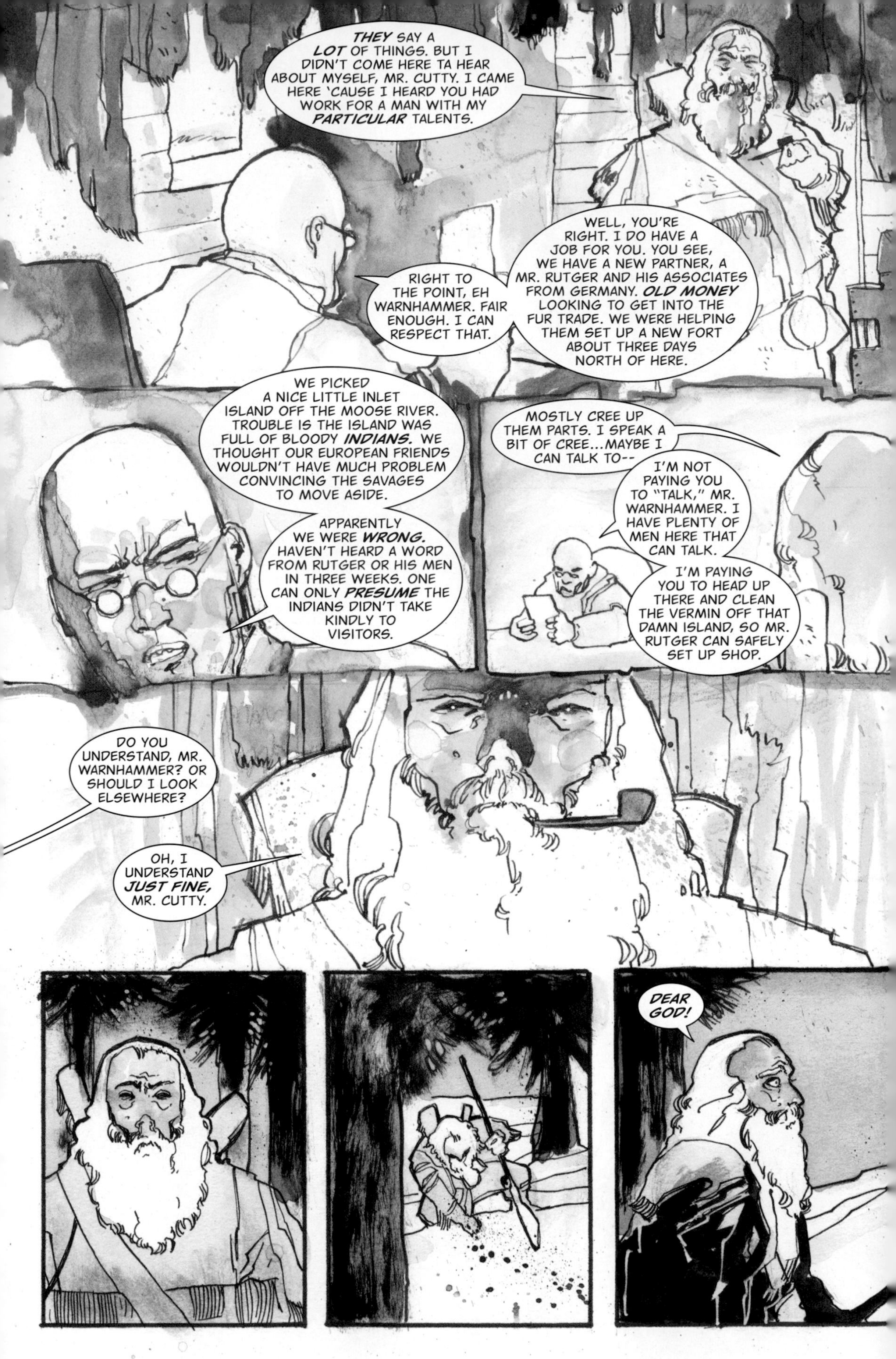
THEY SAY A LOT OF THINGS. BUT I DIDN'T COME HERE TA HEAR ABOUT MYSELF, MR. CUTTY. I CAME HERE 'CAUSE I HEARD YOU HAD WORK FOR A MAN WITH MY PARTICULAR TALENTS.
RIGHT TO THE POINT, EH WARNHAMMER. FAIR ENOUGH. I CAN RESPECT THAT.
WELL, YOU'RE RIGHT. I DO HAVE A JOB FOR YOU. YOU SEE, WE HAVE A NEW PARTNER, A MR. RUTGER AND HIS ASSOCIATES FROM GERMANY. OLD MONEY LOOKING TO GET INTO THE FUR TRADE. WE WERE HELPING THEM SET UP A NEW FORT ABOUT THREE DAYS NORTH OF HERE.
WE PICKED A NICE LITTLE INLET ISLAND OFF THE MOOSE RIVER. TROUBLE IS THE ISLAND WAS FULL OF BLOODY INDIANS. WE THOUGHT OUR EUROPEAN FRIENDS WOULDN'T HAVE MUCH PROBLEM CONVINCING THE SAVAGES TO MOVE ASIDE.
APPARENTLY WE WERE WRONG. HAVEN'T HEARD A WORD FROM RUTGER OR HIS MEN IN THREE WEEKS. ONE CAN ONLY PRESUME THE INDIANS DIDN'T TAKE KINDLY TO VISITORS.
MOSTLY CREE UP THEM PARTS. I SPEAK A BIT OF CREE... MAYBE I CAN TALK TO--
I'M NOT PAYING YOU TO "TALK," MR. WARNHAMMER. I HAVE PLENTY OF MEN HERE THAT CAN TALK.
I'M PAYING YOU TO HEAD UP THERE AND CLEAN THE VERMIN OFF THAT DAMN ISLAND, SO MR. RUTGER CAN SAFELY SET UP SHOP.
DO YOU UNDERSTAND, MR. WARNHAMMER? OR SHOULD I LOOK ELSEWHERE?
OH, I UNDERSTAND JUST FINE, MR. CUTTY.
DEAR GOD!

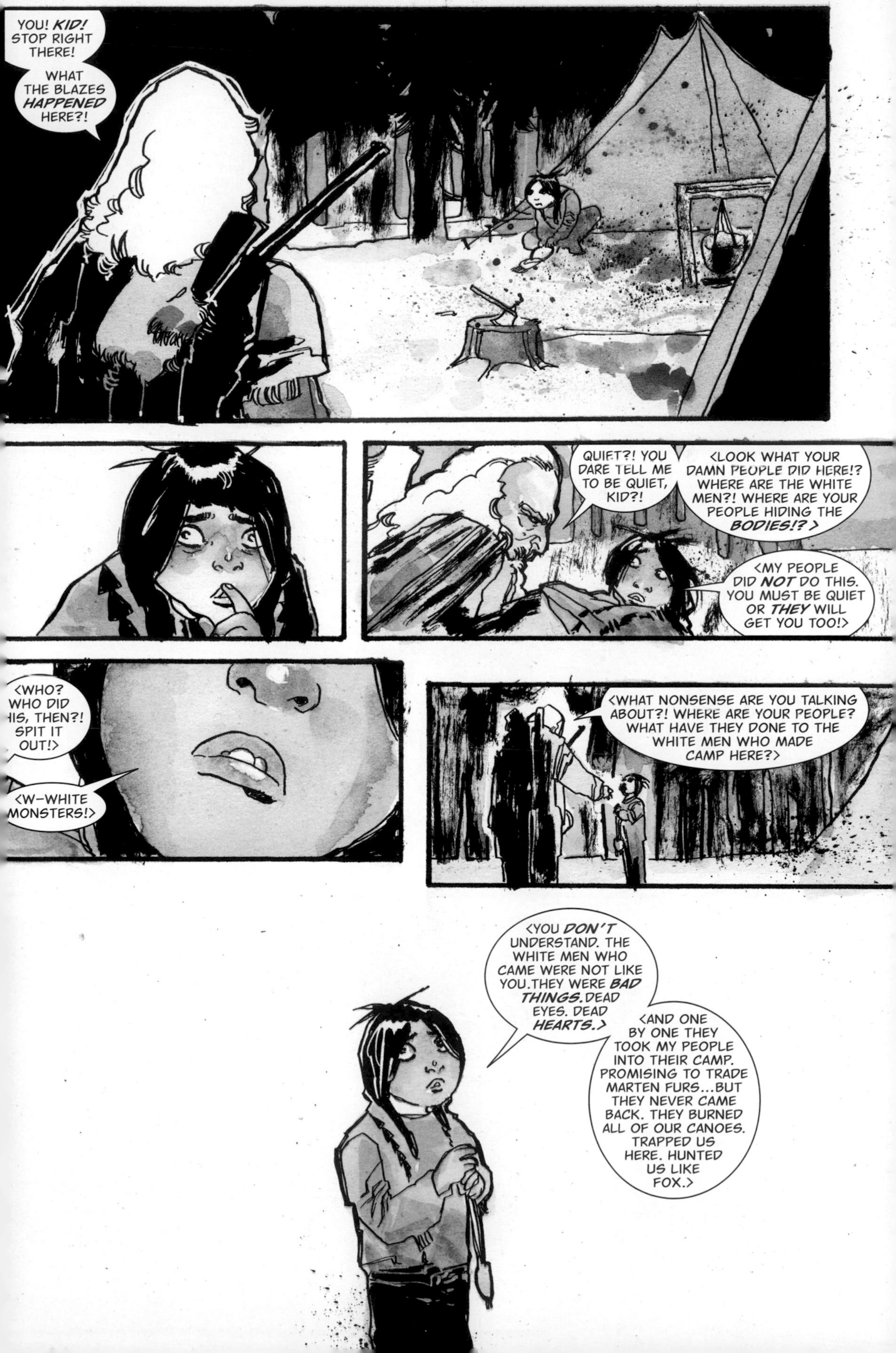
YOU! KID! STOP RIGHT THERE!
WHAT THE BLAZES HAPPENED HERE?!
QUIET?! YOU DARE TELL ME TO BE QUIET, KID?!
<LOOK WHAT YOUR DAMN PEOPLE DID HERE!? WHERE ARE THE WHITE MEN?! WHERE ARE YOUR PEOPLE HIDING THE BODIES!?>
<MY PEOPLE DID NOT DO THIS. YOU MUST BE QUIET OR THEY WILL GET YOU TOO!>
<WHO? WHO DID HIS, THEN?! SPIT IT OUT!>
<W-WHITE MONSTERS!>
<WHAT NONSENSE ARE YOU TALKING ABOUT?! WHERE ARE YOUR PEOPLE? WHAT HAVE THEY DONE TO THE WHITE MEN WHO MADE CAMP HERE?>
<YOU DON'T UNDERSTAND. THE WHITE MEN WHO CAME WERE NOT LIKE YOU.THEY WERE BAD THINGS.DEAD EYES. DEAD HEARTS.>
<AND ONE BY ONE THEY TOOK MY PEOPLE INTO THEIR CAMP. PROMISING TO TRADE MARTEN FURS...BUT THEY NEVER CAME BACK. THEY BURNED ALL OF OUR CANOES. TRAPPED US HERE. HUNTED US LIKE FOX.>

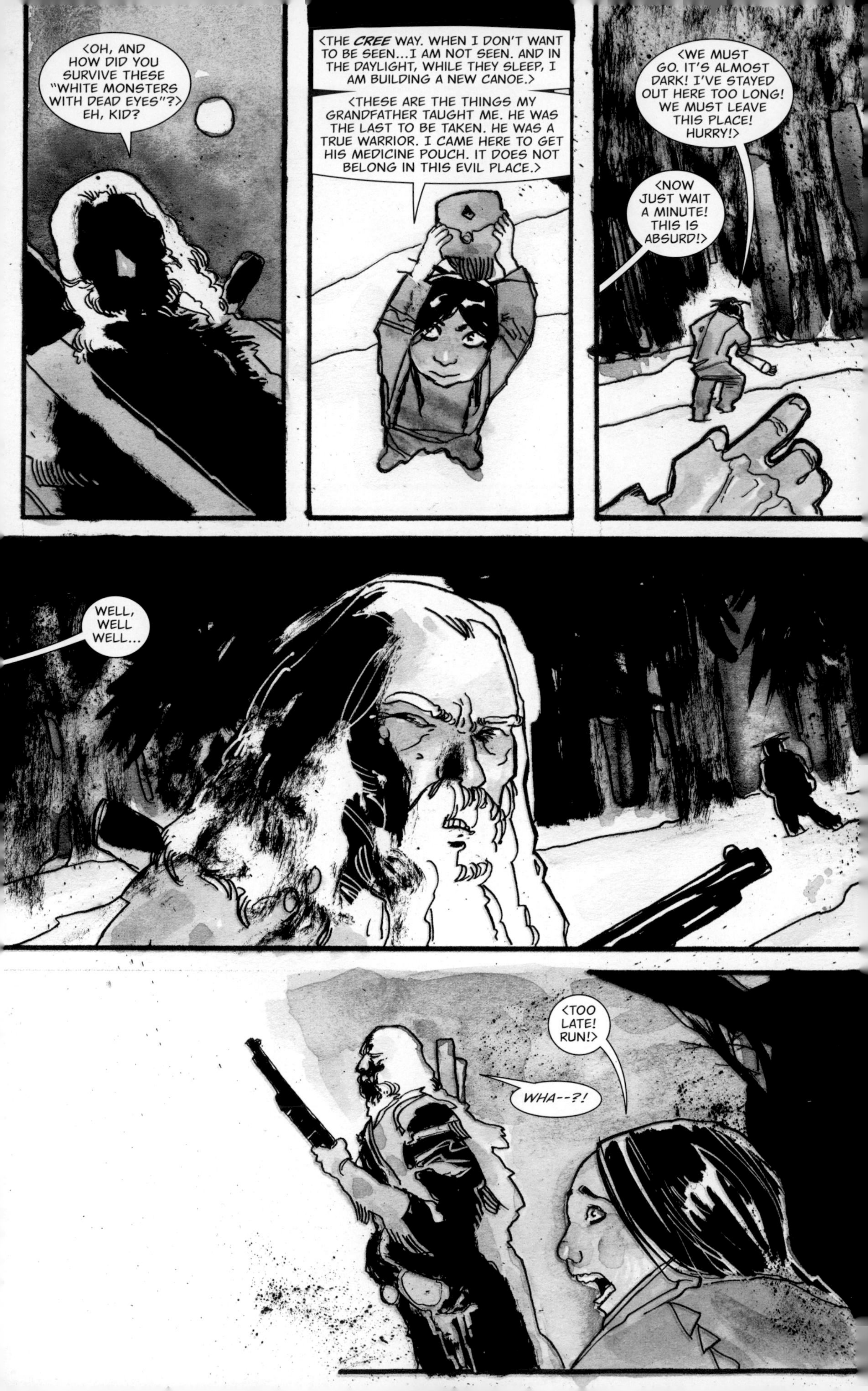
<OH, AND HOW DID YOU SURVIVE THESE "WHITE MONSTERS WITH DEAD EYES"?> EH, KID?
<THE CREE WAY. WHEN I DON'T WANT TO BE SEEN...I AM NOT SEEN. AND IN THE DAYLIGHT, WHILE THEY SLEEP, I AM BUILDING A NEW CANOE.>
<THESE ARE THE THINGS MY GRANDFATHER TAUGHT ME. HE WAS THE LAST TO BE TAKEN. HE WAS A TRUE WARRIOR. I CAME HERE TO GET HIS MEDICINE POUCH. IT DOES NOT BELONG IN THIS EVIL PLACE.>
<WE MUST GO. IT'S ALMOST DARK! I'VE STAYED OUT HERE TOO LONG! WE MUST LEAVE THIS PLACE! HURRY!>
<NOW JUST WAIT A MINUTE! THIS IS ABSURD!>
WELL, WELL WELL...
<TOO LATE! RUN!>
WHA--?!

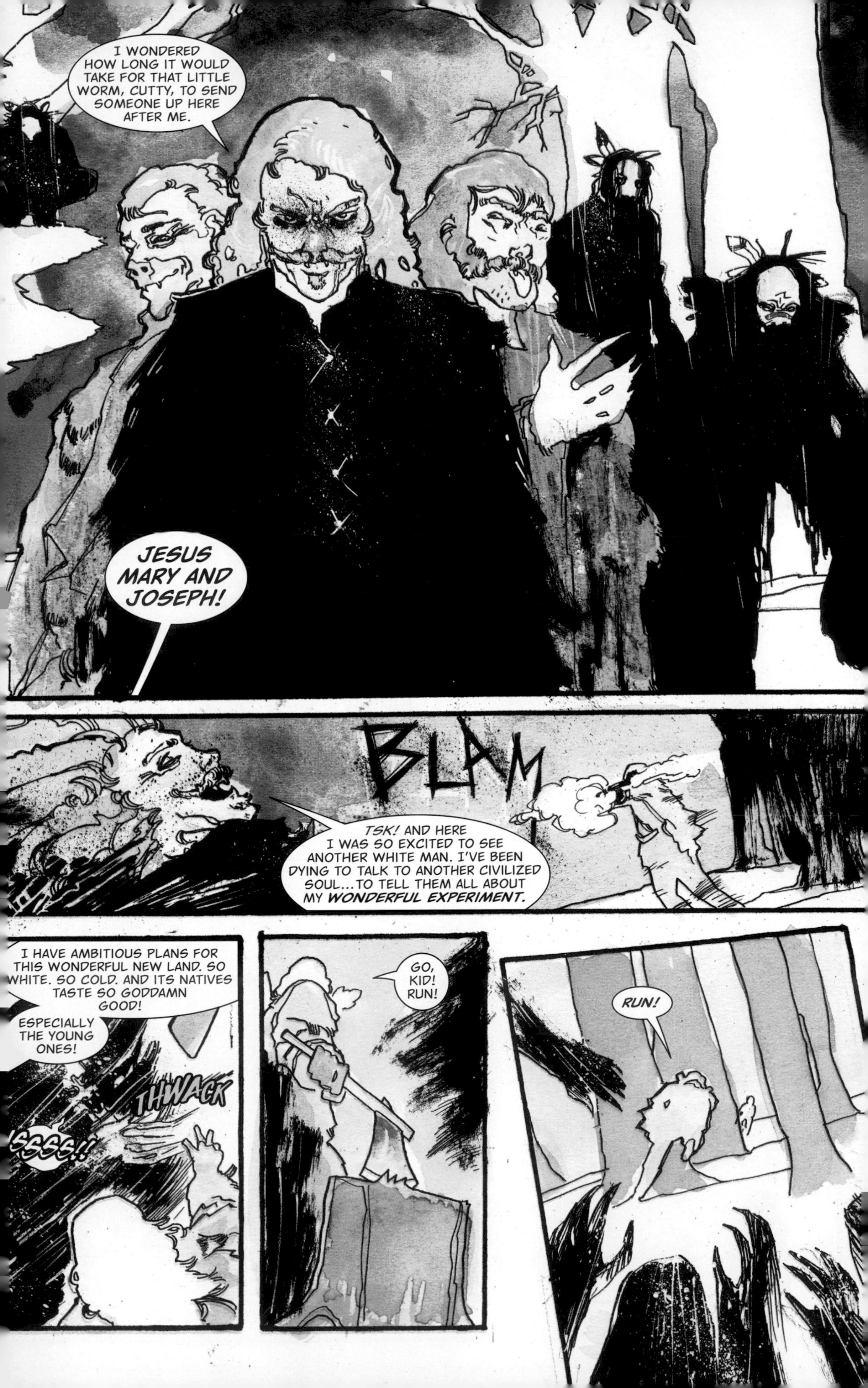
I WONDERED HOW LONG IT WOULD TAKE FOR THAT LITTLE WORM, CUTTY, TO SEND SOMEONE UP HERE AFTER ME.
JESUS MARY AND JOSEPH!
BLAM
TSK! AND HERE I WAS SO EXCITED TO SEE ANOTHER WHITE MAN. I'VE BEEN DYING TO TALK TO ANOTHER CIVILIZED SOUL...TO TELL THEM ALL ABOUT MY WONDERFUL EXPERIMENT.
I HAVE AMBITIOUS PLANS FOR THIS WONDERFUL NEW LAND. SO WHITE. SO COLD. AND ITS NATIVES TASTE SO GODDAMN GOOD!
ESPECIALLY THE YOUNG ONES!
THWACK
SSSS!!
GO, KID! RUN!
RUN!

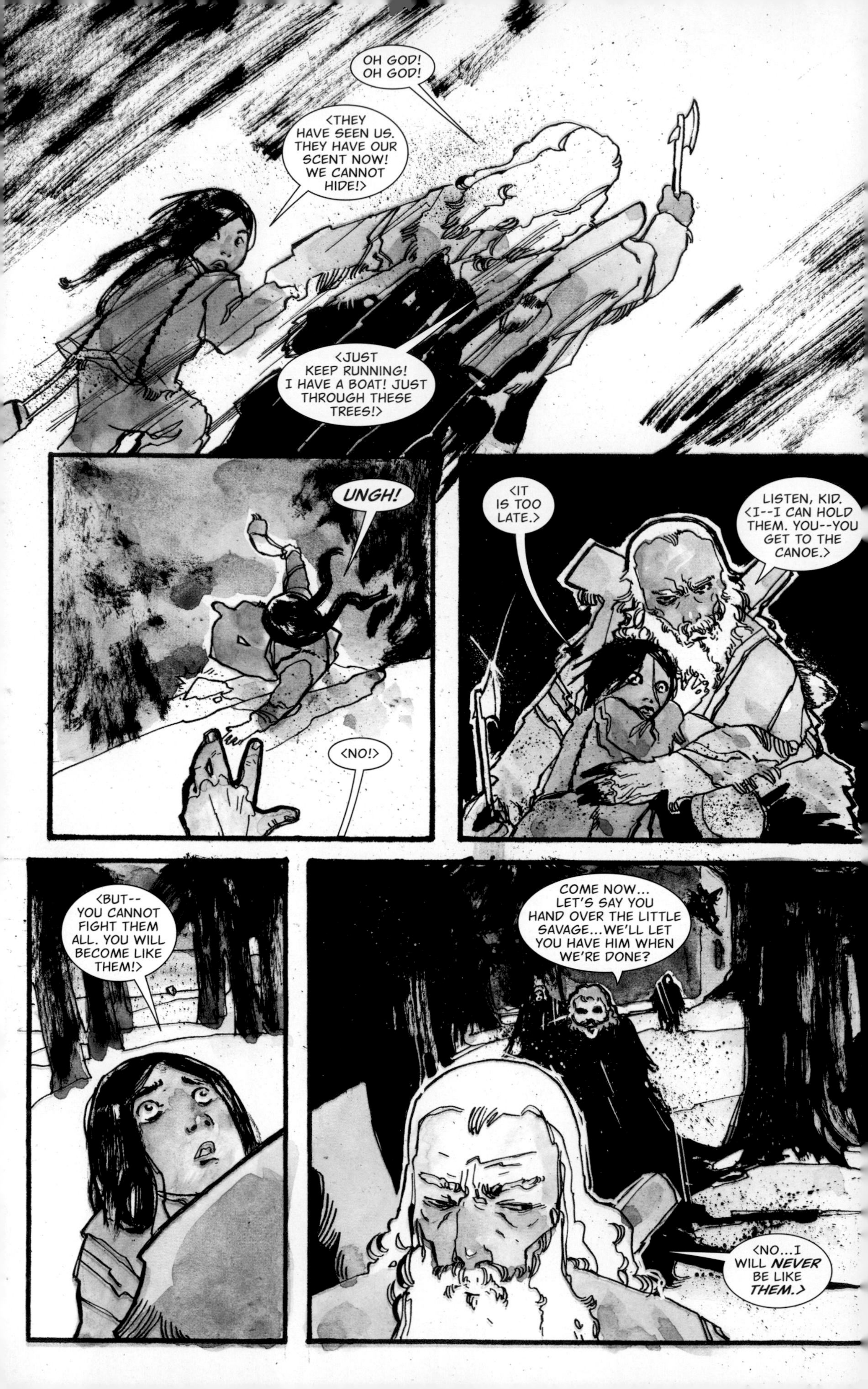
OH GOD! OH GOD!
<THEY HAVE SEEN US. THEY HAVE OUR SCENT NOW! WE CANNOT HIDE!>
<JUST KEEP RUNNING! I HAVE A BOAT! JUST THROUGH THESE TREES!>
UNGH!
<NO!>
<IT IS TOO LATE.>
LISTEN, KID. <I--I CAN HOLD THEM. YOU--YOU GET TO THE CANOE.>
<BUT--YOU CANNOT FIGHT THEM ALL. YOU WILL BECOME LIKE THEM!>
COME NOW... LET'S SAY YOU HAND OVER THE LITTLE SAVAGE...WE'LL LET YOU HAVE HIM WHEN WE'RE DONE?
<NO...I WILL *NEVER* BE LIKE *THEM*.>

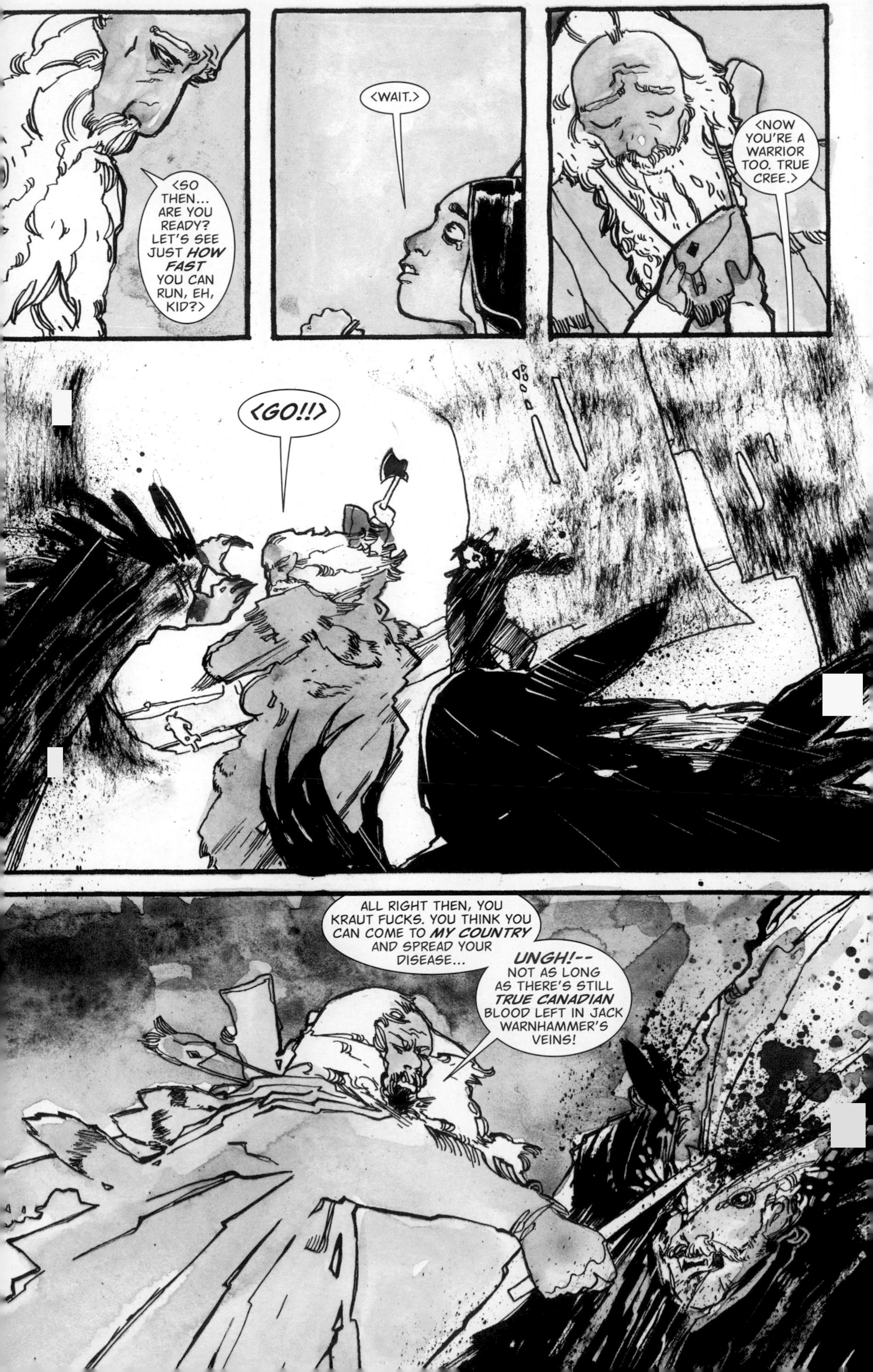

<SO THEN... ARE YOU READY? LET'S SEE JUST HOW FAST YOU CAN RUN, EH, KID?>
<WAIT.>
<NOW YOU'RE A WARRIOR TOO. TRUE CREE.>
<GO!!>
ALL RIGHT THEN, YOU KRAUT FUCKS. YOU THINK YOU CAN COME TO MY COUNTRY AND SPREAD YOUR DISEASE...
UNGH!-- NOT AS LONG AS THERE'S STILL TRUE CANADIAN BLOOD LEFT IN JACK WARNHAMMER'S VEINS!

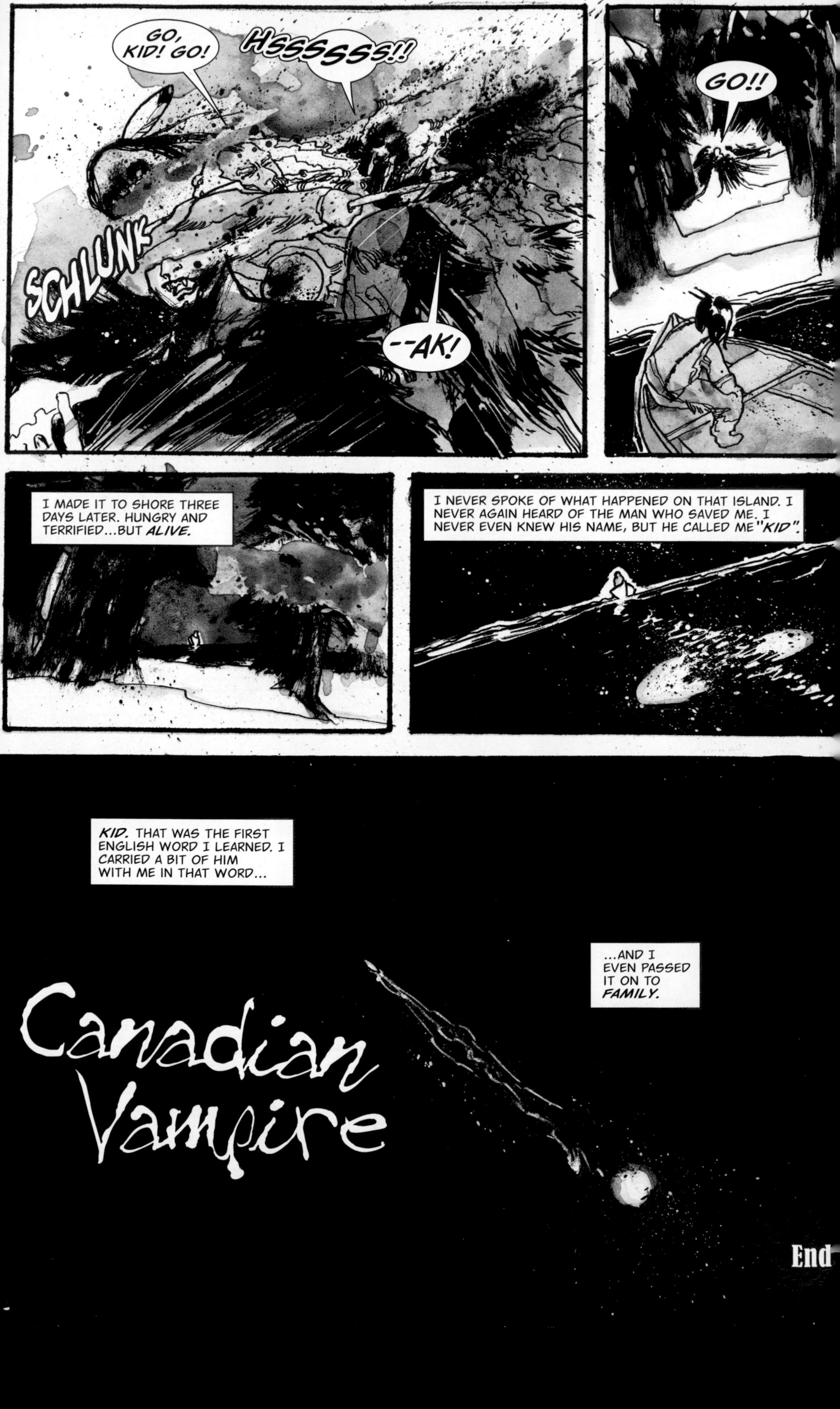
GO, KID! GO!
HSSSSSS!!
SCHLUNK
--AK!
GO!!
I MADE IT TO SHORE THREE DAYS LATER. HUNGRY AND TERRIFIED...BUT *ALIVE.*
I NEVER SPOKE OF WHAT HAPPENED ON THAT ISLAND. I NEVER AGAIN HEARD OF THE MAN WHO SAVED ME. I NEVER EVEN KNEW HIS NAME, BUT HE CALLED ME "*KID*".
KID. THAT WAS THE FIRST ENGLISH WORD I LEARNED. I CARRIED A BIT OF HIM WITH ME IN THAT WORD...
...AND I EVEN PASSED IT ON TO *FAMILY.*
Canadian Vampire
End

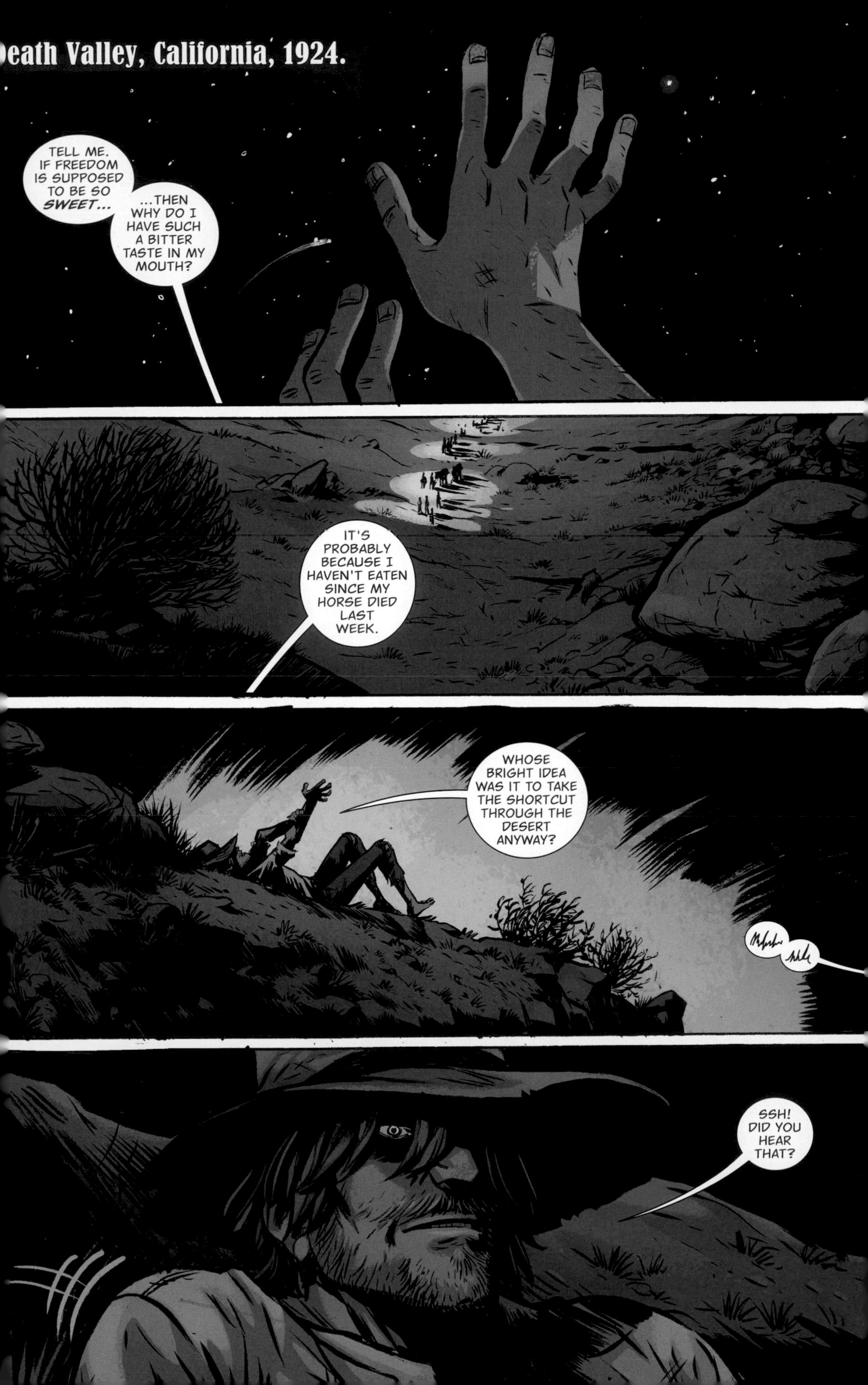
Death Valley, California, 1924.
TELL ME. IF FREEDOM IS SUPPOSED TO BE SO SWEET...
...THEN WHY DO I HAVE SUCH A BITTER TASTE IN MY MOUTH?
IT'S PROBABLY BECAUSE I HAVEN'T EATEN SINCE MY HORSE DIED LAST WEEK.
WHOSE BRIGHT IDEA WAS IT TO TAKE THE SHORTCUT THROUGH THE DESERT ANYWAY?
SSH! DID YOU HEAR THAT?

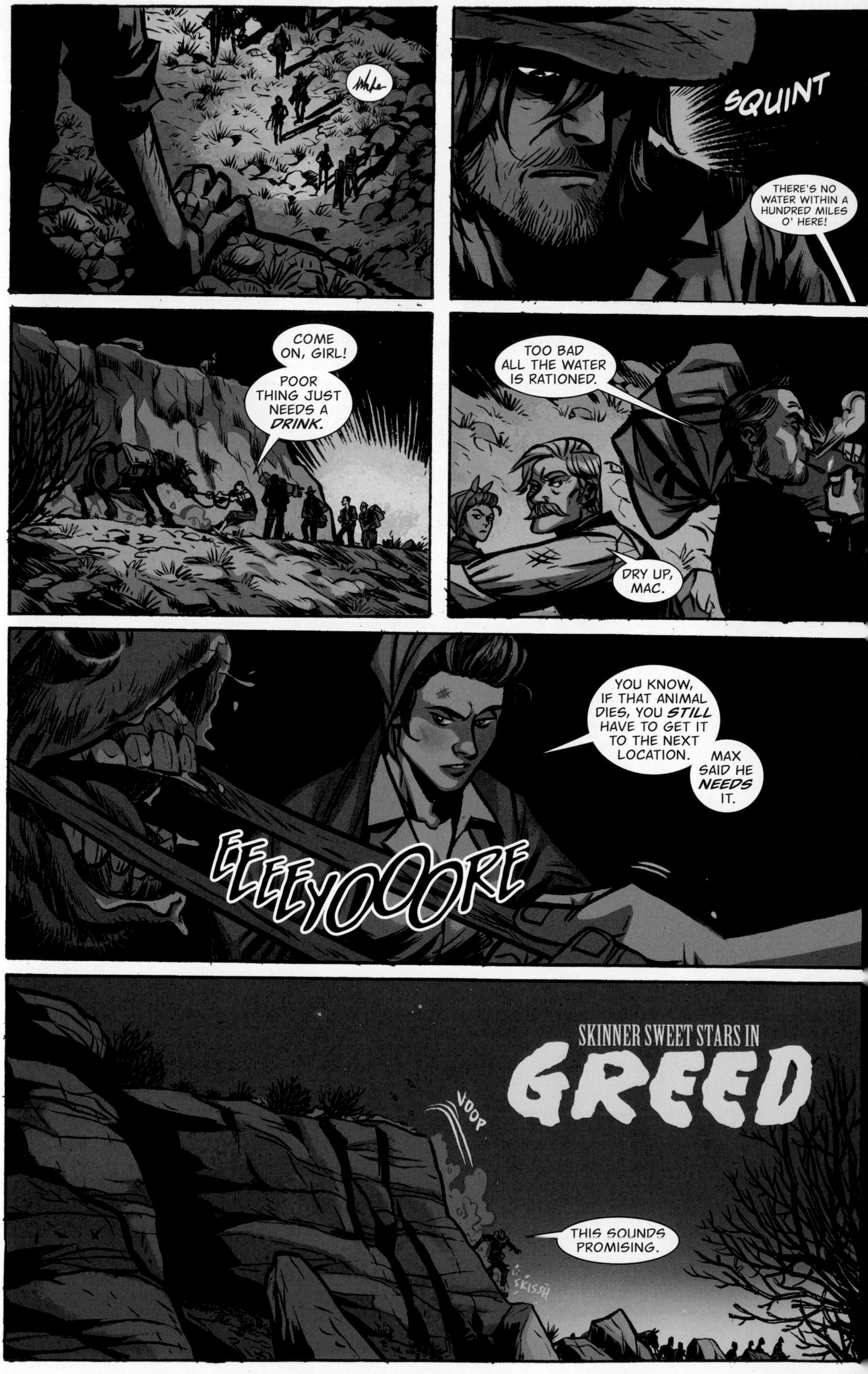
SQUINT
THERE'S NO WATER WITHIN A HUNDRED MILES O' HERE!
COME ON, GIRL!
POOR THING JUST NEEDS A DRINK.
TOO BAD ALL THE WATER IS RATIONED.
DRY UP, MAC.
YOU KNOW, IF THAT ANIMAL DIES, YOU STILL HAVE TO GET IT TO THE NEXT LOCATION.
MAX SAID HE NEEDS IT.
EEEEYOOOORE
SKINNER SWEET STARS IN
GREED
VOOP
THIS SOUNDS PROMISING.
SKISSH

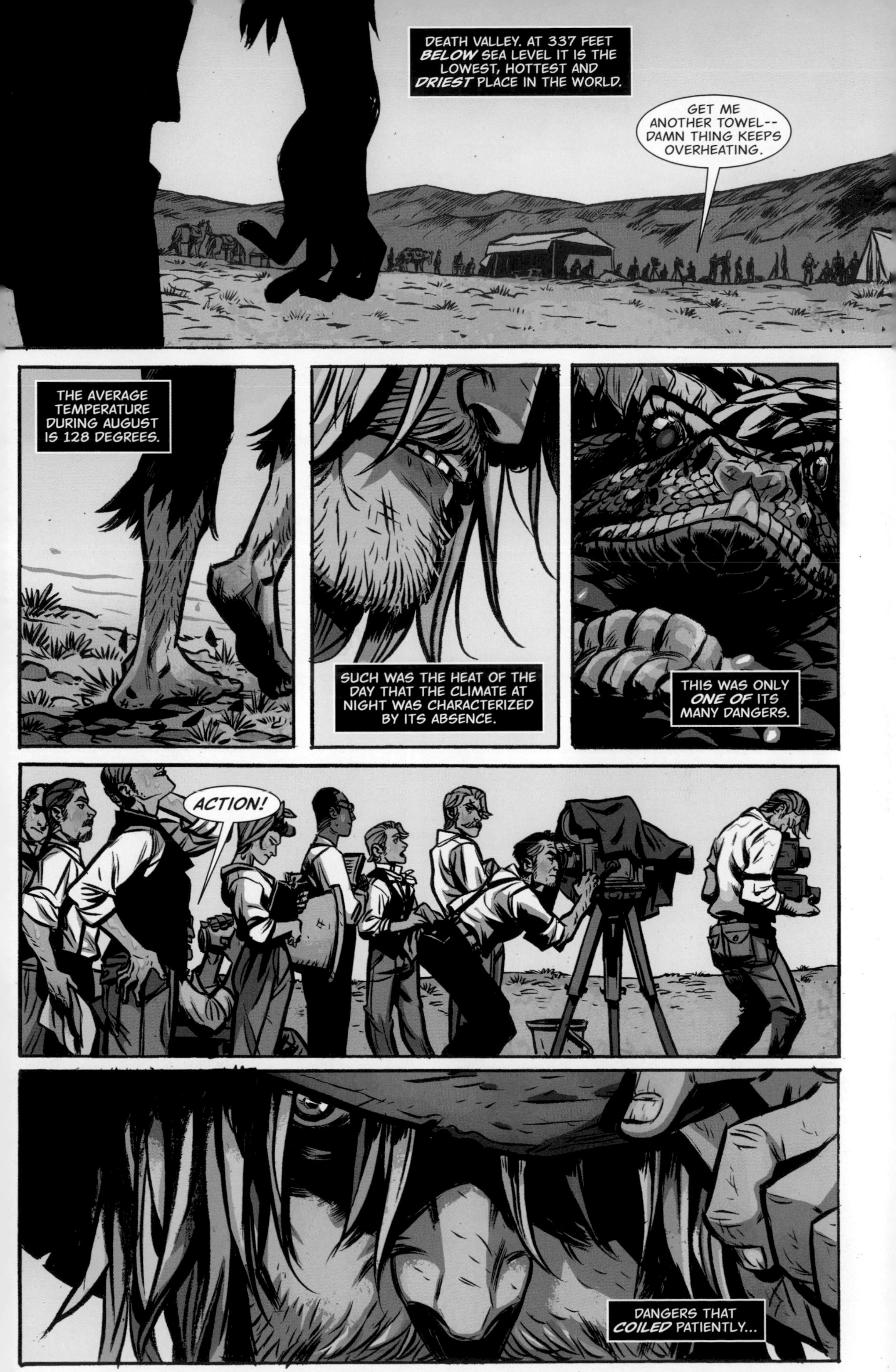
DEATH VALLEY. AT 337 FEET BELOW SEA LEVEL IT IS THE LOWEST, HOTTEST AND DRIEST PLACE IN THE WORLD.
GET ME ANOTHER TOWEL-- DAMN THING KEEPS OVERHEATING.
THE AVERAGE TEMPERATURE DURING AUGUST IS 128 DEGREES.
SUCH WAS THE HEAT OF THE DAY THAT THE CLIMATE AT NIGHT WAS CHARACTERIZED BY ITS ABSENCE.
THIS WAS ONLY ONE OF ITS MANY DANGERS.
ACTION!
DANGERS THAT COILED PATIENTLY...

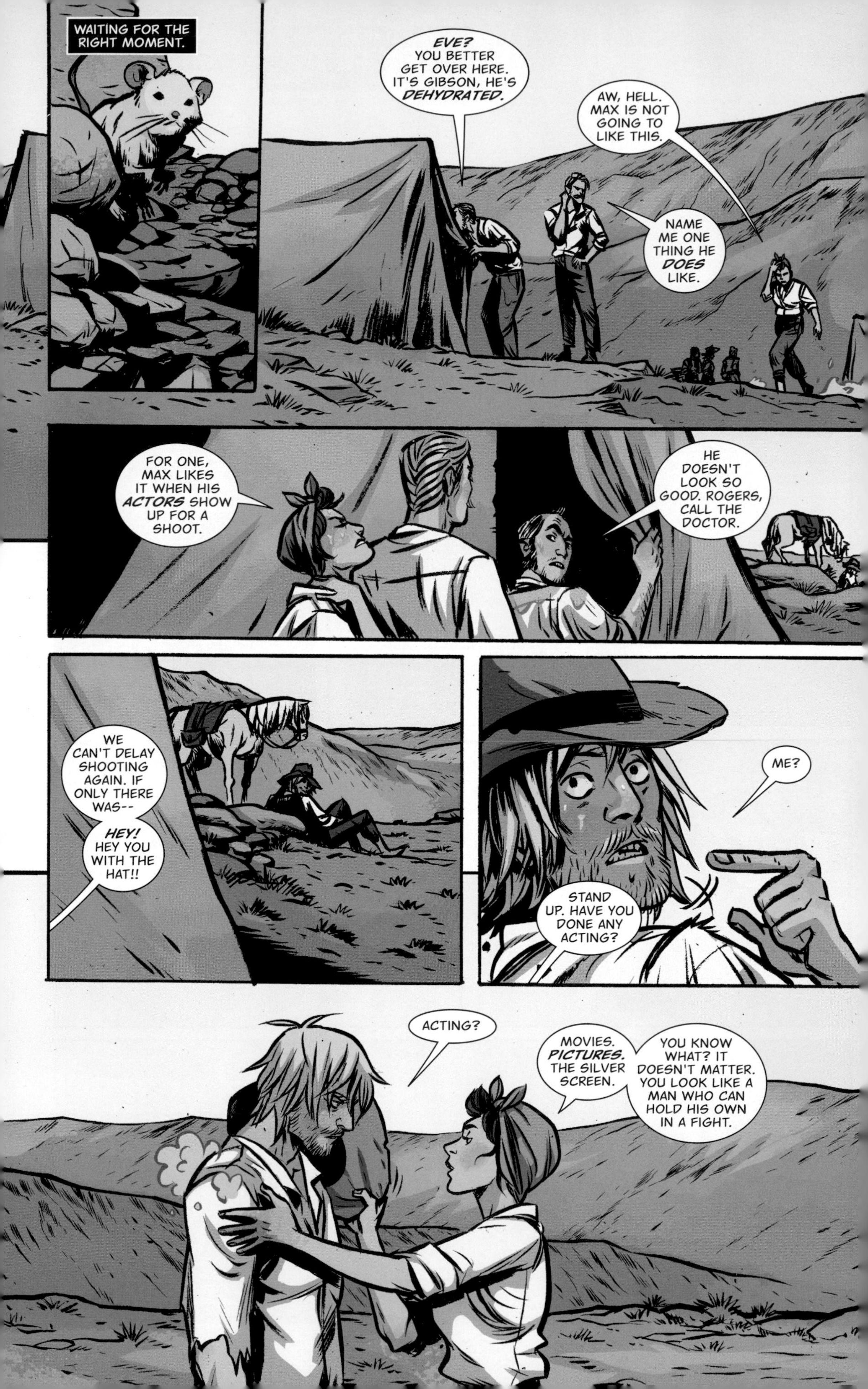
WAITING FOR THE RIGHT MOMENT.
EVE? YOU BETTER GET OVER HERE. IT'S GIBSON, HE'S DEHYDRATED.
AW, HELL. MAX IS NOT GOING TO LIKE THIS.
NAME ME ONE THING HE DOES LIKE.
FOR ONE, MAX LIKES IT WHEN HIS ACTORS SHOW UP FOR A SHOOT.
HE DOESN'T LOOK SO GOOD. ROGERS, CALL THE DOCTOR.
WE CAN'T DELAY SHOOTING AGAIN. IF ONLY THERE WAS--
HEY! HEY YOU WITH THE HAT!!
ME?
STAND UP. HAVE YOU DONE ANY ACTING?
ACTING?
MOVIES. PICTURES. THE SILVER SCREEN.
YOU KNOW WHAT? IT DOESN'T MATTER. YOU LOOK LIKE A MAN WHO CAN HOLD HIS OWN IN A FIGHT.

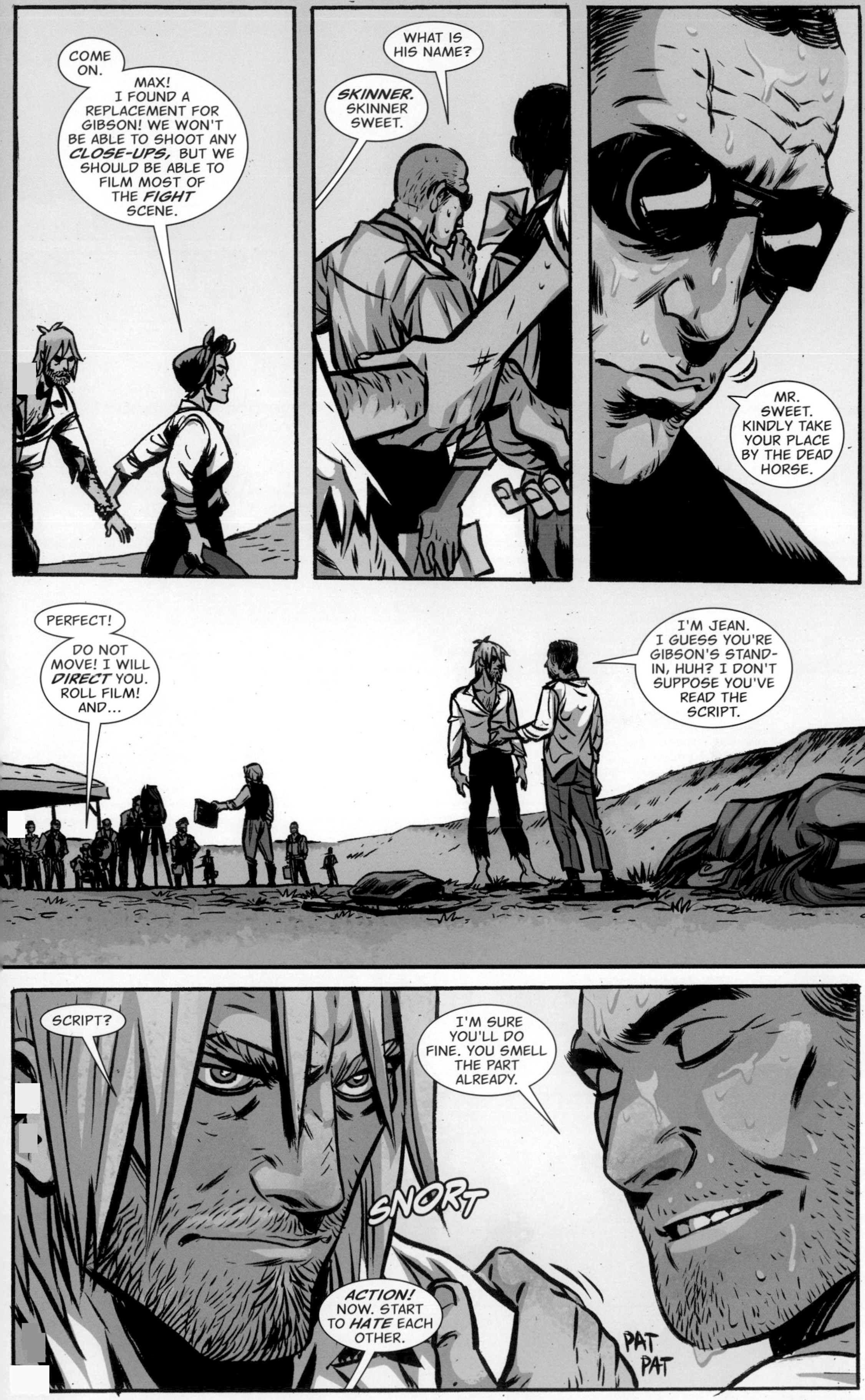

COME ON.
MAX! I FOUND A REPLACEMENT FOR GIBSON! WE WON'T BE ABLE TO SHOOT ANY CLOSE-UPS, BUT WE SHOULD BE ABLE TO FILM MOST OF THE FIGHT SCENE.
WHAT IS HIS NAME?
SKINNER. SKINNER SWEET.
MR. SWEET. KINDLY TAKE YOUR PLACE BY THE DEAD HORSE.
PERFECT!
DO NOT MOVE! I WILL DIRECT YOU. ROLL FILM! AND...
I'M JEAN. I GUESS YOU'RE GIBSON'S STAND-IN, HUH? I DON'T SUPPOSE YOU'VE READ THE SCRIPT.
SCRIPT?
I'M SURE YOU'LL DO FINE. YOU SMELL THE PART ALREADY.
SNORT
ACTION! NOW. START TO HATE EACH OTHER.
PAT PAT

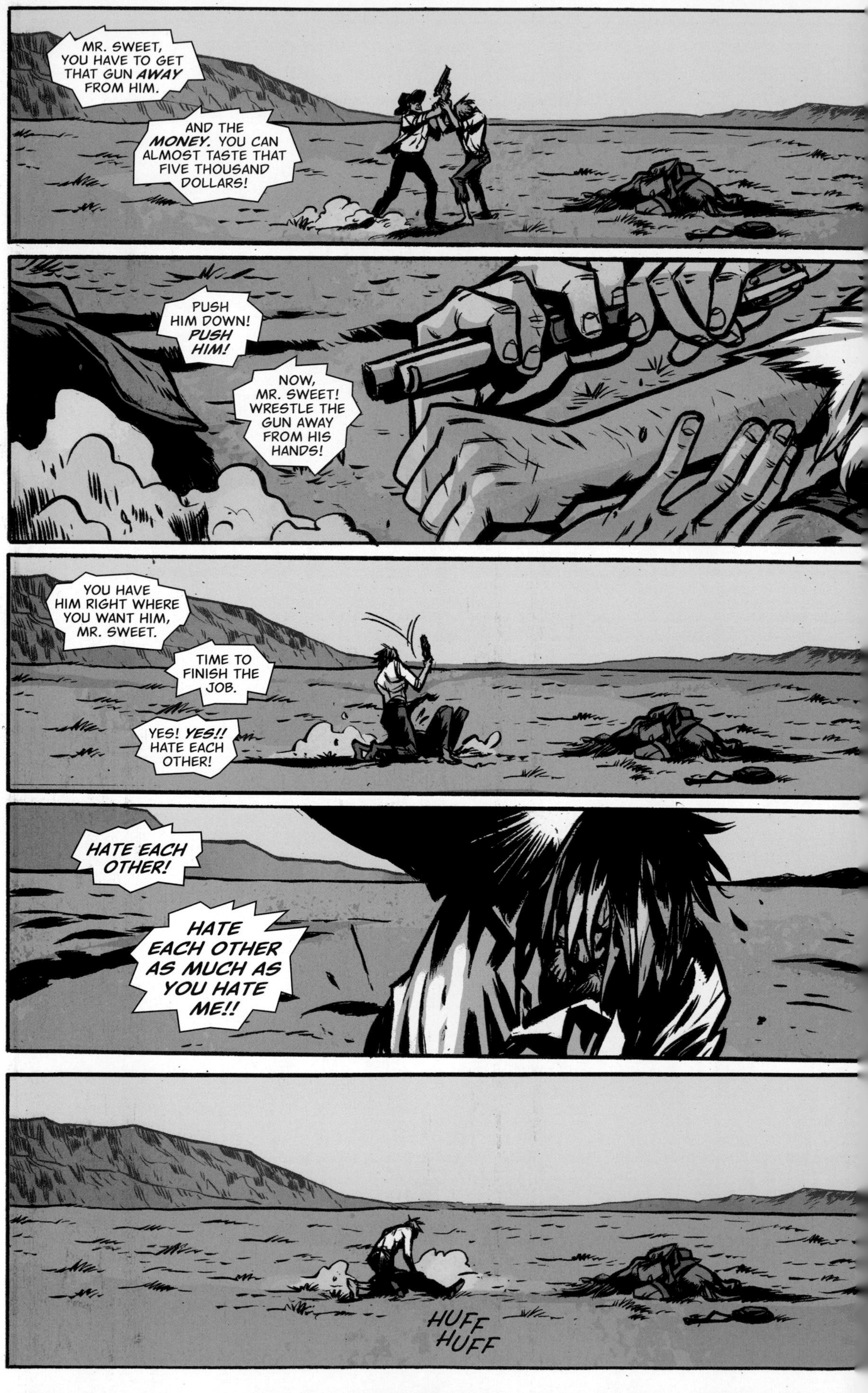
MR. SWEET, YOU HAVE TO GET THAT GUN *AWAY* FROM HIM.
AND THE *MONEY.* YOU CAN ALMOST TASTE THAT FIVE THOUSAND DOLLARS!
PUSH HIM DOWN! *PUSH HIM!*
NOW, MR. SWEET! WRESTLE THE GUN AWAY FROM HIS HANDS!
YOU HAVE HIM RIGHT WHERE YOU WANT HIM, MR. SWEET.
TIME TO FINISH THE JOB.
YES! *YES!!* HATE EACH OTHER!
HATE EACH OTHER!
HATE EACH OTHER AS MUCH AS YOU HATE ME!!
HUFF HUFF

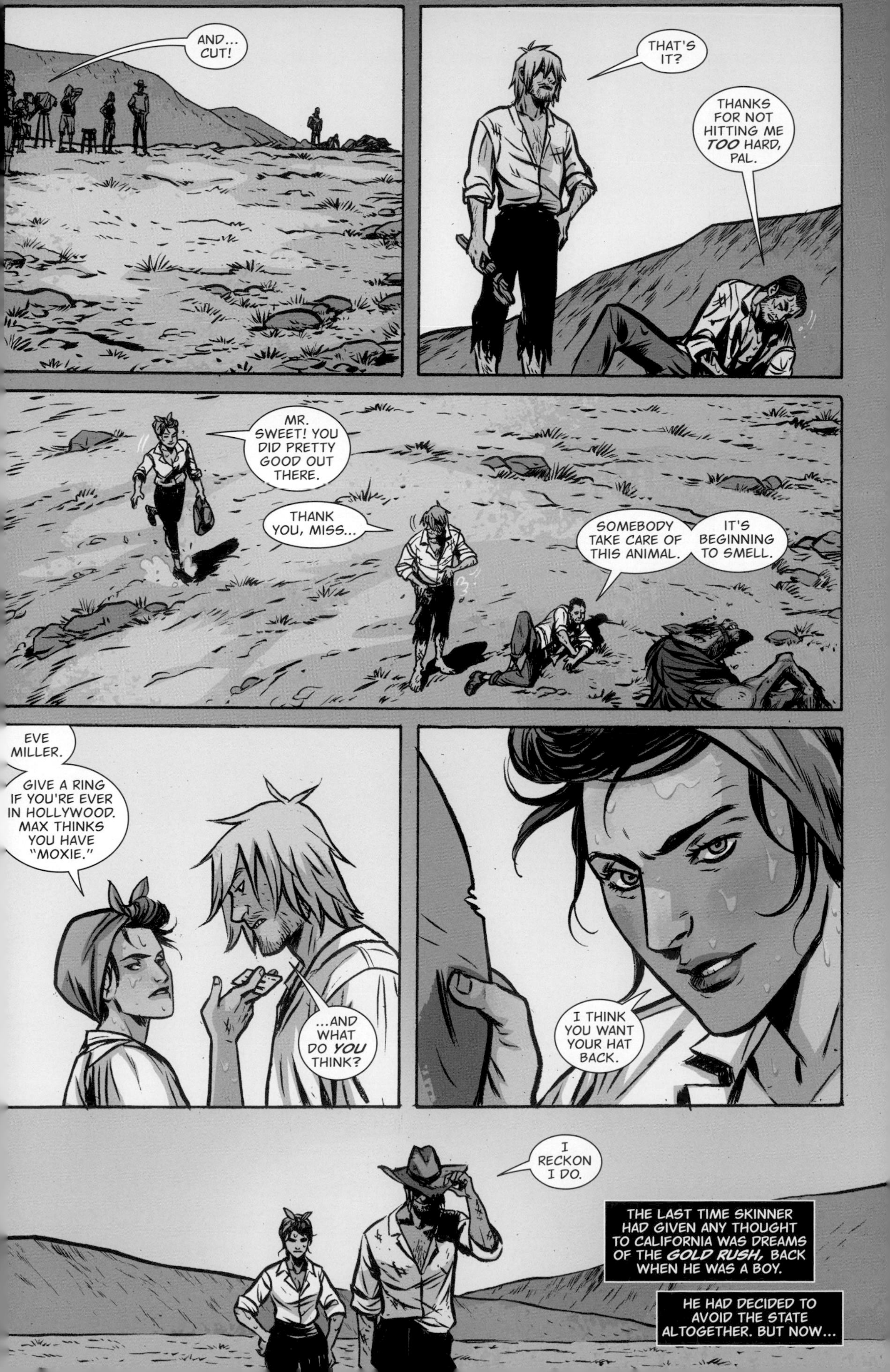
AND... CUT!
THAT'S IT?
THANKS FOR NOT HITTING ME TOO HARD, PAL.
MR. SWEET! YOU DID PRETTY GOOD OUT THERE.
THANK YOU, MISS...
SOMEBODY TAKE CARE OF THIS ANIMAL.
IT'S BEGINNING TO SMELL.
EVE MILLER.
GIVE A RING IF YOU'RE EVER IN HOLLYWOOD. MAX THINKS YOU HAVE "MOXIE."
...AND WHAT DO YOU THINK?
I THINK YOU WANT YOUR HAT BACK.
I RECKON I DO.
THE LAST TIME SKINNER HAD GIVEN ANY THOUGHT TO CALIFORNIA WAS DREAMS OF THE GOLD RUSH, BACK WHEN HE WAS A BOY.
HE HAD DECIDED TO AVOID THE STATE ALTOGETHER. BUT NOW...

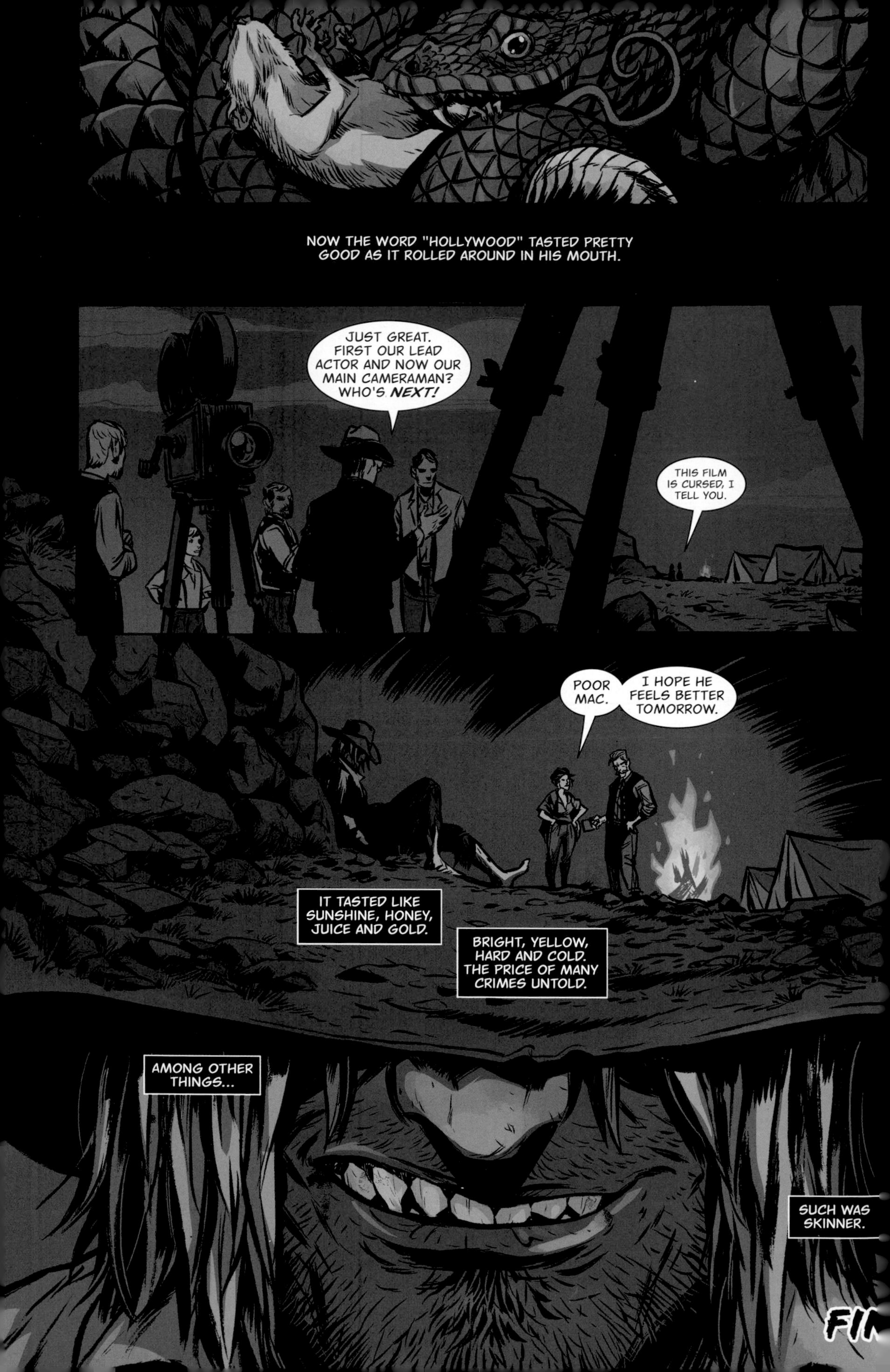
NOW THE WORD "HOLLYWOOD" TASTED PRETTY GOOD AS IT ROLLED AROUND IN HIS MOUTH.
JUST GREAT. FIRST OUR LEAD ACTOR AND NOW OUR MAIN CAMERAMAN? WHO'S ***NEXT!***
THIS FILM IS CURSED, I TELL YOU.
POOR MAC.
I HOPE HE FEELS BETTER TOMORROW.
IT TASTED LIKE SUNSHINE, HONEY, JUICE AND GOLD.
BRIGHT, YELLOW, HARD AND COLD. THE PRICE OF MANY CRIMES UNTOLD.
AMONG OTHER THINGS...
SUCH WAS SKINNER.

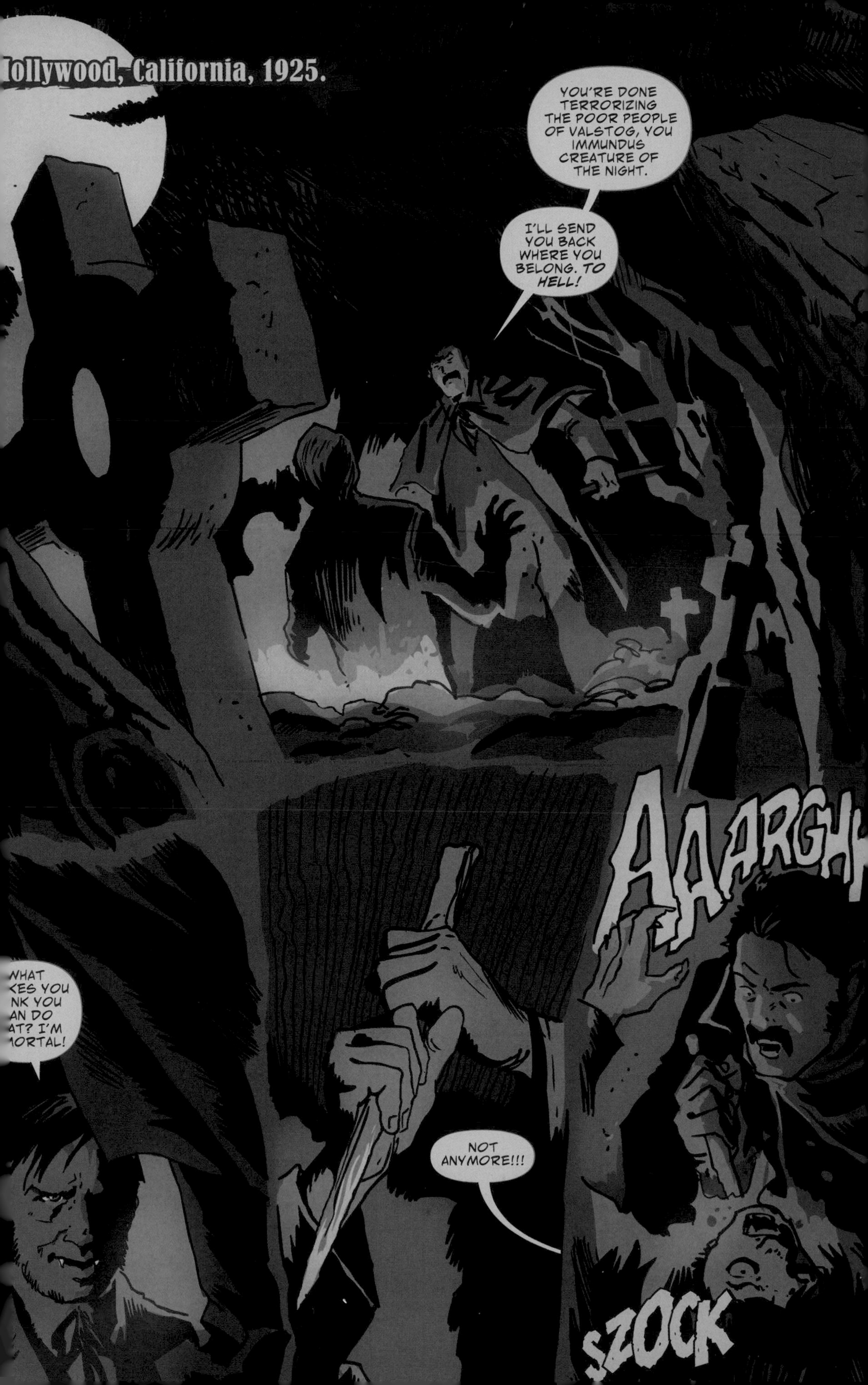
ollywood, California, 1925.
YOU'RE DONE TERRORIZING THE POOR PEOPLE OF VALSTOG, YOU IMMUNDUS CREATURE OF THE NIGHT.
I'LL SEND YOU BACK WHERE YOU BELONG. TO HELL!
AAARGH
NOT ANYMORE!!!
SZOCK

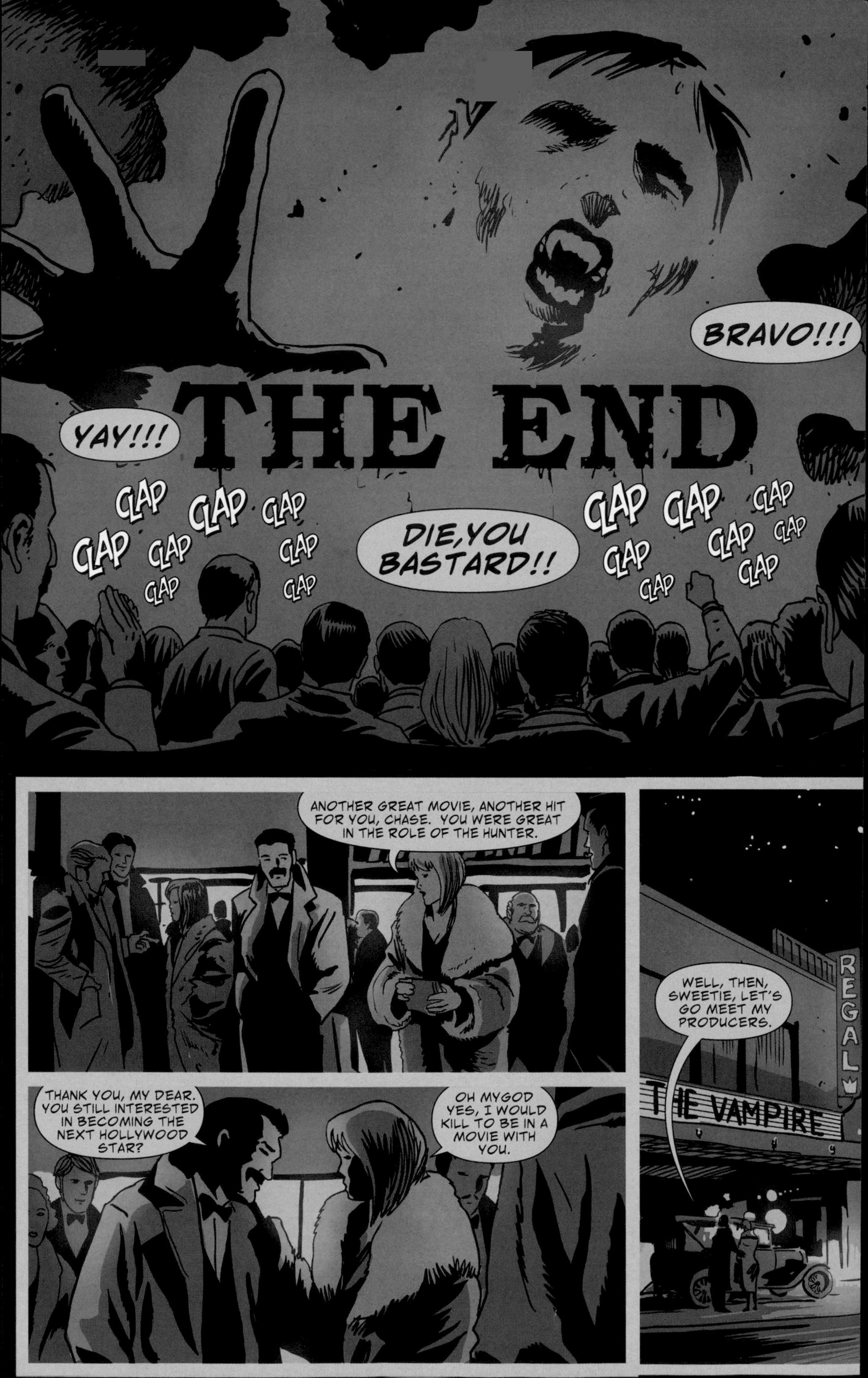
THE END
BRAVO!!!
YAY!!!
CLAP CLAP CLAP CLAP CLAP CLAP CLAP CLAP CLAP
DIE,YOU BASTARD!!
CLAP CLAP CLAP CLAP CLAP CLAP CLAP CLAP
ANOTHER GREAT MOVIE, ANOTHER HIT FOR YOU, CHASE. YOU WERE GREAT IN THE ROLE OF THE HUNTER.
THANK YOU, MY DEAR. YOU STILL INTERESTED IN BECOMING THE NEXT HOLLYWOOD STAR?
OH MYGOD YES, I WOULD KILL TO BE IN A MOVIE WITH YOU.
REGAL
THE VAMPIRE
WELL, THEN, SWEETIE, LET'S GO MEET MY PRODUCERS.

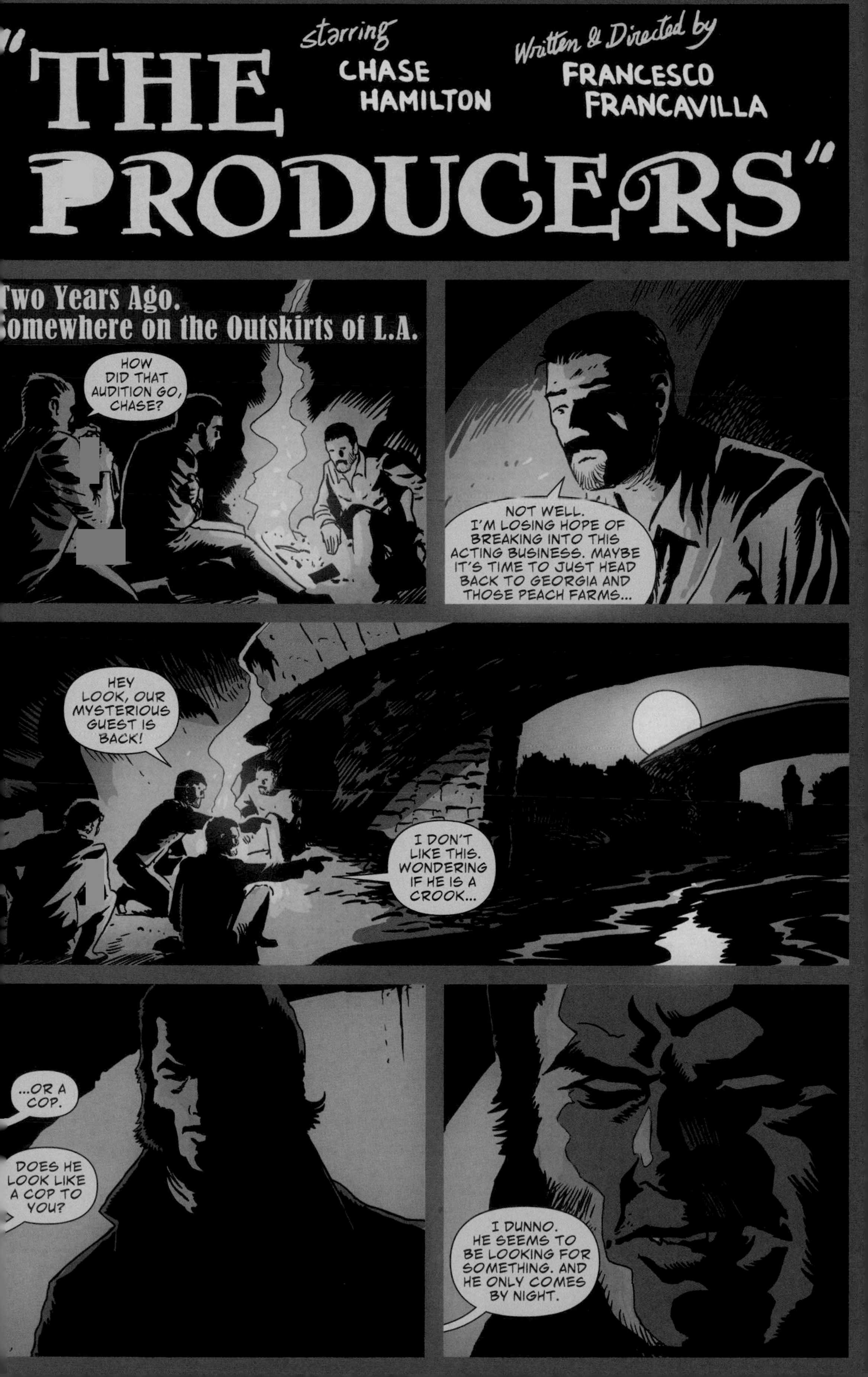
"THE PRODUCERS"
starring CHASE HAMILTON
Written & Directed by FRANCESCO FRANCAVILLA
Two Years Ago. Somewhere on the Outskirts of L.A.
HOW DID THAT AUDITION GO, CHASE?
NOT WELL. I'M LOSING HOPE OF BREAKING INTO THIS ACTING BUSINESS. MAYBE IT'S TIME TO JUST HEAD BACK TO GEORGIA AND THOSE PEACH FARMS...
HEY LOOK, OUR MYSTERIOUS GUEST IS BACK!
I DON'T LIKE THIS. WONDERING IF HE IS A CROOK...
...OR A COP.
DOES HE LOOK LIKE A COP TO YOU?
I DUNNO. HE SEEMS TO BE LOOKING FOR SOMETHING. AND HE ONLY COMES BY NIGHT.

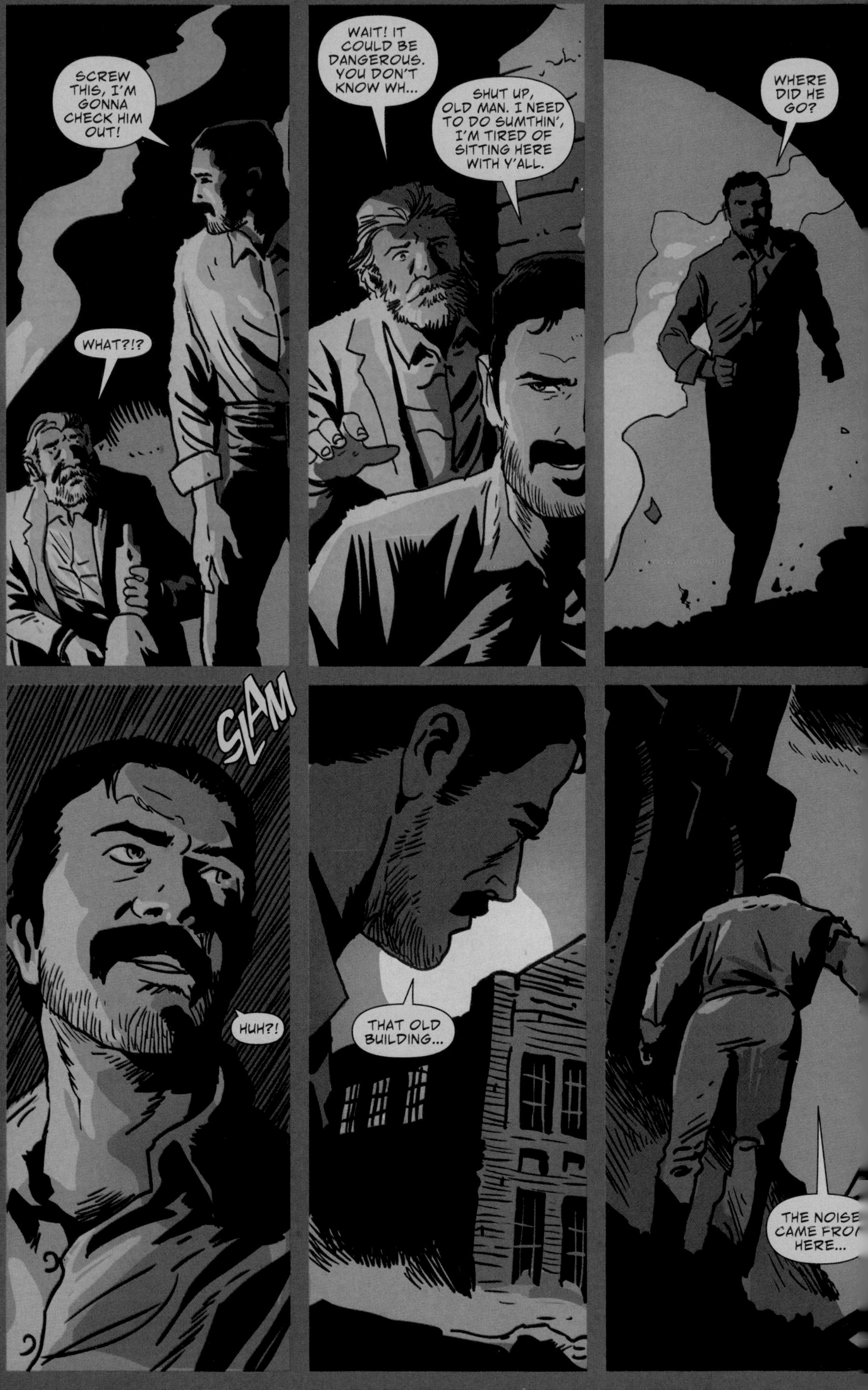
SCREW THIS, I'M GONNA CHECK HIM OUT!
WHAT?!?
WAIT! IT COULD BE DANGEROUS. YOU DON'T KNOW WH...
SHUT UP, OLD MAN. I NEED TO DO SUMTHIN', I'M TIRED OF SITTING HERE WITH Y'ALL.
WHERE DID HE GO?
SLAM
HUH?!
THAT OLD BUILDING...
THE NOISE CAME FRO HERE...

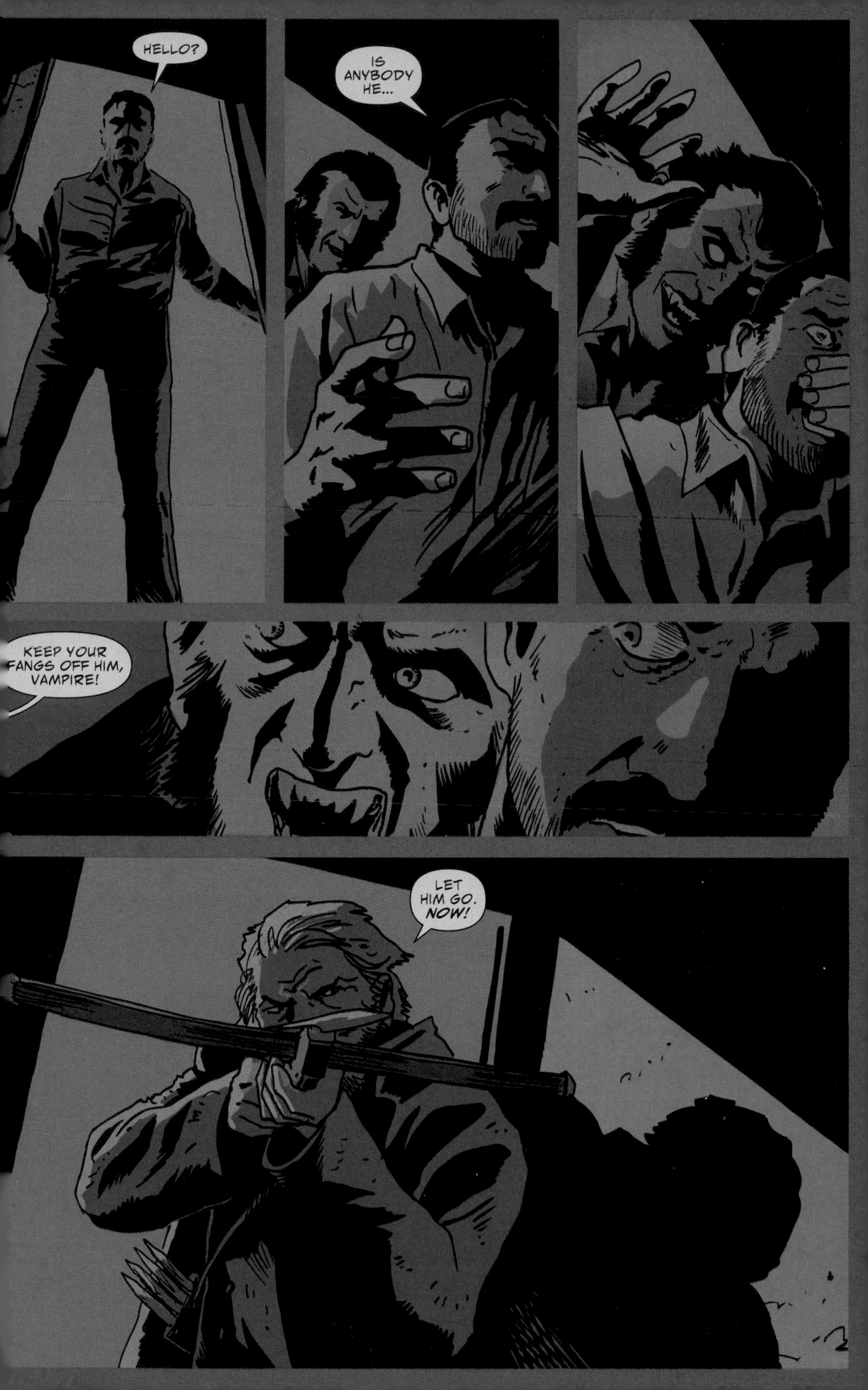
HELLO?
IS ANYBODY HE...
KEEP YOUR FANGS OFF HIM, VAMPIRE!
LET HIM GO. NOW!

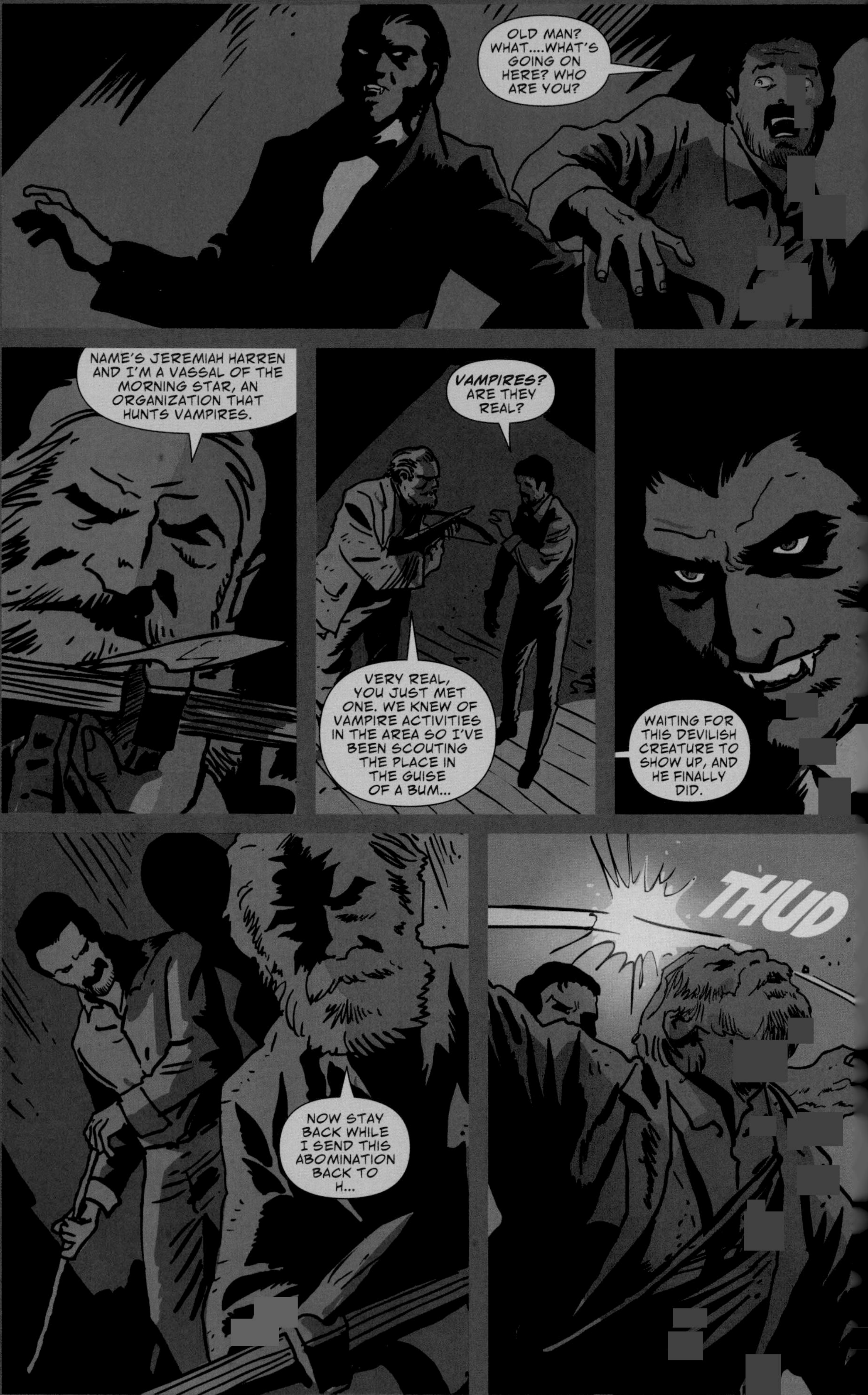
OLD MAN? WHAT....WHAT'S GOING ON HERE? WHO ARE YOU?
NAME'S JEREMIAH HARREN AND I'M A VASSAL OF THE MORNING STAR, AN ORGANIZATION THAT HUNTS VAMPIRES.
VAMPIRES? ARE THEY REAL?
VERY REAL, YOU JUST MET ONE. WE KNEW OF VAMPIRE ACTIVITIES IN THE AREA SO I'VE BEEN SCOUTING THE PLACE IN THE GUISE OF A BUM...
WAITING FOR THIS DEVILISH CREATURE TO SHOW UP, AND HE FINALLY DID.
NOW STAY BACK WHILE I SEND THIS ABOMINATION BACK TO H...
THUD

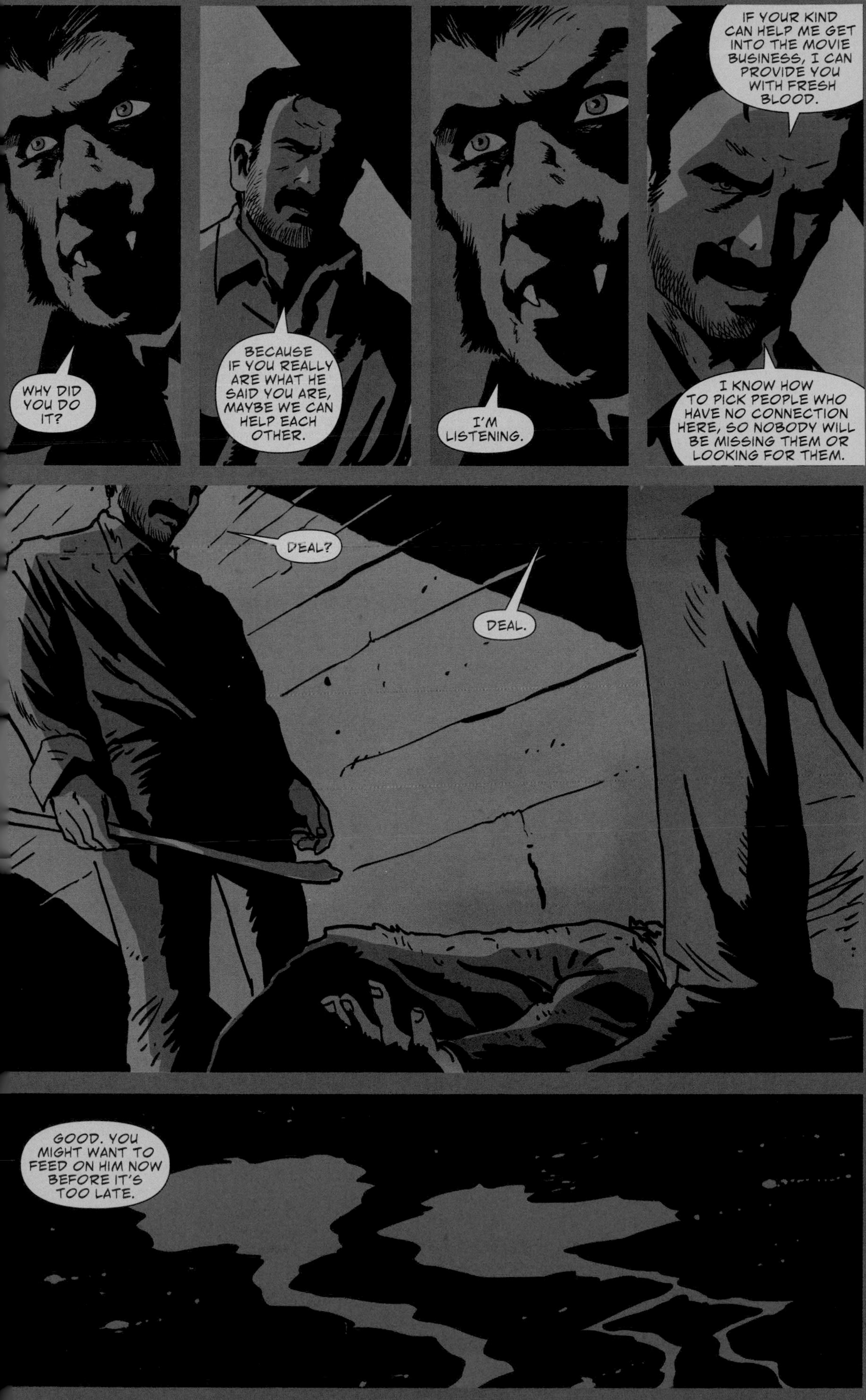

WHY DID YOU DO IT?
BECAUSE IF YOU REALLY ARE WHAT HE SAID YOU ARE, MAYBE WE CAN HELP EACH OTHER.
I'M LISTENING.
IF YOUR KIND CAN HELP ME GET INTO THE MOVIE BUSINESS, I CAN PROVIDE YOU WITH FRESH BLOOD.
I KNOW HOW TO PICK PEOPLE WHO HAVE NO CONNECTION HERE, SO NOBODY WILL BE MISSING THEM OR LOOKING FOR THEM.
DEAL?
DEAL.
GOOD. YOU MIGHT WANT TO FEED ON HIM NOW BEFORE IT'S TOO LATE.

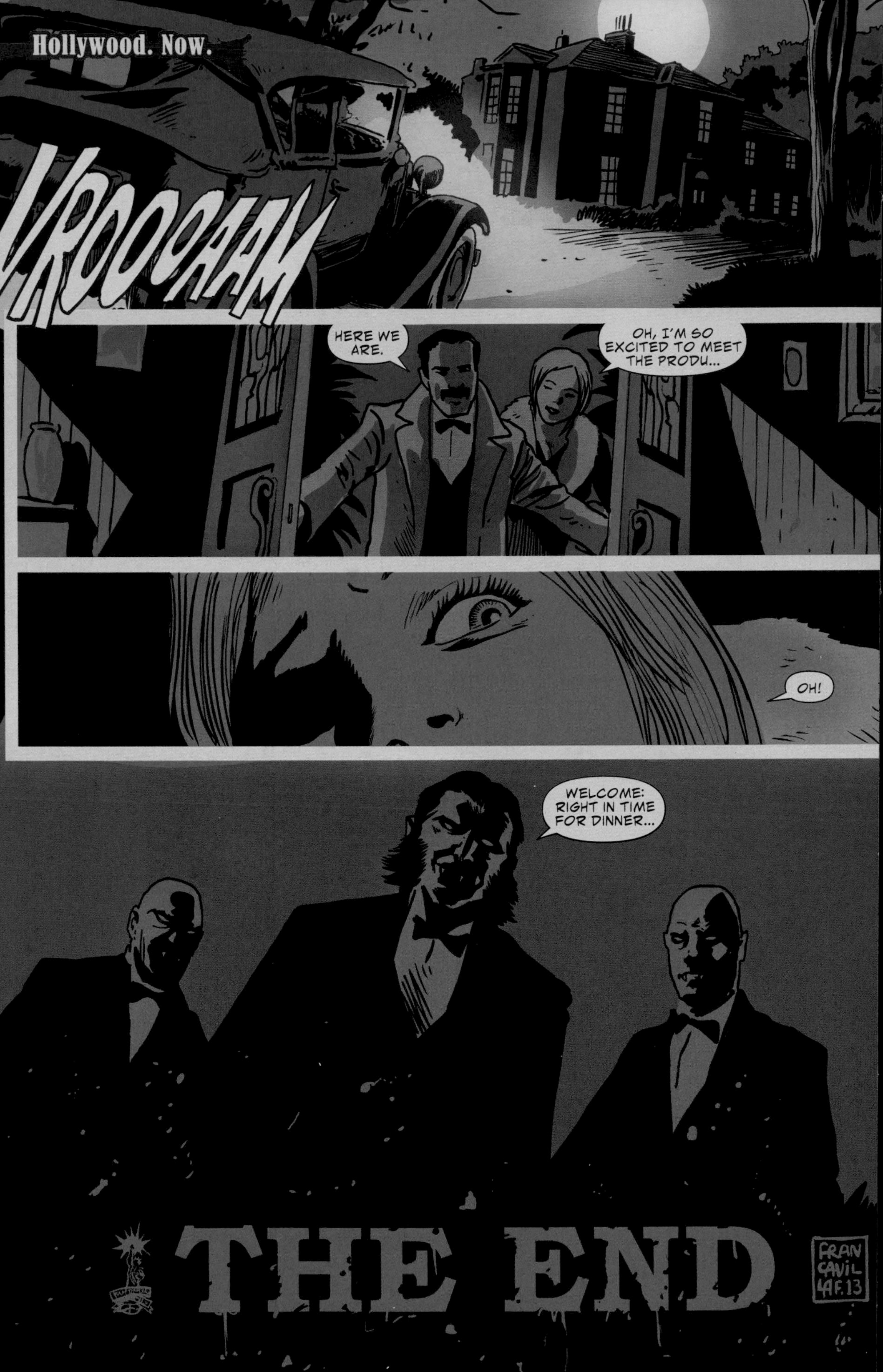
Hollywood. Now.
VROOOAAM
HERE WE ARE.
OH, I'M SO EXCITED TO MEET THE PRODU...
OH!
WELCOME: RIGHT IN TIME FOR DINNER...
THE END
FRAN CAVIL LA F.13

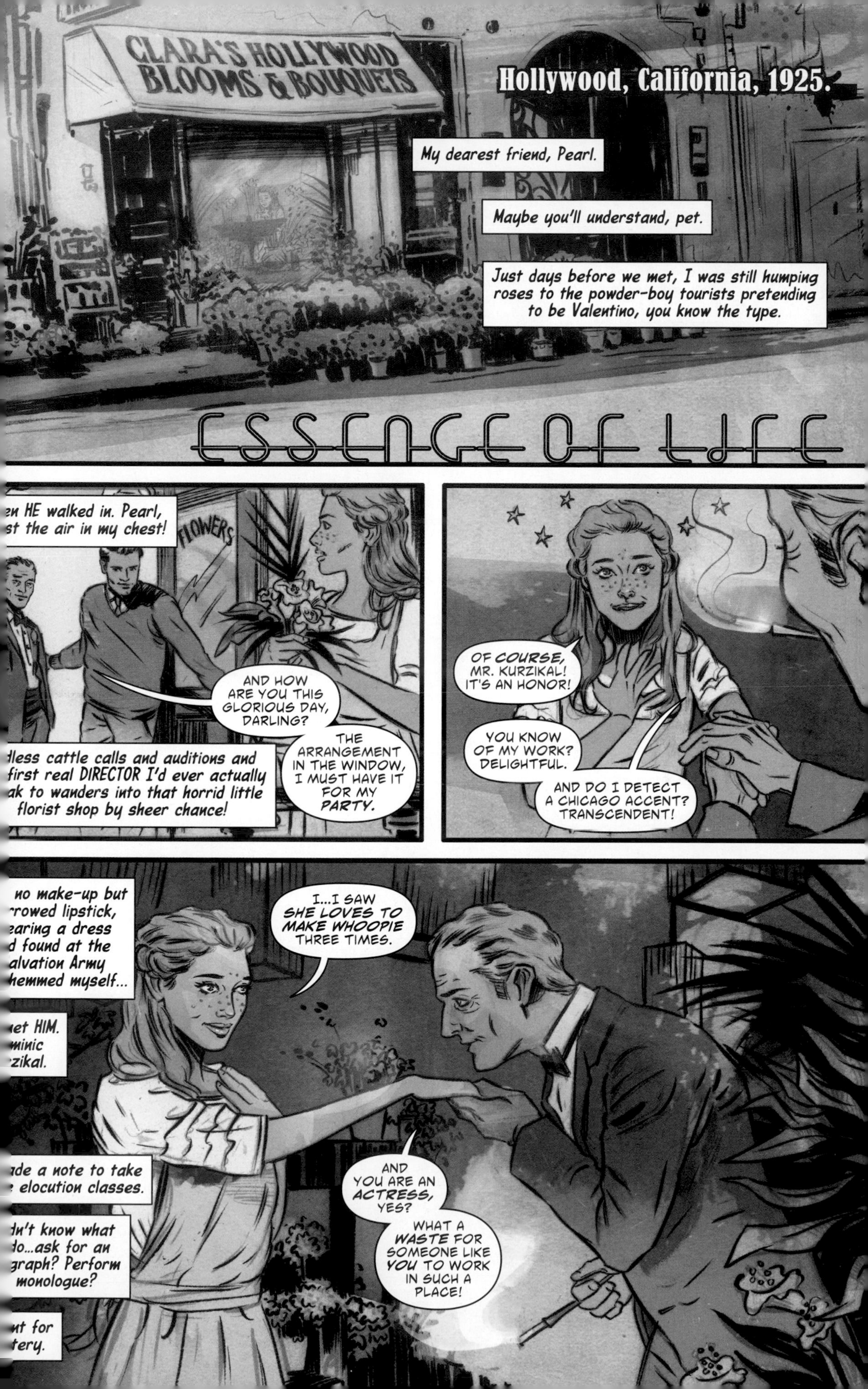

CLARA'S HOLLYWOOD BLOOMS & BOUQUETS
Hollywood, California, 1925.
My dearest friend, Pearl.
Maybe you'll understand, pet.
Just days before we met, I was still humping roses to the powder-boy tourists pretending to be Valentino, you know the type.
ESSENCE OF LIFE
en HE walked in. Pearl, st the air in my chest!
FLOWERS
AND HOW ARE YOU THIS GLORIOUS DAY, DARLING?
dless cattle calls and auditions and first real DIRECTOR I'd ever actually ak to wanders into that horrid little florist shop by sheer chance!
THE ARRANGEMENT IN THE WINDOW, I MUST HAVE IT FOR MY PARTY.
OF COURSE, MR. KURZIKAL! IT'S AN HONOR!
YOU KNOW OF MY WORK? DELIGHTFUL.
AND DO I DETECT A CHICAGO ACCENT? TRANSCENDENT!
no make-up but rrowed lipstick, earing a dress d found at the alvation Army hemmed myself...
I...I SAW SHE LOVES TO MAKE WHOOPIE THREE TIMES.
net HIM. minic zikal.
ade a note to take e elocution classes.
dn't know what do...ask for an graph? Perform monologue?
AND YOU ARE AN ACTRESS, YES?
WHAT A WASTE FOR SOMEONE LIKE YOU TO WORK IN SUCH A PLACE!
nt for tery.

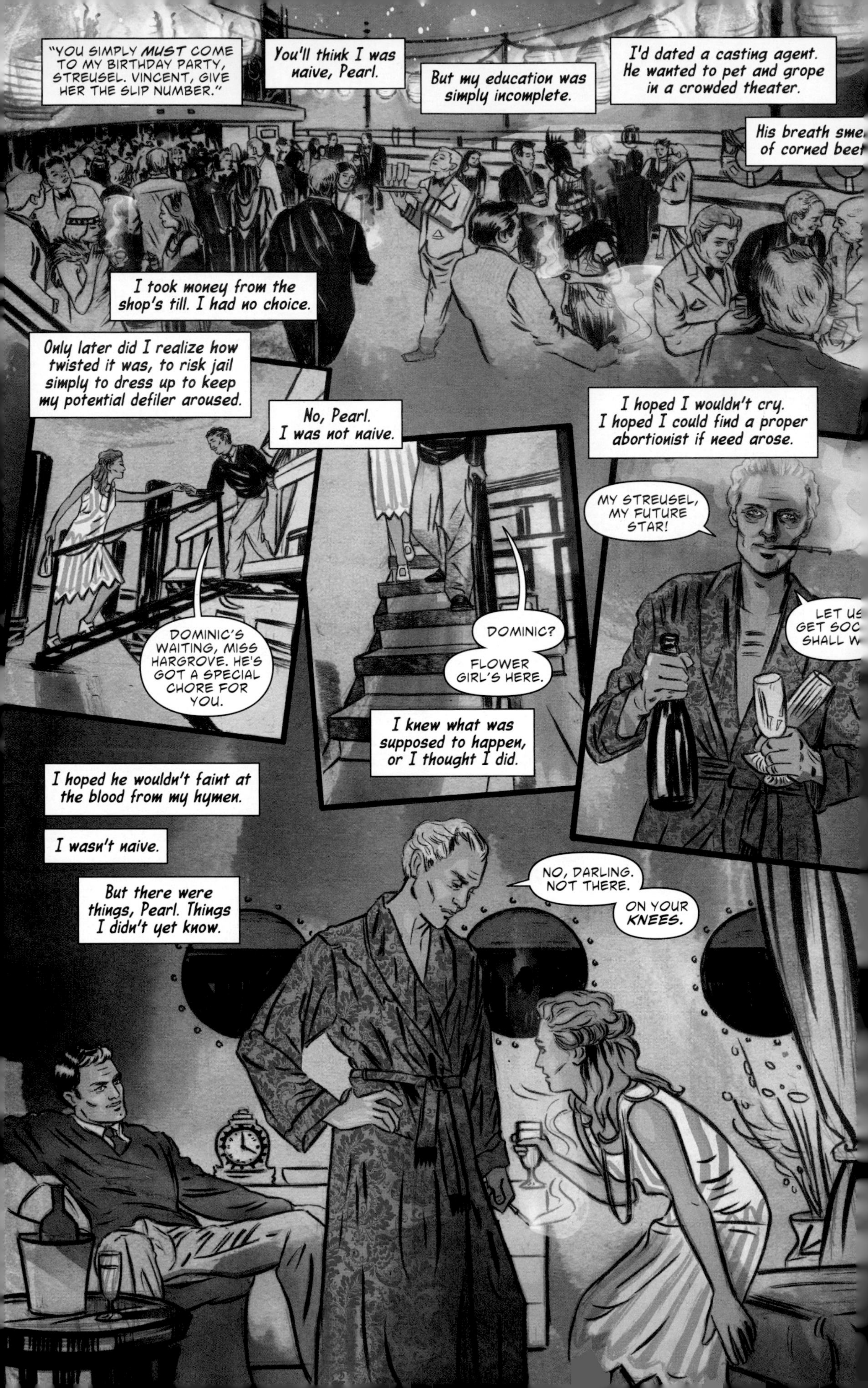
"YOU SIMPLY MUST COME TO MY BIRTHDAY PARTY, STREUSEL. VINCENT, GIVE HER THE SLIP NUMBER."
You'll think I was naive, Pearl.
But my education was simply incomplete.
I'd dated a casting agent. He wanted to pet and grope in a crowded theater.
I took money from the shop's till. I had no choice.
Only later did I realize how twisted it was, to risk jail simply to dress up to keep my potential defiler aroused.
DOMINIC'S WAITING, MISS HARGROVE. HE'S GOT A SPECIAL CHORE FOR YOU.
No, Pearl. I was not naive.
DOMINIC?
FLOWER GIRL'S HERE.
I knew what was supposed to happen, or I thought I did.
I hoped I wouldn't cry. I hoped I could find a proper abortionist if need arose.
MY STREUSEL, MY FUTURE STAR!
I hoped he wouldn't faint at the blood from my hymen.
I wasn't naive.
But there were things, Pearl. Things I didn't yet know.
NO, DARLING. NOT THERE.
ON YOUR KNEES.

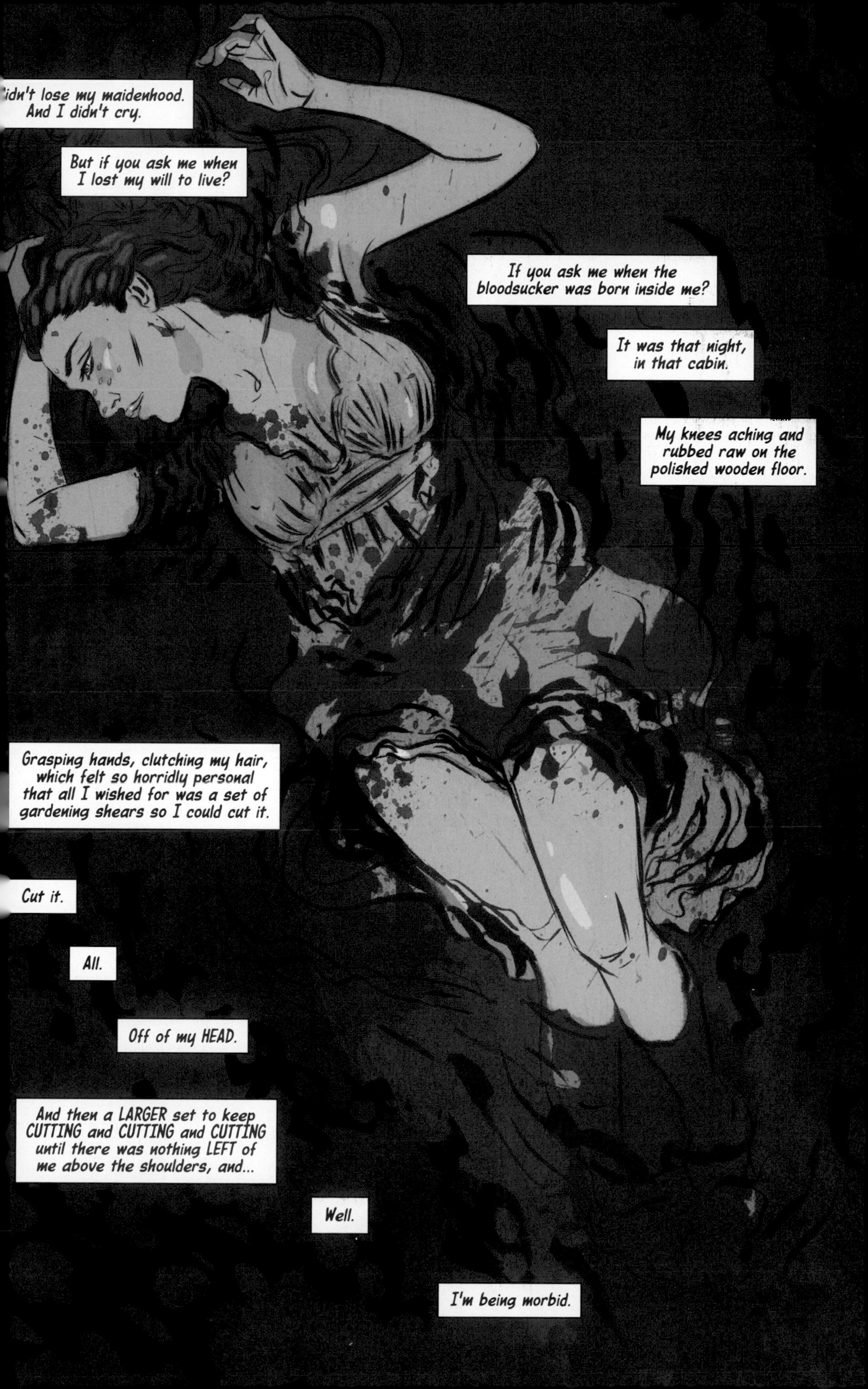
idn't lose my maidenhood. And I didn't cry.
But if you ask me when I lost my will to live?
If you ask me when the bloodsucker was born inside me?
It was that night, in that cabin.
My knees aching and rubbed raw on the polished wooden floor.
Grasping hands, clutching my hair, which felt so horridly personal that all I wished for was a set of gardening shears so I could cut it.
Cut it.
All.
Off of my HEAD.
And then a LARGER set to keep CUTTING and CUTTING and CUTTING until there was nothing LEFT of me above the shoulders, and...
Well.
I'm being morbid.

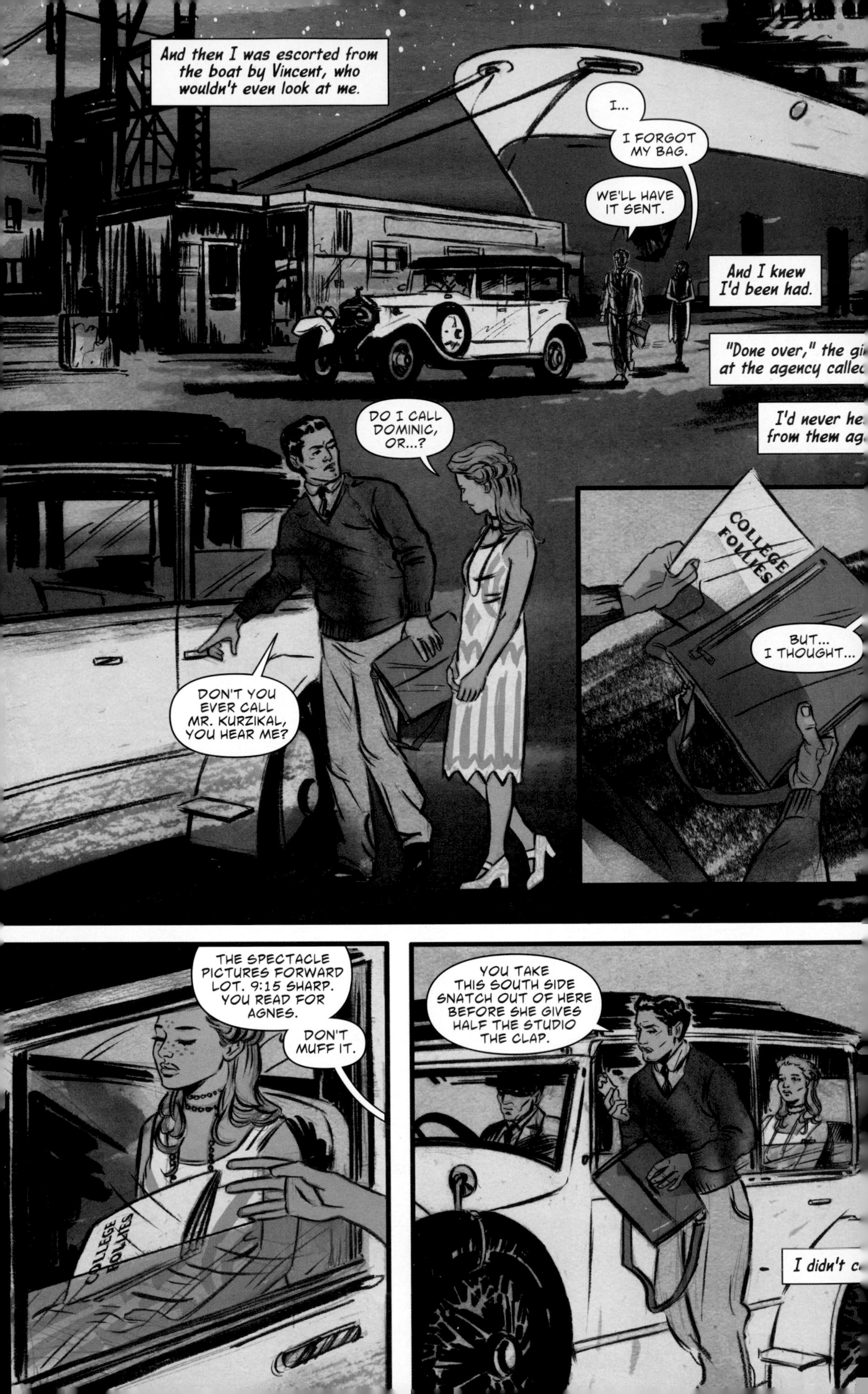
And then I was escorted from the boat by Vincent, who wouldn't even look at me.
I...
I FORGOT MY BAG.
WE'LL HAVE IT SENT.
And I knew I'd been had.
"Done over," the gi at the agency calle
I'd never he from them ag
DO I CALL DOMINIC, OR...?
DON'T YOU EVER CALL MR. KURZIKAL, YOU HEAR ME?
COLLEGE FOLLIES
BUT... I THOUGHT...
THE SPECTACLE PICTURES FORWARD LOT. 9:15 SHARP. YOU READ FOR AGNES.
DON'T MUFF IT.
COLLEGE FOLLIES
YOU TAKE THIS SOUTH SIDE SNATCH OUT OF HERE BEFORE SHE GIVES HALF THE STUDIO THE CLAP.
I didn't c

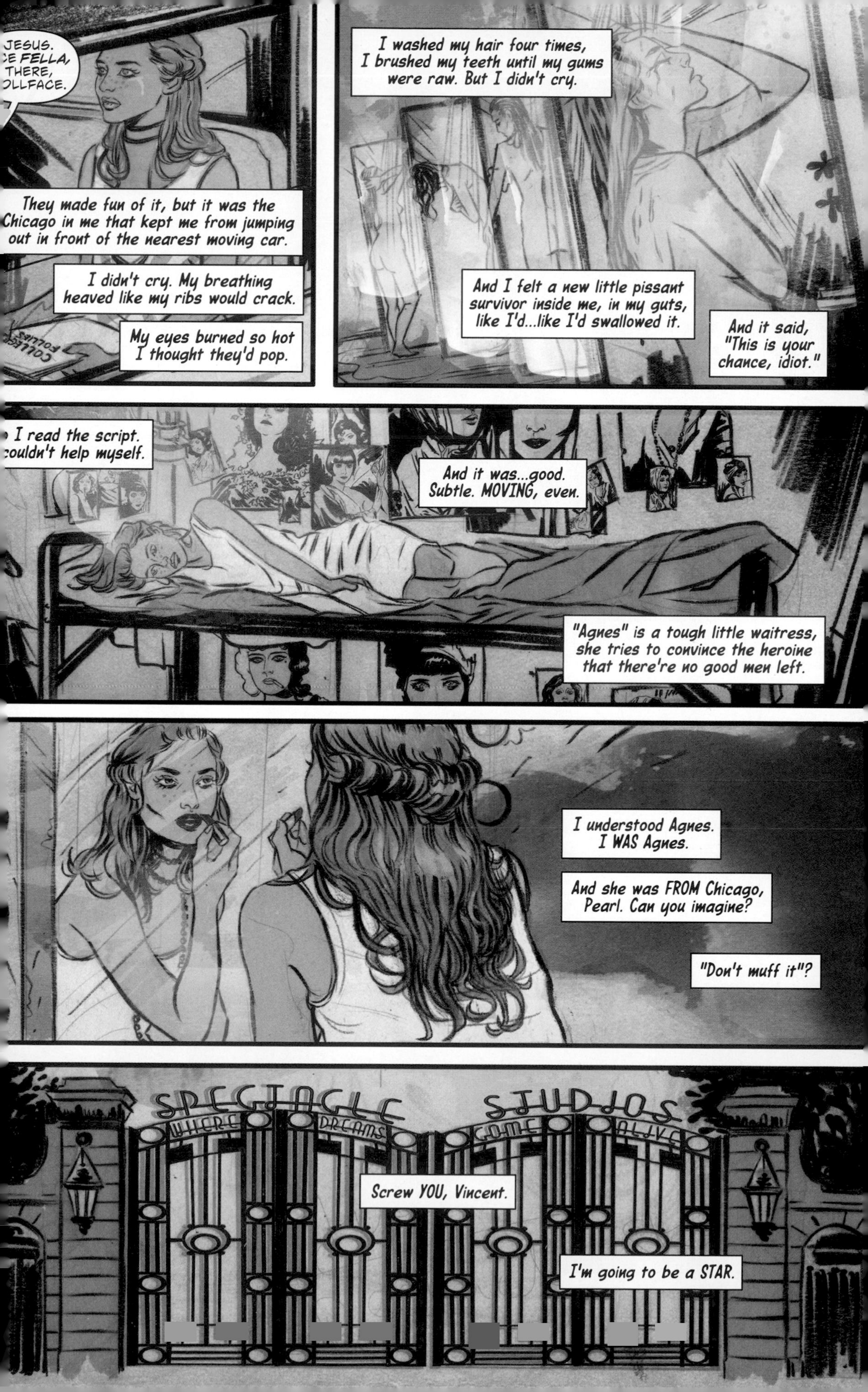
JESUS.
CE FELLA,
THERE,
OLLFACE.
They made fun of it, but it was the Chicago in me that kept me from jumping out in front of the nearest moving car.
I didn't cry. My breathing heaved like my ribs would crack.
My eyes burned so hot I thought they'd pop.
COLLEGE FOLLIES
I washed my hair four times, I brushed my teeth until my gums were raw. But I didn't cry.
And I felt a new little pissant survivor inside me, in my guts, like I'd...like I'd swallowed it.
And it said, "This is your chance, idiot."
I read the script.
ouldn't help myself.
And it was...good. Subtle. MOVING, even.
"Agnes" is a tough little waitress, she tries to convince the heroine that there're no good men left.
I understood Agnes. I WAS Agnes.
And she was FROM Chicago, Pearl. Can you imagine?
"Don't muff it"?
SPECTACLE STUDIOS
WHERE DREAMS COME ALIVE
Screw YOU, Vincent.
I'm going to be a STAR.

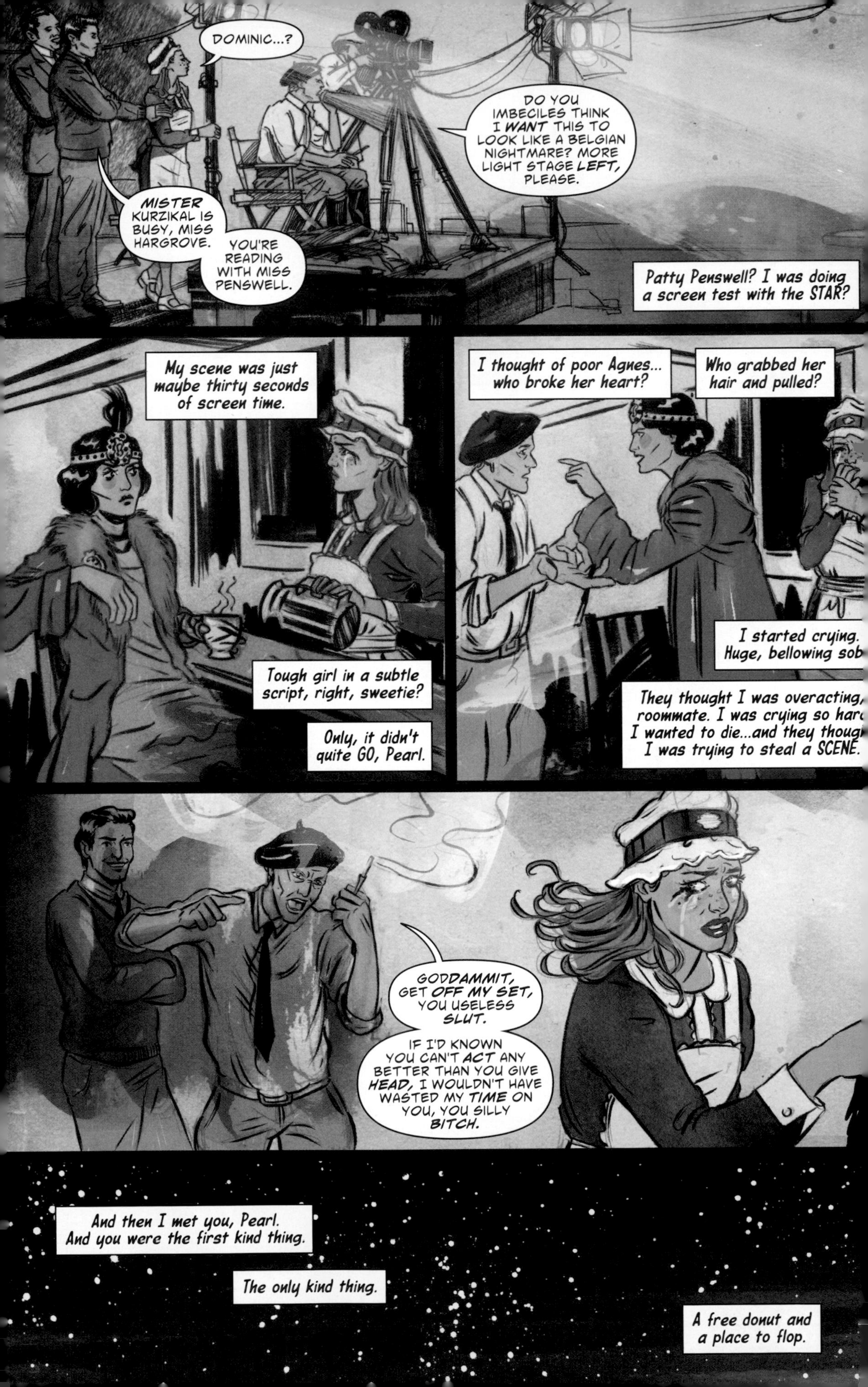
DOMINIC...?
DO YOU IMBECILES THINK I WANT THIS TO LOOK LIKE A BELGIAN NIGHTMARE? MORE LIGHT STAGE LEFT, PLEASE.
MISTER KURZIKAL IS BUSY, MISS HARGROVE.
YOU'RE READING WITH MISS PENSWELL.
Patty Penswell? I was doing a screen test with the STAR?
My scene was just maybe thirty seconds of screen time.
Tough girl in a subtle script, right, sweetie?
Only, it didn't quite GO, Pearl.
I thought of poor Agnes... who broke her heart?
Who grabbed her hair and pulled?
I started crying. Huge, bellowing sob
They thought I was overacting, roommate. I was crying so hard I wanted to die...and they thought I was trying to steal a SCENE.
GODDAMMIT, GET OFF MY SET, YOU USELESS SLUT.
IF I'D KNOWN YOU CAN'T ACT ANY BETTER THAN YOU GIVE HEAD, I WOULDN'T HAVE WASTED MY TIME ON YOU, YOU SILLY BITCH.
And then I met you, Pearl. And you were the first kind thing.
The only kind thing.
A free donut and a place to flop.

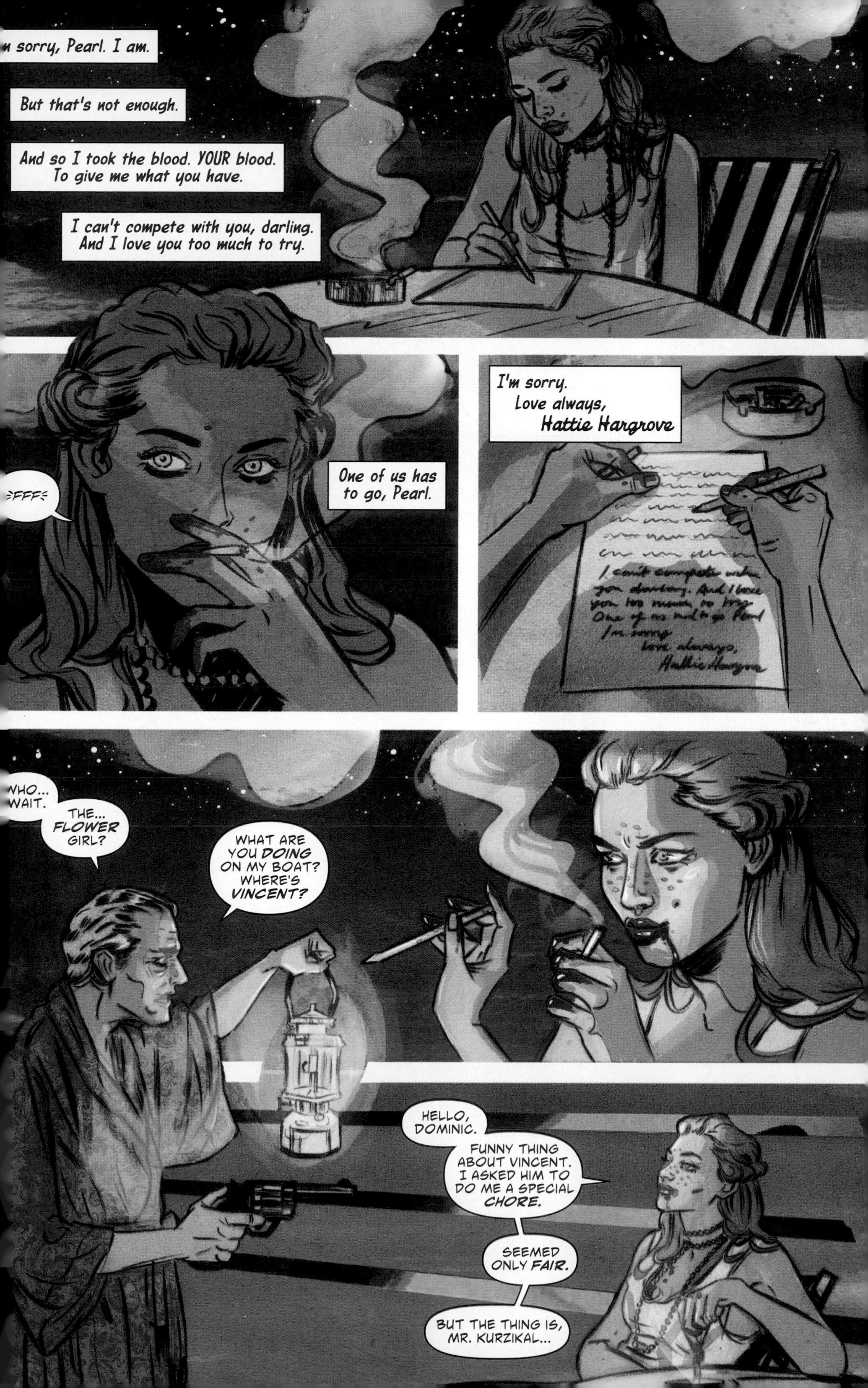
m sorry, Pearl. I am.
But that's not enough.
And so I took the blood. YOUR blood. To give me what you have.
I can't compete with you, darling. And I love you too much to try.
FFF
One of us has to go, Pearl.
I'm sorry. Love always, Hattie Hargrove
WHO... WAIT.
THE... FLOWER GIRL?
WHAT ARE YOU DOING ON MY BOAT? WHERE'S VINCENT?
HELLO, DOMINIC.
FUNNY THING ABOUT VINCENT. I ASKED HIM TO DO ME A SPECIAL CHORE.
SEEMED ONLY FAIR.
BUT THE THING IS, MR. KURZIKAL...

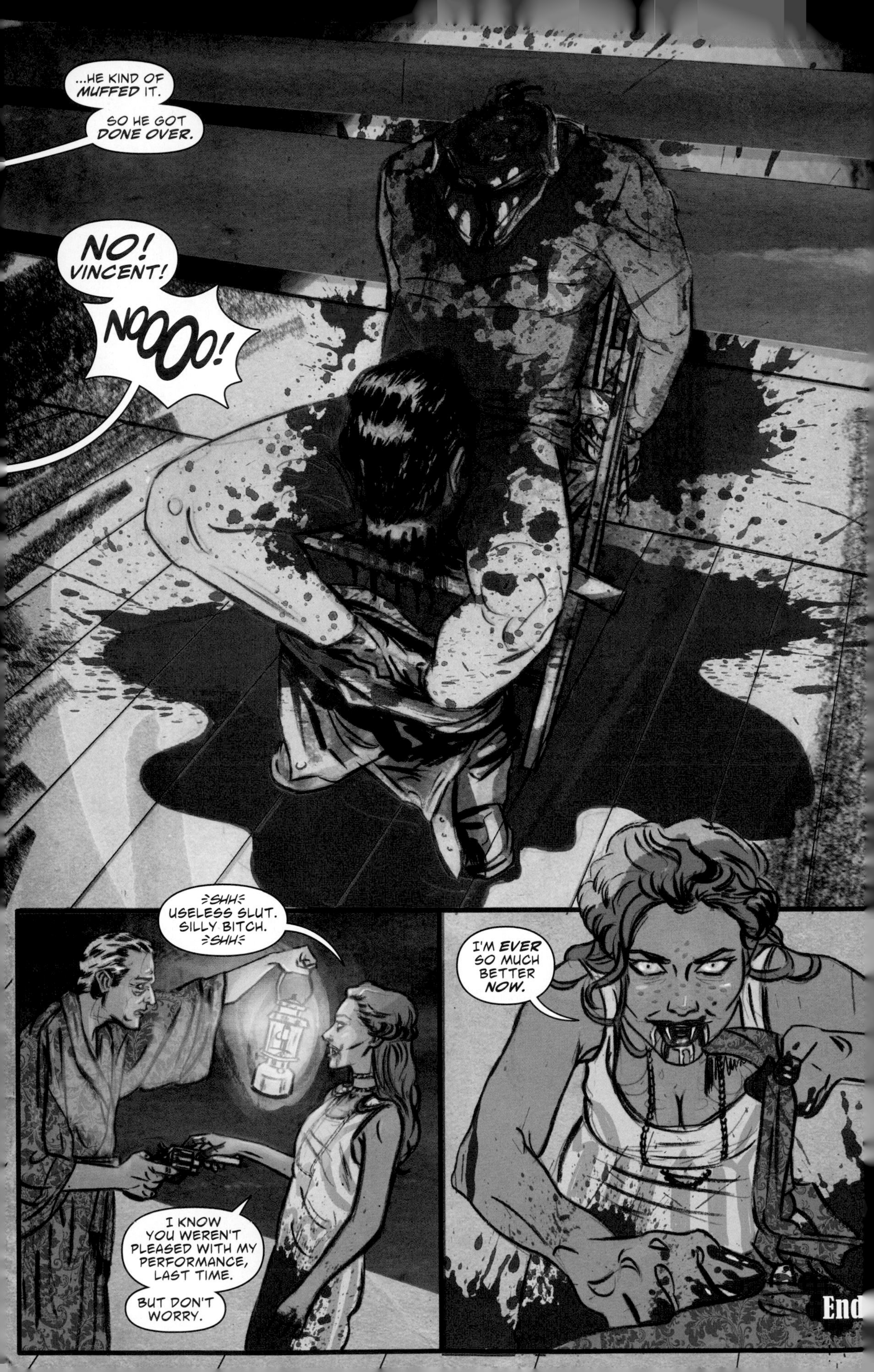

...HE KIND OF MUFFED IT.
SO HE GOT DONE OVER.
NO! VINCENT!
NOOOO!
SHH
USELESS SLUT. SILLY BITCH.
SHH
I KNOW YOU WEREN'T PLEASED WITH MY PERFORMANCE, LAST TIME.
BUT DON'T WORRY.
I'M EVER SO MUCH BETTER NOW.
End

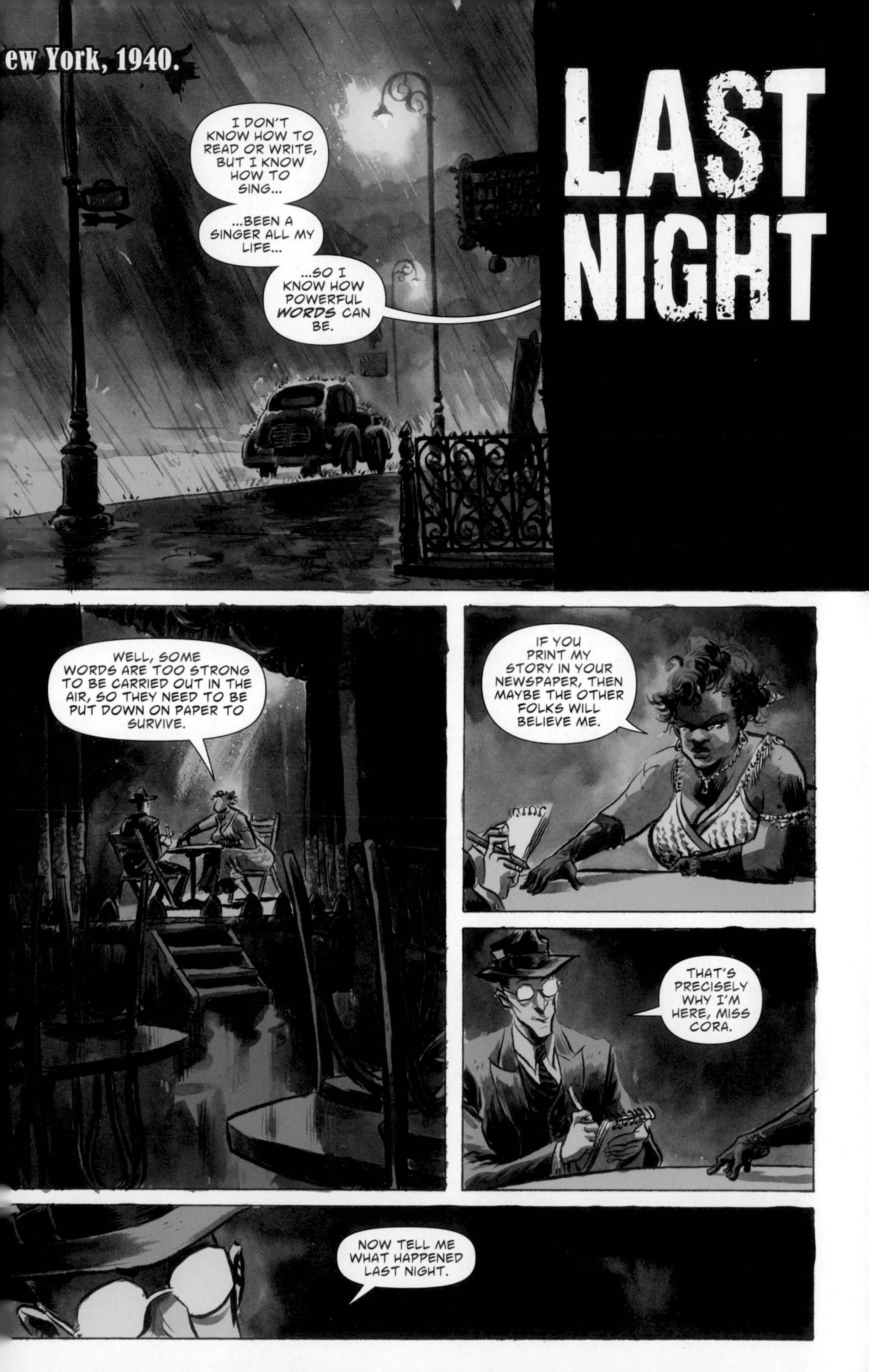
ew York, 1940.
LAST NIGHT
I DON'T KNOW HOW TO READ OR WRITE, BUT I KNOW HOW TO SING...
...BEEN A SINGER ALL MY LIFE...
...SO I KNOW HOW POWERFUL WORDS CAN BE.
WELL, SOME WORDS ARE TOO STRONG TO BE CARRIED OUT IN THE AIR, SO THEY NEED TO BE PUT DOWN ON PAPER TO SURVIVE.
IF YOU PRINT MY STORY IN YOUR NEWSPAPER, THEN MAYBE THE OTHER FOLKS WILL BELIEVE ME.
THAT'S PRECISELY WHY I'M HERE, MISS CORA.
NOW TELL ME WHAT HAPPENED LAST NIGHT.

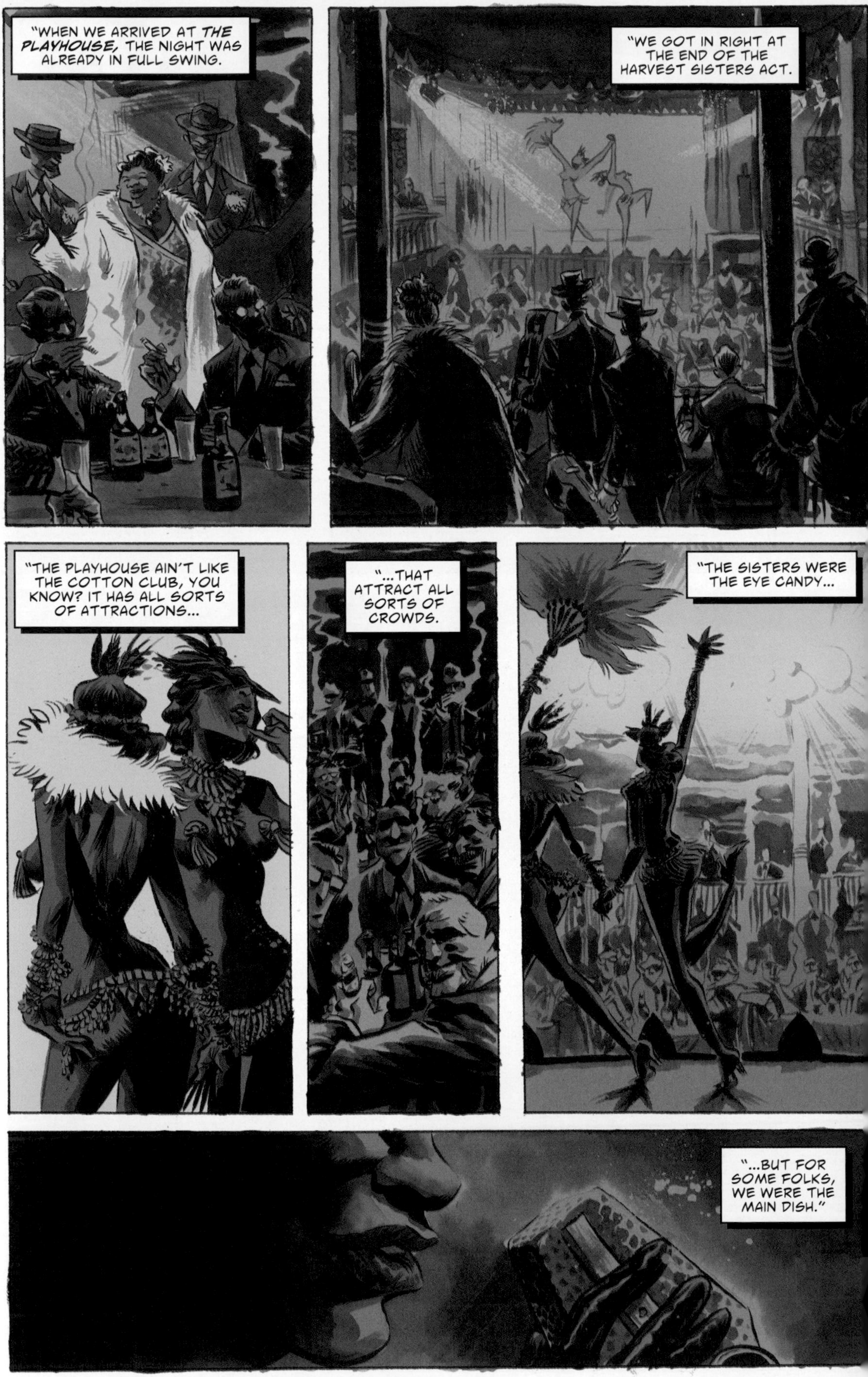
"WHEN WE ARRIVED AT *THE PLAYHOUSE,* THE NIGHT WAS ALREADY IN FULL SWING.
"WE GOT IN RIGHT AT THE END OF THE HARVEST SISTERS ACT.
"THE PLAYHOUSE AIN'T LIKE THE COTTON CLUB, YOU KNOW? IT HAS ALL SORTS OF ATTRACTIONS...
"...THAT ATTRACT ALL SORTS OF CROWDS.
"THE SISTERS WERE THE EYE CANDY...
"...BUT FOR SOME FOLKS, WE WERE THE MAIN DISH."

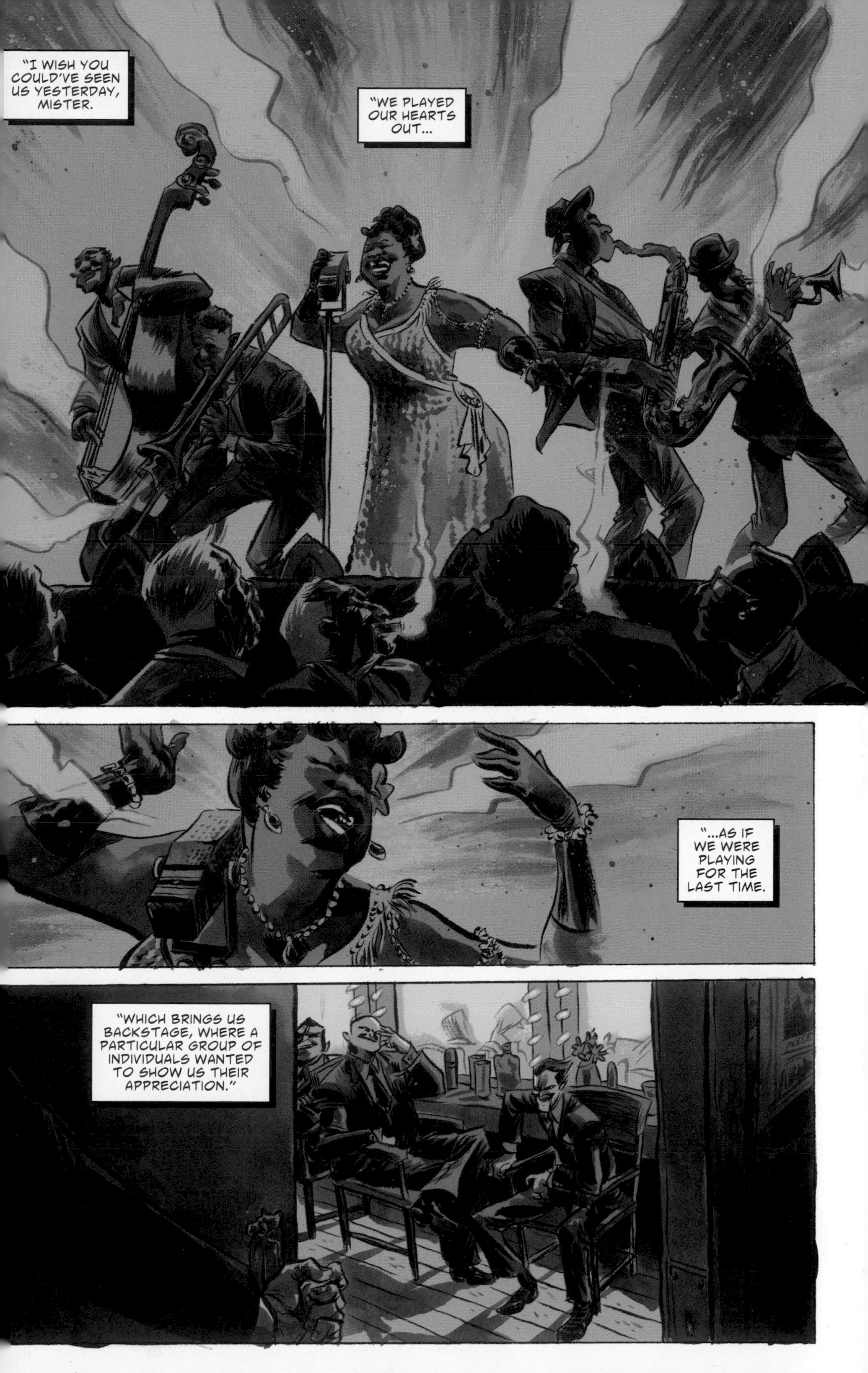
"I WISH YOU COULD'VE SEEN US YESTERDAY, MISTER.
"WE PLAYED OUR HEARTS OUT...
"...AS IF WE WERE PLAYING FOR THE LAST TIME.
"WHICH BRINGS US BACKSTAGE, WHERE A PARTICULAR GROUP OF INDIVIDUALS WANTED TO SHOW US THEIR APPRECIATION."

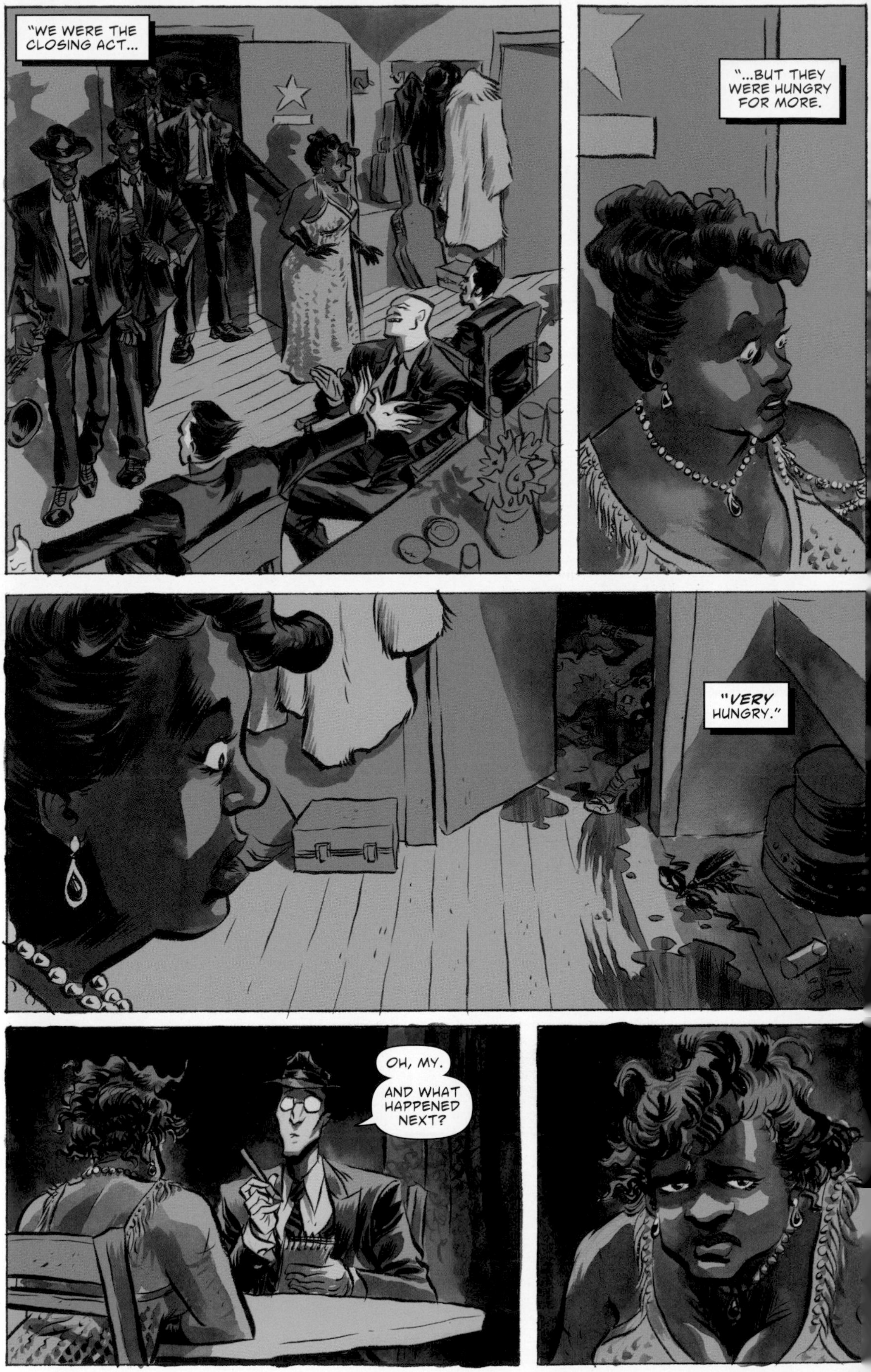
"WE WERE THE CLOSING ACT...
"...BUT THEY WERE HUNGRY FOR MORE.
"VERY HUNGRY."
OH, MY.
AND WHAT HAPPENED NEXT?

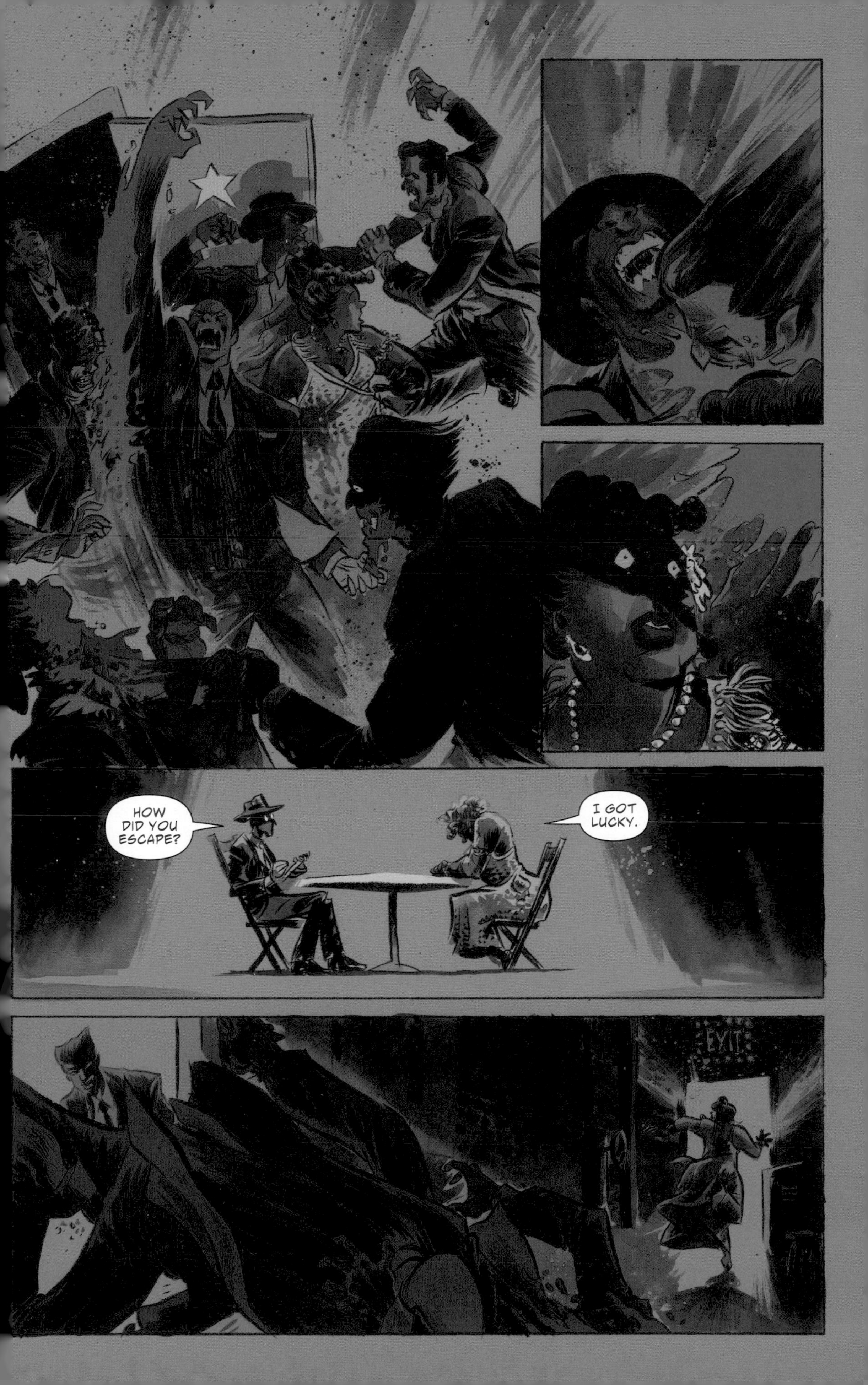
HOW DID YOU ESCAPE?
I GOT LUCKY.
EXIT

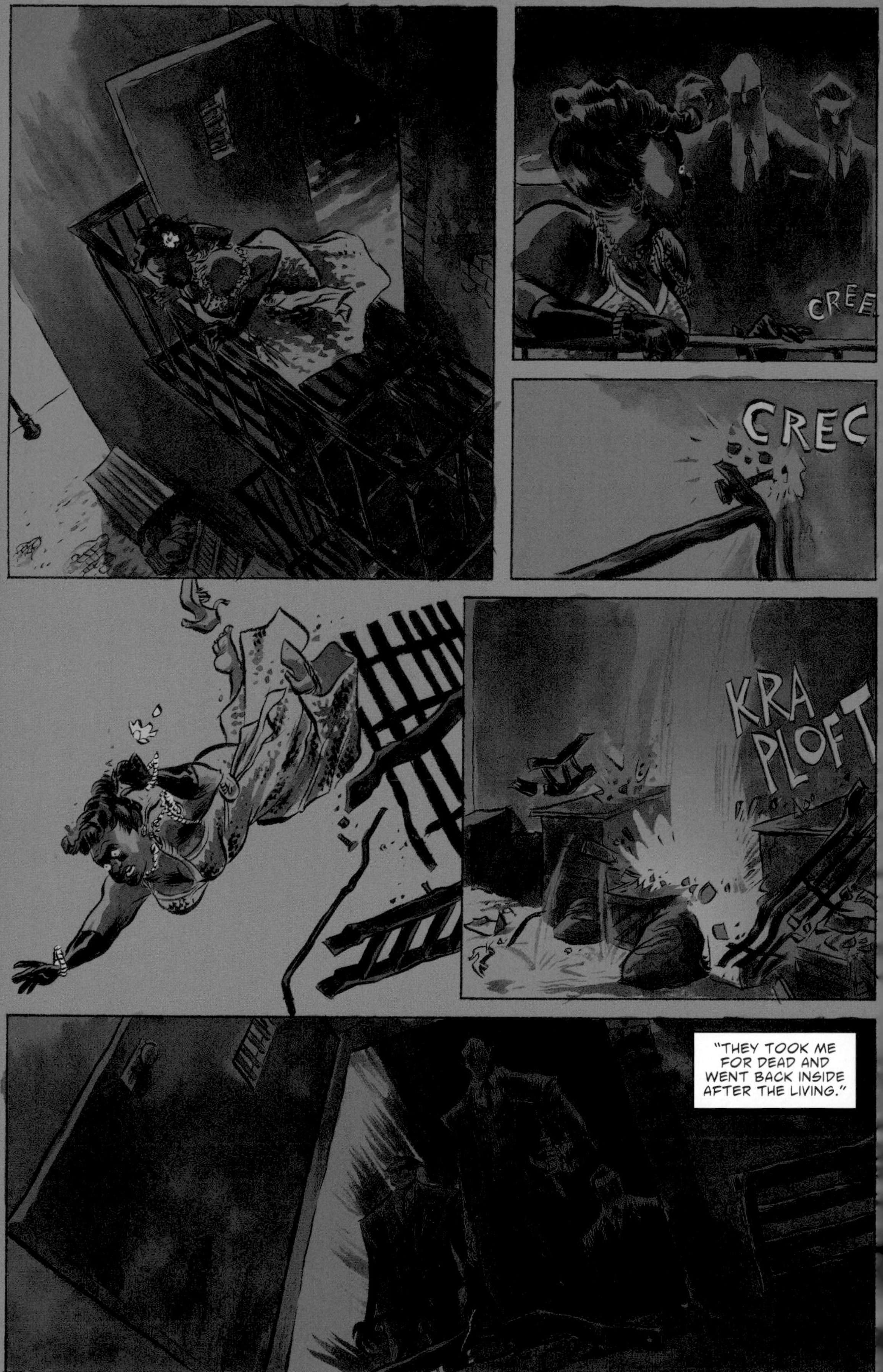
CREE
CREC
KRA PLOFT
"THEY TOOK ME FOR DEAD AND WENT BACK INSIDE AFTER THE LIVING."

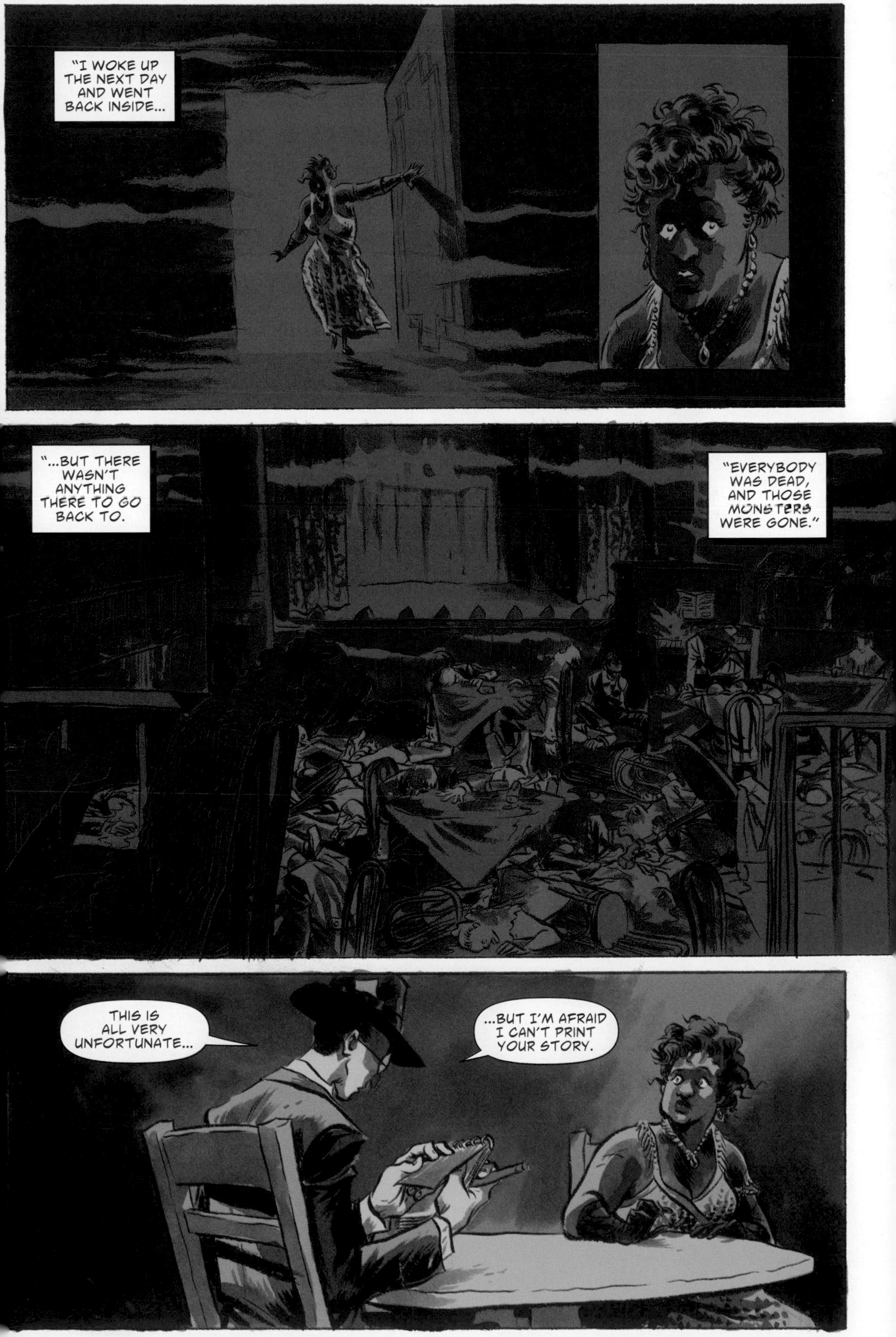
"I WOKE UP THE NEXT DAY AND WENT BACK INSIDE...
"...BUT THERE WASN'T ANYTHING THERE TO GO BACK TO.
"EVERYBODY WAS DEAD, AND THOSE MONSTERS WERE GONE."
THIS IS ALL VERY UNFORTUNATE...
...BUT I'M AFRAID I CAN'T PRINT YOUR STORY.

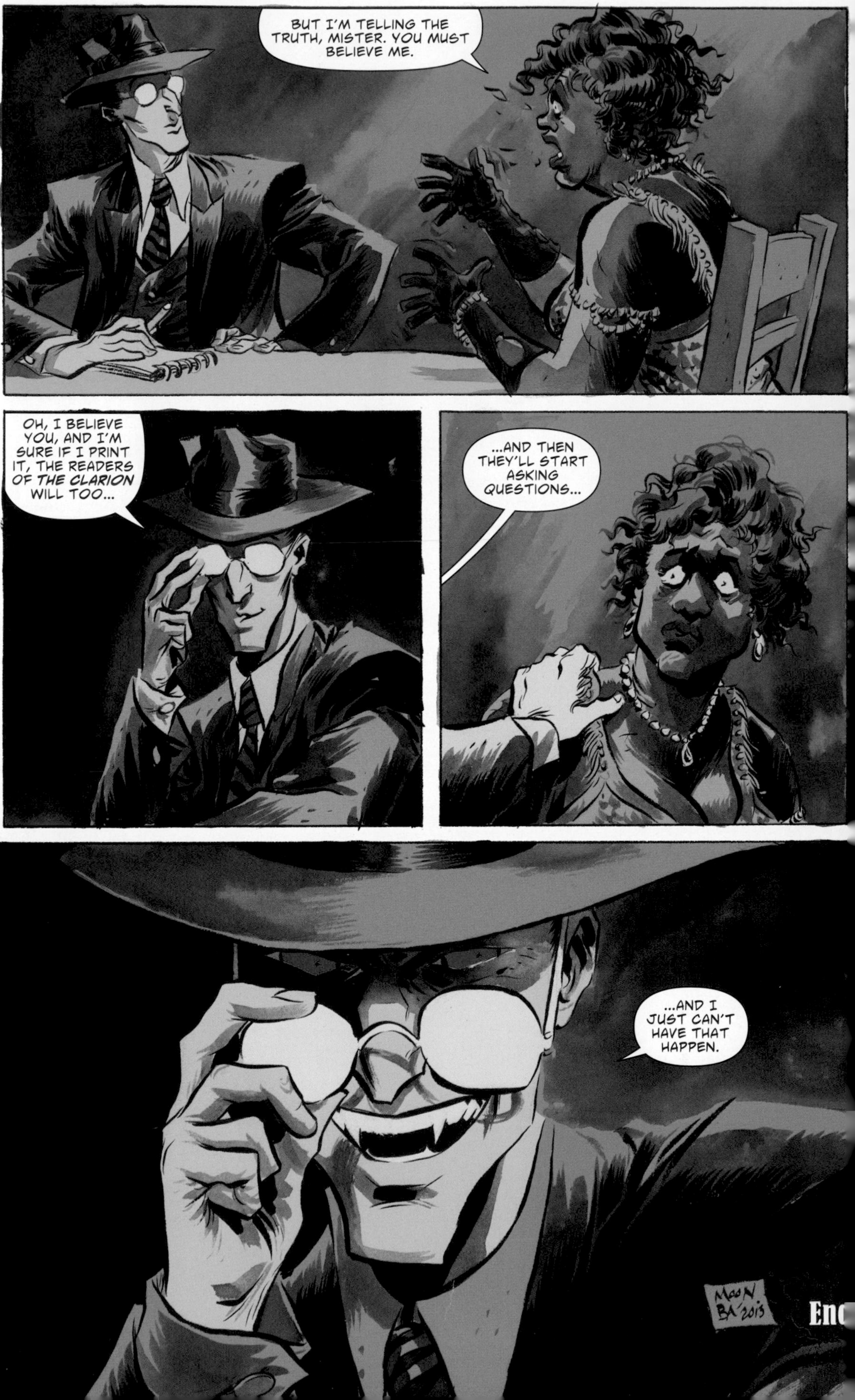
BUT I'M TELLING THE TRUTH, MISTER. YOU MUST BELIEVE ME.
OH, I BELIEVE YOU, AND I'M SURE IF I PRINT IT, THE READERS OF *THE CLARION* WILL TOO...
...AND THEN THEY'LL START ASKING QUESTIONS...
...AND I JUST CAN'T HAVE THAT HAPPEN.

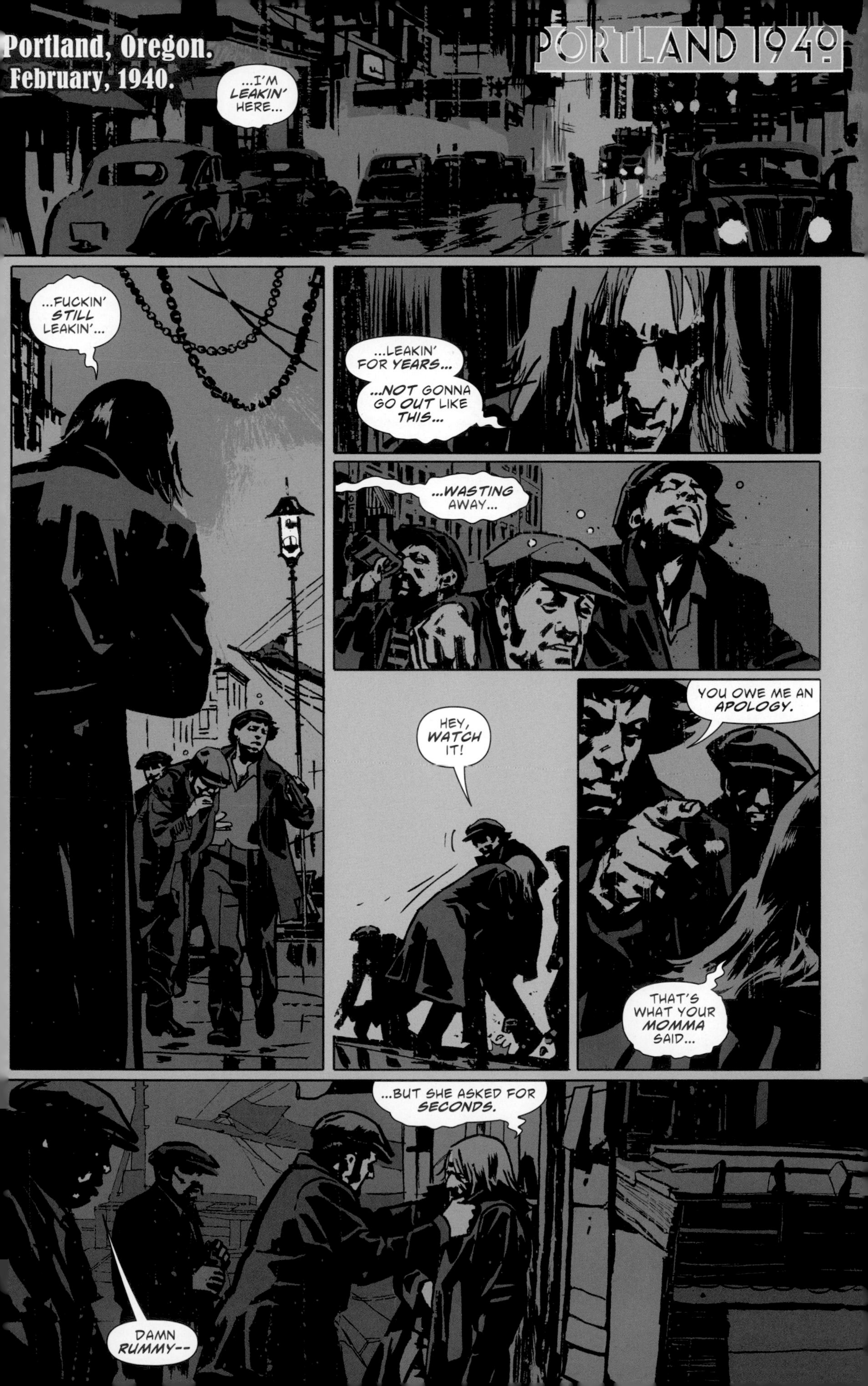
Portland, Oregon. February, 1940.
PORTLAND 1940
...I'M LEAKIN' HERE...
...FUCKIN' STILL LEAKIN'...
...LEAKIN' FOR YEARS...
...NOT GONNA GO OUT LIKE THIS...
...WASTING AWAY...
HEY, WATCH IT!
YOU OWE ME AN APOLOGY.
THAT'S WHAT YOUR MOMMA SAID...
...BUT SHE ASKED FOR SECONDS.
DAMN RUMMY--

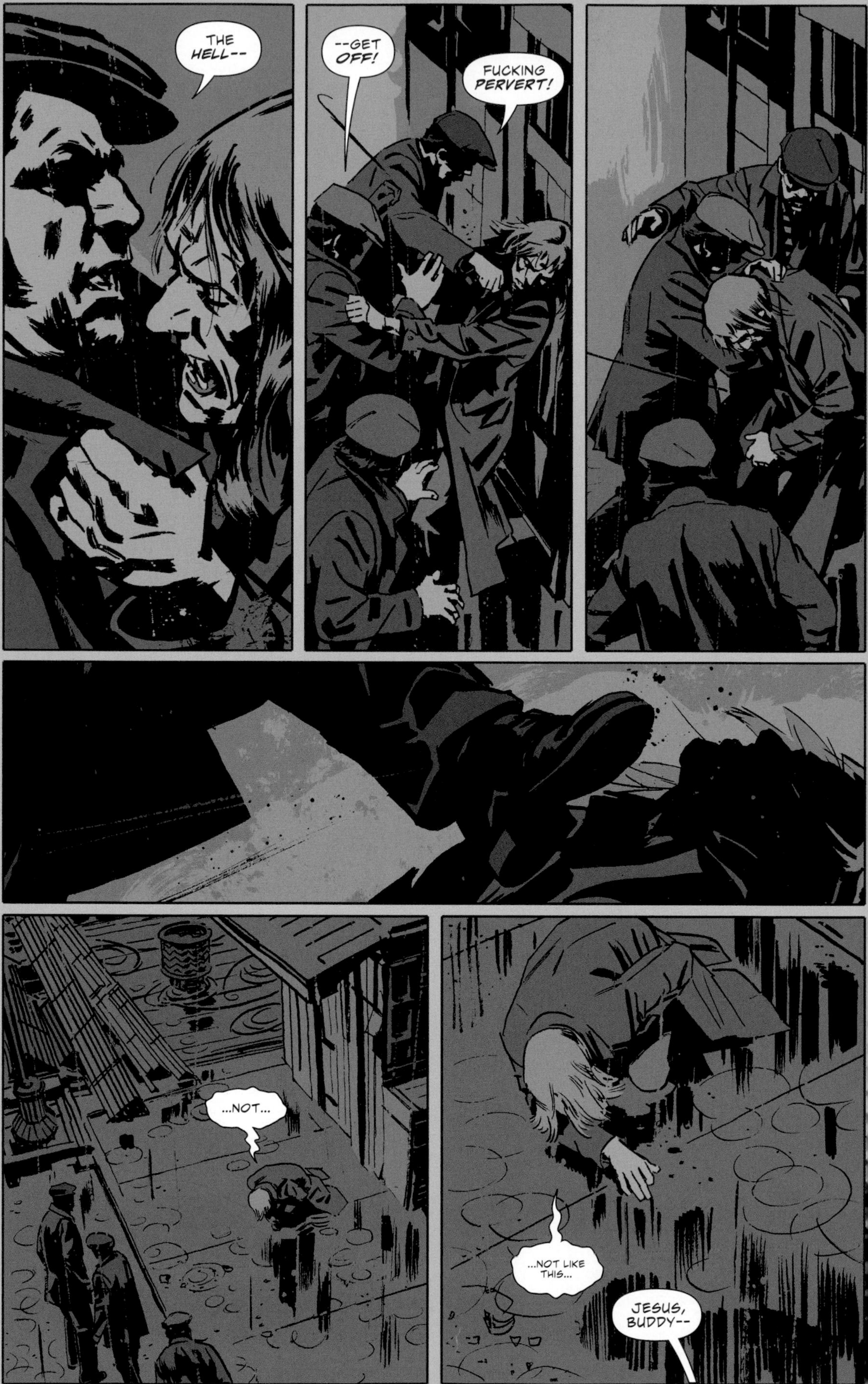
THE HELL--
--GET OFF!
FUCKING PERVERT!
...NOT...
...NOT LIKE THIS...
JESUS, BUDDY--

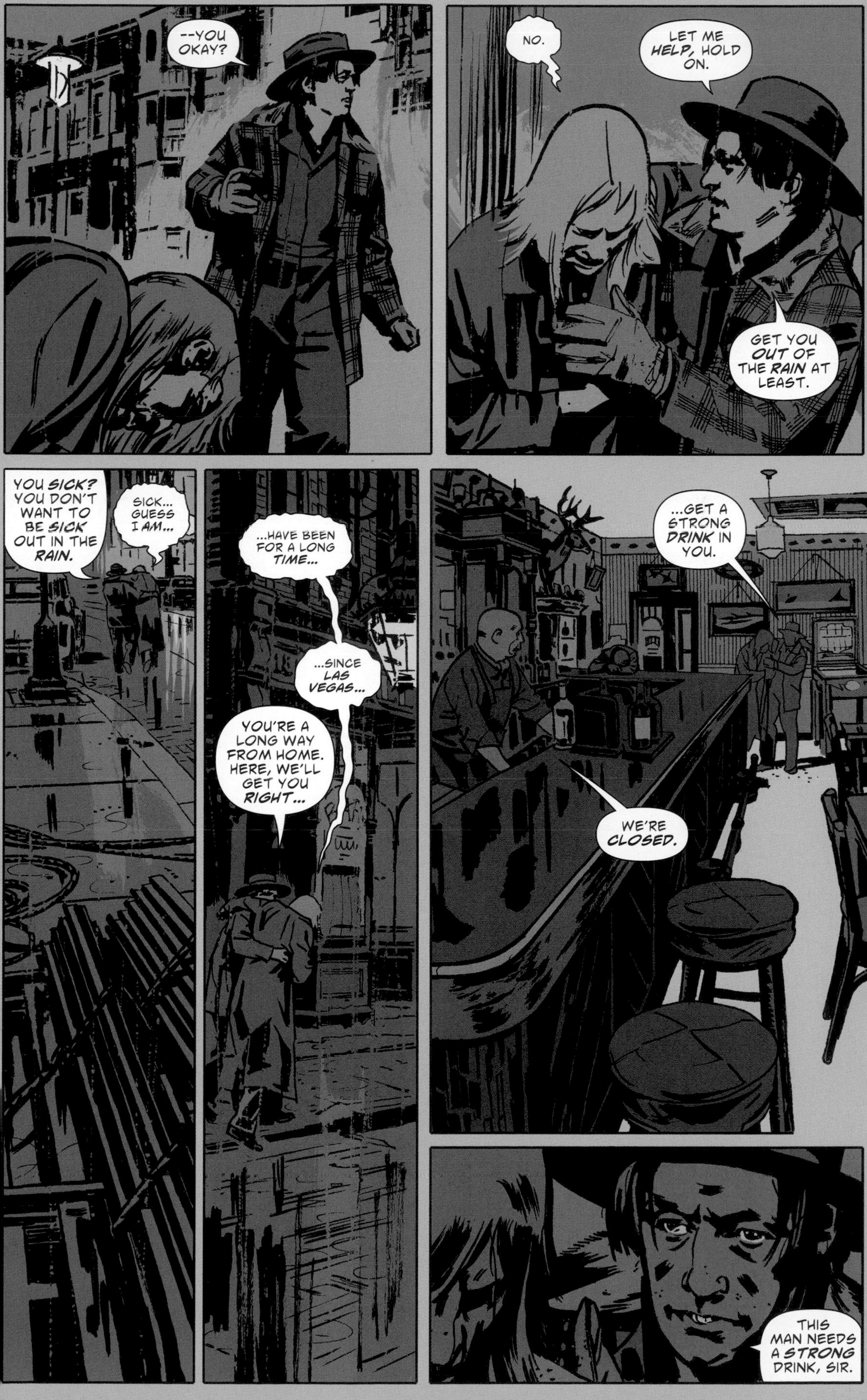
--YOU OKAY?
NO.
LET ME HELP, HOLD ON.
GET YOU OUT OF THE RAIN AT LEAST.
YOU SICK? YOU DON'T WANT TO BE SICK OUT IN THE RAIN.
SICK... GUESS I AM...
...HAVE BEEN FOR A LONG TIME...
...SINCE LAS VEGAS...
YOU'RE A LONG WAY FROM HOME. HERE, WE'LL GET YOU RIGHT...
...GET A STRONG DRINK IN YOU.
WE'RE CLOSED.
THIS MAN NEEDS A STRONG DRINK, SIR.

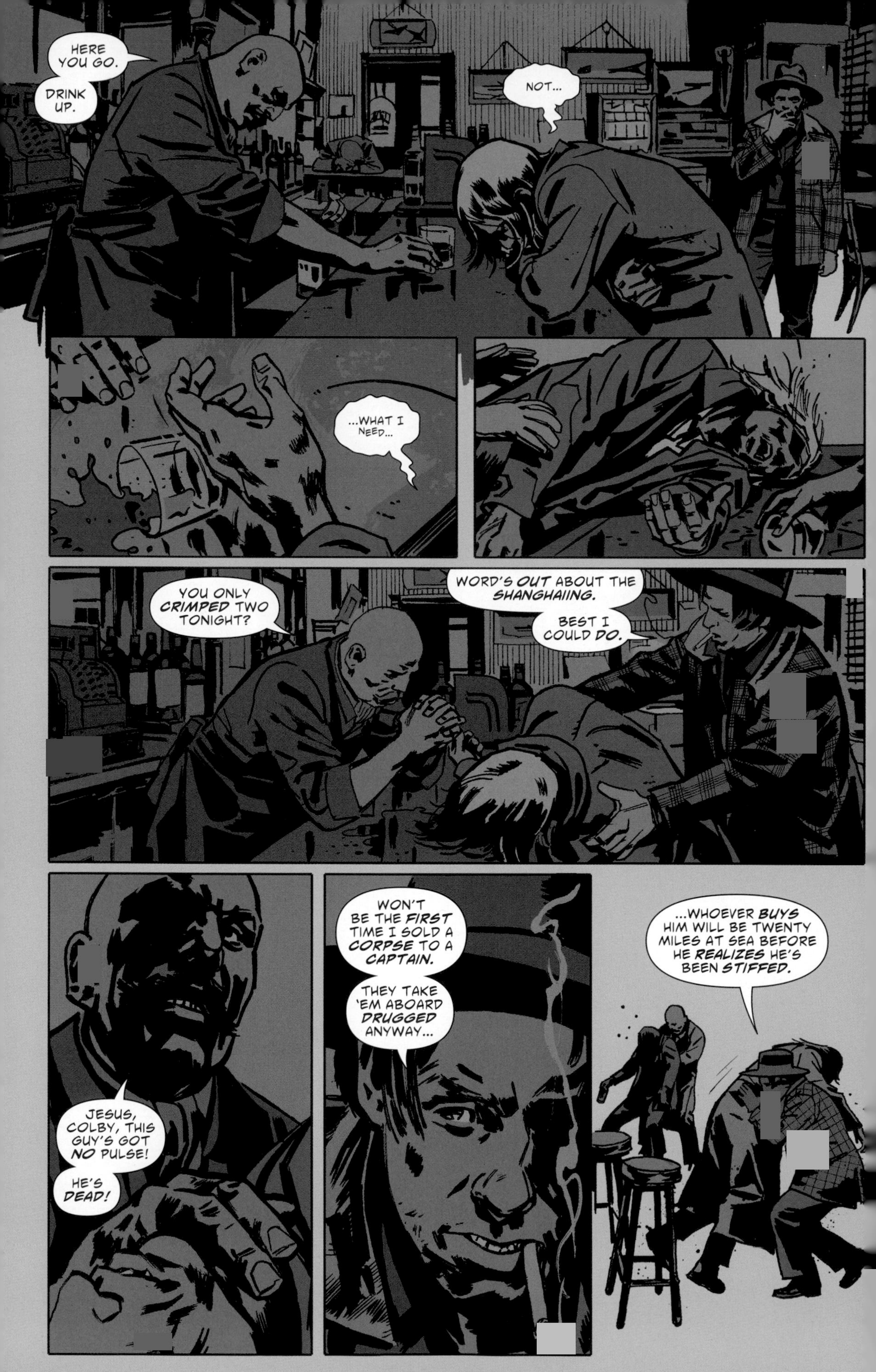
HERE YOU GO.
DRINK UP.
NOT...
...WHAT I NEED...
YOU ONLY CRIMPED TWO TONIGHT?
WORD'S OUT ABOUT THE SHANGHAIING.
BEST I COULD DO.
JESUS, COLBY, THIS GUY'S GOT NO PULSE!
HE'S DEAD!
WON'T BE THE FIRST TIME I SOLD A CORPSE TO A CAPTAIN.
THEY TAKE 'EM ABOARD DRUGGED ANYWAY...
...WHOEVER BUYS HIM WILL BE TWENTY MILES AT SEA BEFORE HE REALIZES HE'S BEEN STIFFED.

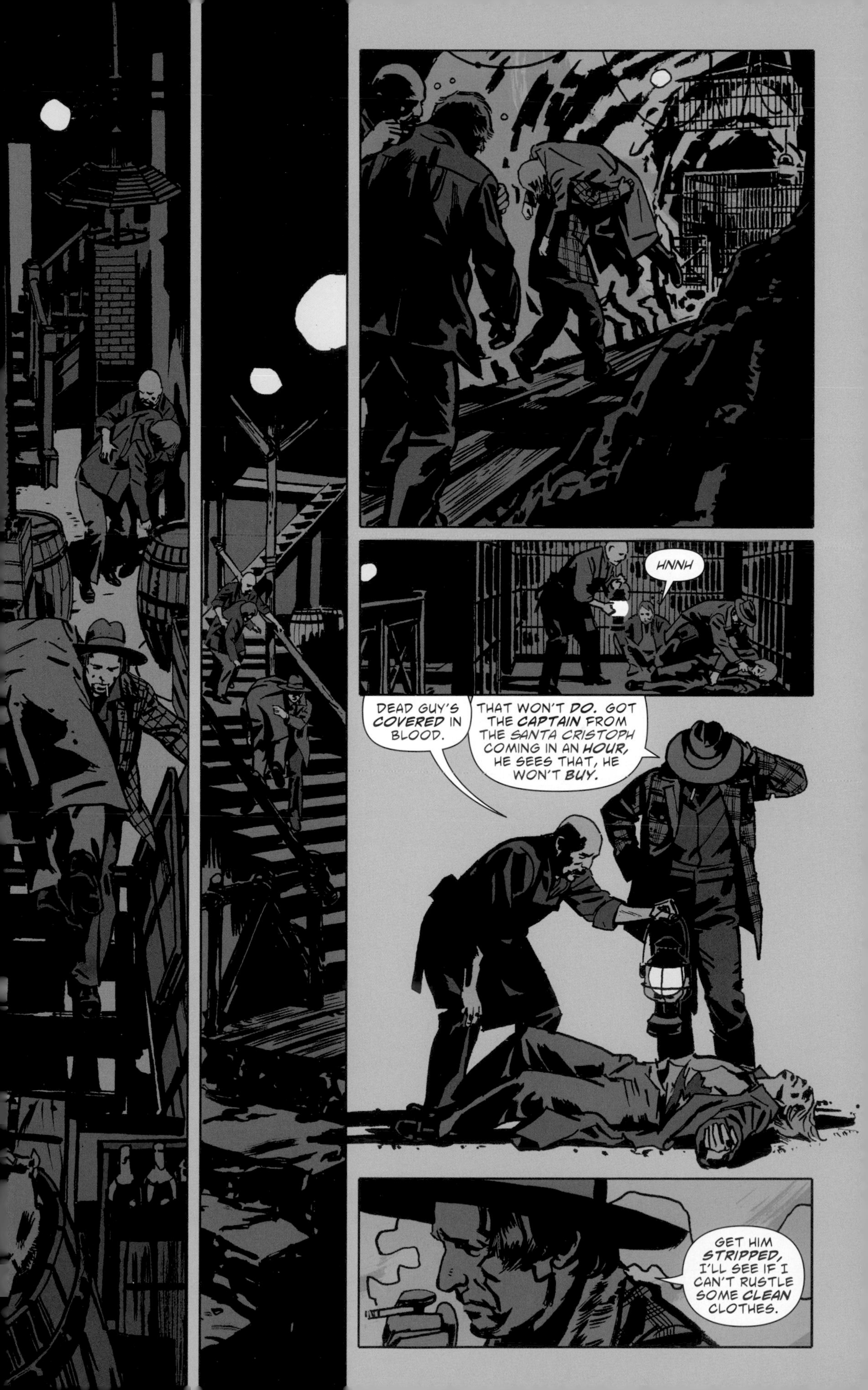
HNNH
DEAD GUY'S COVERED IN BLOOD.
THAT WON'T DO. GOT THE CAPTAIN FROM THE SANTA CRISTOPH COMING IN AN HOUR, HE SEES THAT, HE WON'T BUY.
GET HIM STRIPPED, I'LL SEE IF I CAN'T RUSTLE SOME CLEAN CLOTHES.

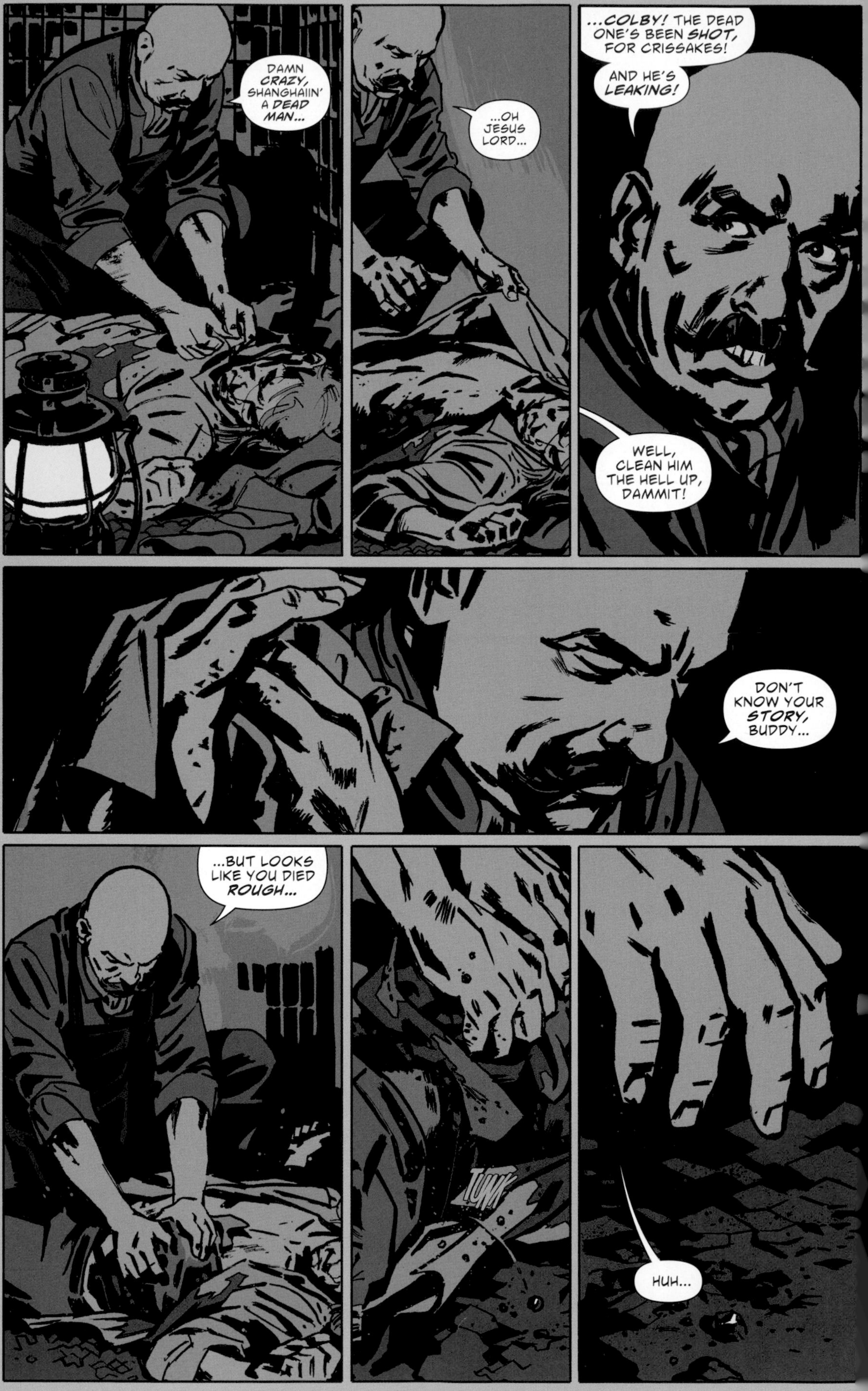
DAMN CRAZY, SHANGHAIIN' A DEAD MAN...
...OH JESUS LORD...
...COLBY! THE DEAD ONE'S BEEN SHOT, FOR CRISSAKES!
AND HE'S LEAKING!
WELL, CLEAN HIM THE HELL UP, DAMMIT!
DON'T KNOW YOUR STORY, BUDDY...
...BUT LOOKS LIKE YOU DIED ROUGH...
TUNK
HUH...

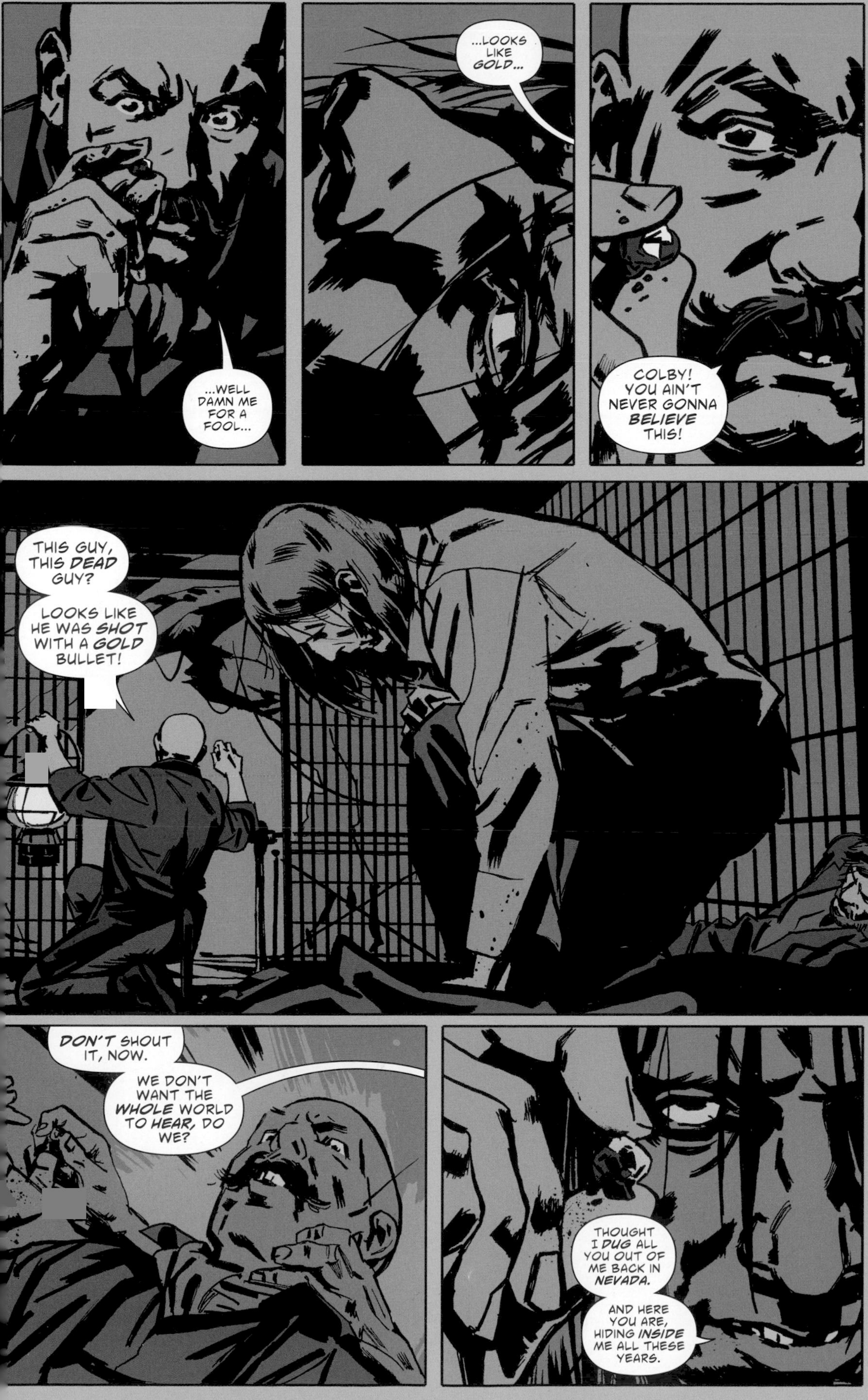
...WELL DAMN ME FOR A FOOL...
...LOOKS LIKE GOLD...
COLBY! YOU AIN'T NEVER GONNA BELIEVE THIS!
THIS GUY, THIS DEAD GUY?
LOOKS LIKE HE WAS SHOT WITH A GOLD BULLET!
DON'T SHOUT IT, NOW.
WE DON'T WANT THE WHOLE WORLD TO HEAR, DO WE?
THOUGHT I DUG ALL YOU OUT OF ME BACK IN NEVADA.
AND HERE YOU ARE, HIDING INSIDE ME ALL THESE YEARS.

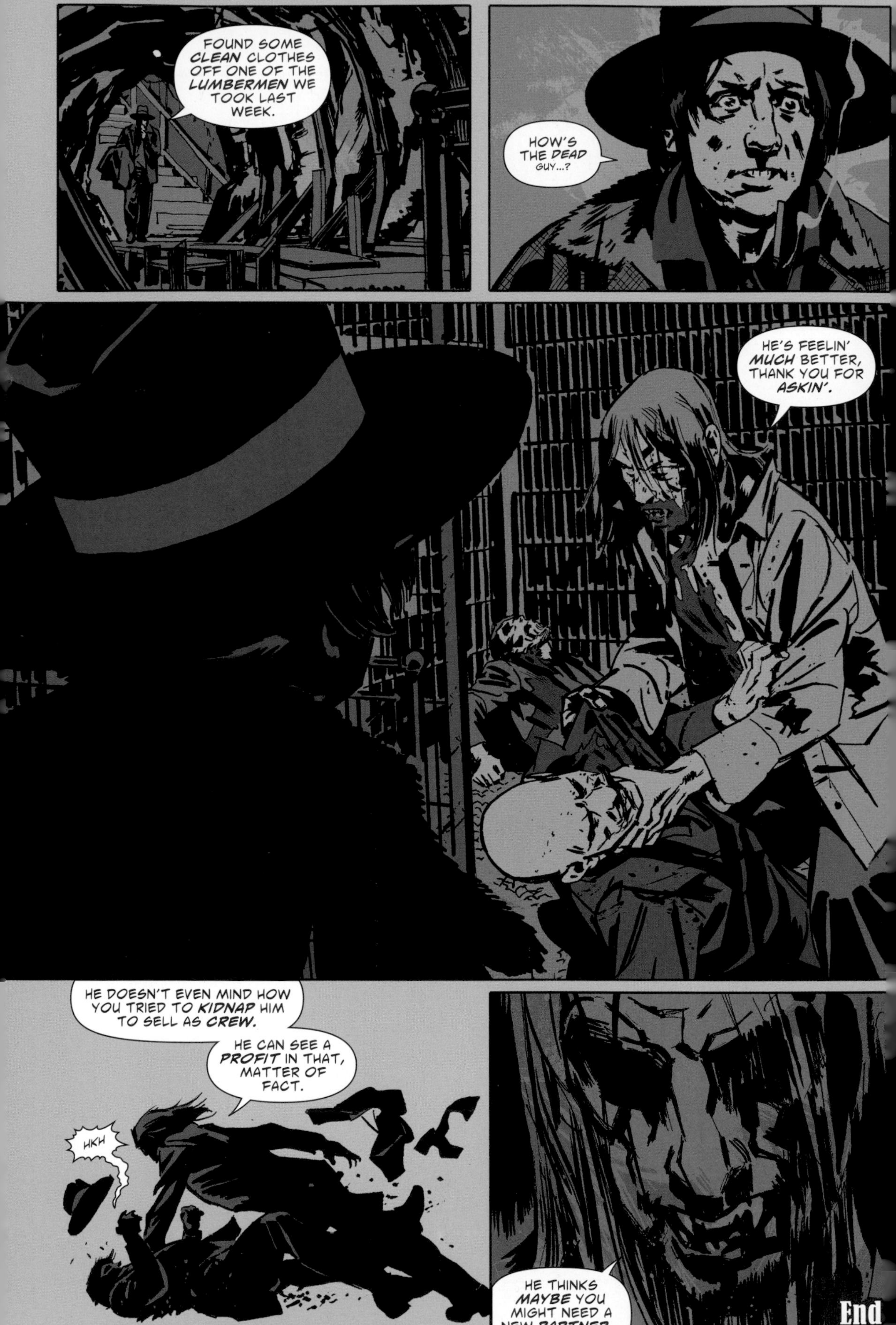
FOUND SOME CLEAN CLOTHES OFF ONE OF THE LUMBERMEN WE TOOK LAST WEEK.
HOW'S THE DEAD GUY...?
HE'S FEELIN' MUCH BETTER, THANK YOU FOR ASKIN'.
HE DOESN'T EVEN MIND HOW YOU TRIED TO KIDNAP HIM TO SELL AS CREW.
HE CAN SEE A PROFIT IN THAT, MATTER OF FACT.
HKH
HE THINKS MAYBE YOU MIGHT NEED A NEW PARTNER...
End

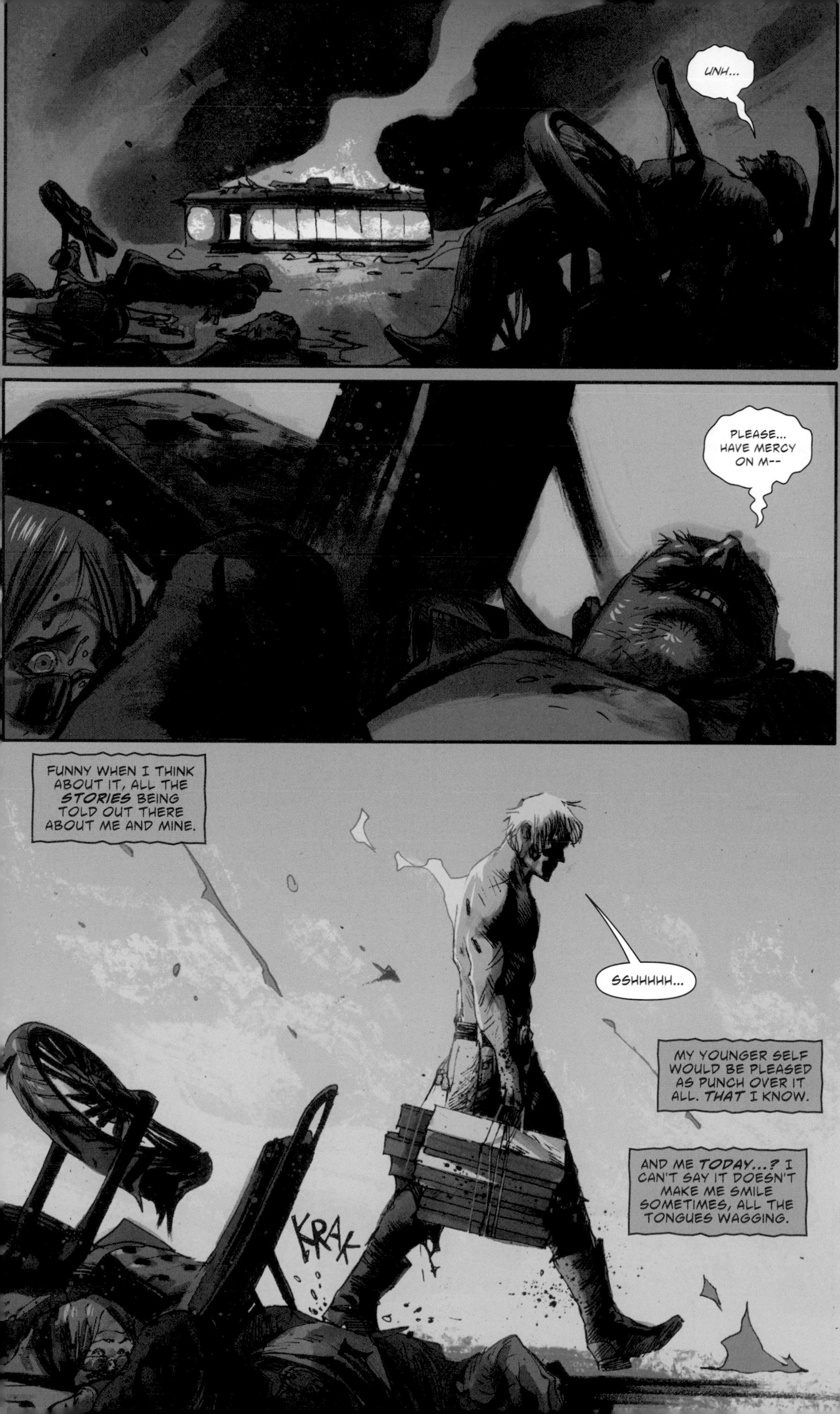
UNH...
PLEASE... HAVE MERCY ON M--
FUNNY WHEN I THINK ABOUT IT, ALL THE STORIES BEING TOLD OUT THERE ABOUT ME AND MINE.
SSHHHHH...
MY YOUNGER SELF WOULD BE PLEASED AS PUNCH OVER IT ALL. THAT I KNOW.
AND ME TODAY...? I CAN'T SAY IT DOESN'T MAKE ME SMILE SOMETIMES, ALL THE TONGUES WAGGING.
KRAK

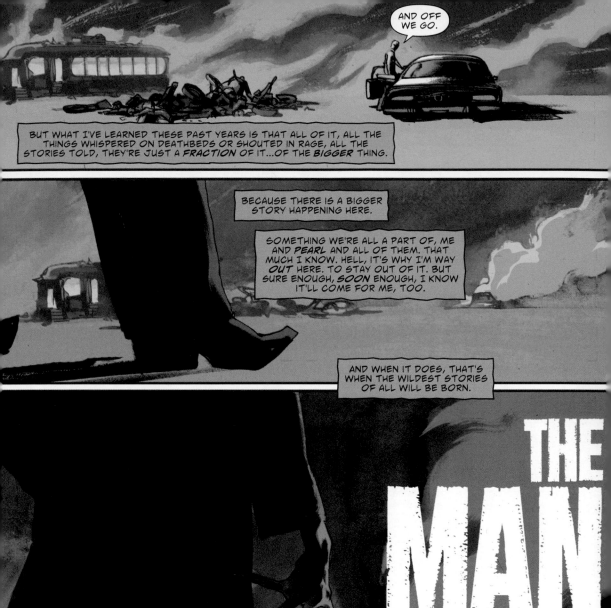

AND OFF WE GO.

BUT WHAT I'VE LEARNED THESE PAST YEARS IS THAT ALL OF IT, ALL THE THINGS WHISPERED ON DEATHBEDS OR SHOUTED IN RAGE, ALL THE STORIES TOLD, THEY'RE JUST A *FRACTION* OF IT...OF THE *BIGGER* THING.

BECAUSE THERE IS A BIGGER STORY HAPPENING HERE.

SOMETHING WE'RE ALL A PART OF, ME AND *PEARL* AND ALL OF THEM. THAT MUCH I KNOW. HELL, IT'S WHY I'M WAY *OUT* HERE. TO STAY OUT OF IT. BUT SURE ENOUGH, *SOON* ENOUGH, I KNOW IT'LL COME FOR ME, TOO.

AND WHEN IT DOES, THAT'S WHEN THE WILDEST STORIES OF ALL WILL BE BORN.

THE MAN COMES AROUND

END.

SNYDER / ALBUQUERQUE

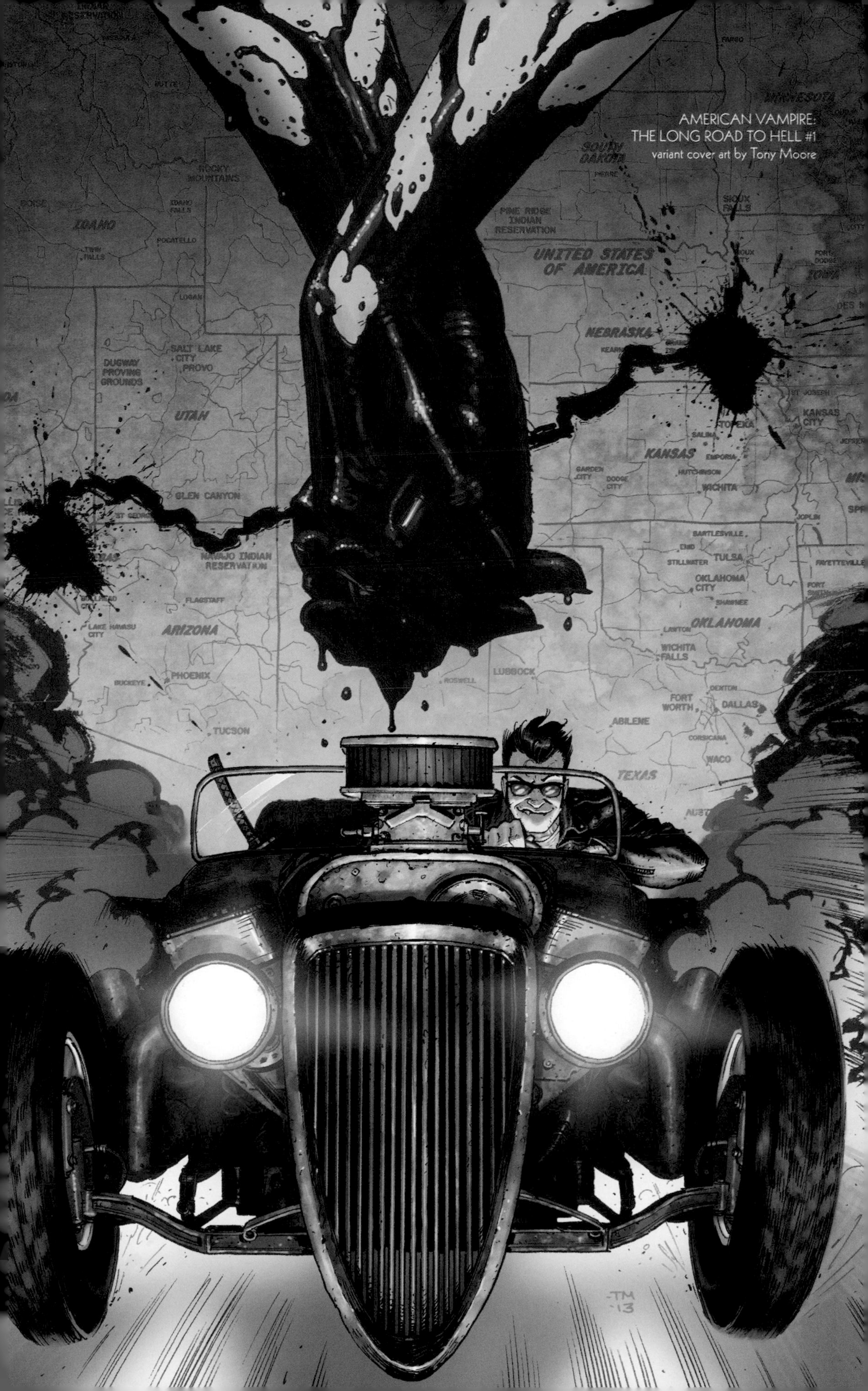
UNITED STATES OF AMERICA
IDAHO
BOISE
POCATELLO
TWIN FALLS
IDAHO FALLS
ROCKY MOUNTAINS
SOUTH DAKOTA
PIERRE
PINE RIDGE INDIAN RESERVATION
SIOUX FALLS
SIOUX CITY
MINNESOTA
FARGO
BUTTE
LOGAN
SALT LAKE CITY
PROVO
DUGWAY PROVING GROUNDS
UTAH
NEBRASKA
KEARNEY
KANSAS
TOPEKA
KANSAS CITY
SALINA
EMPORIA
HUTCHINSON
WICHITA
GARDEN CITY
DODGE CITY
GLEN CANYON
NAVAJO INDIAN RESERVATION
FLAGSTAFF
ARIZONA
LAKE HAVASU CITY
PHOENIX
BUCKEYE
TUCSON
ROSWELL
LUBBOCK
BARTLESVILLE
ENID
STILLWATER
TULSA
OKLAHOMA CITY
SHAWNEE
OKLAHOMA
LAWTON
WICHITA FALLS
JOPLIN
FAYETTEVILLE
DENTON
FORT WORTH
DALLAS
ABILENE
CORSICANA
WACO
TEXAS
TM
'13

AMERICAN VAMPIRE:
THE LONG ROAD TO HELL #1
variant cover art by Tony Moore

SKETCHES AND DESIGNS BY RAFAEL ALBUQUERQUE

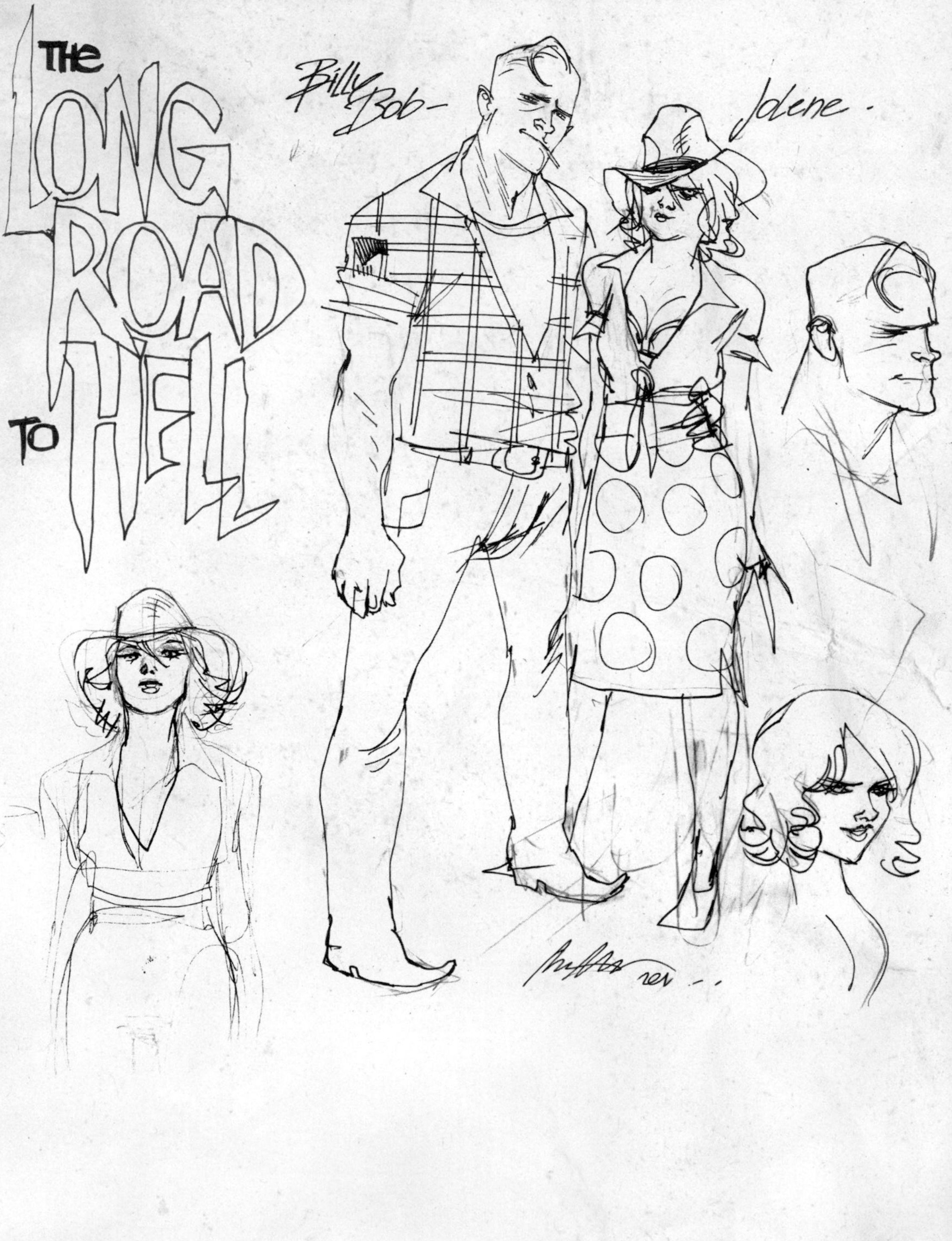
THE LONG ROAD TO HELL
Billy Bob-
Jolene-

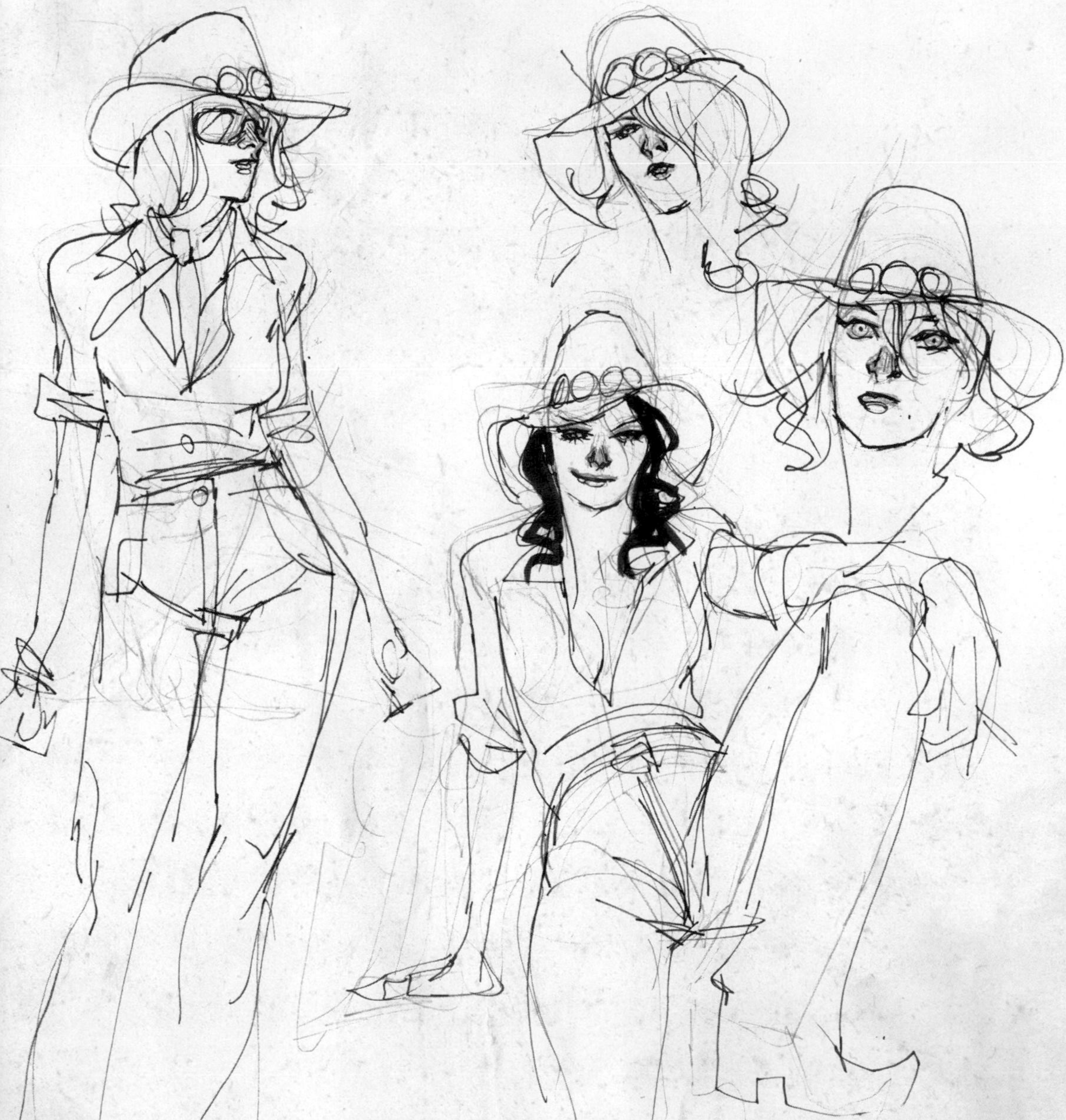

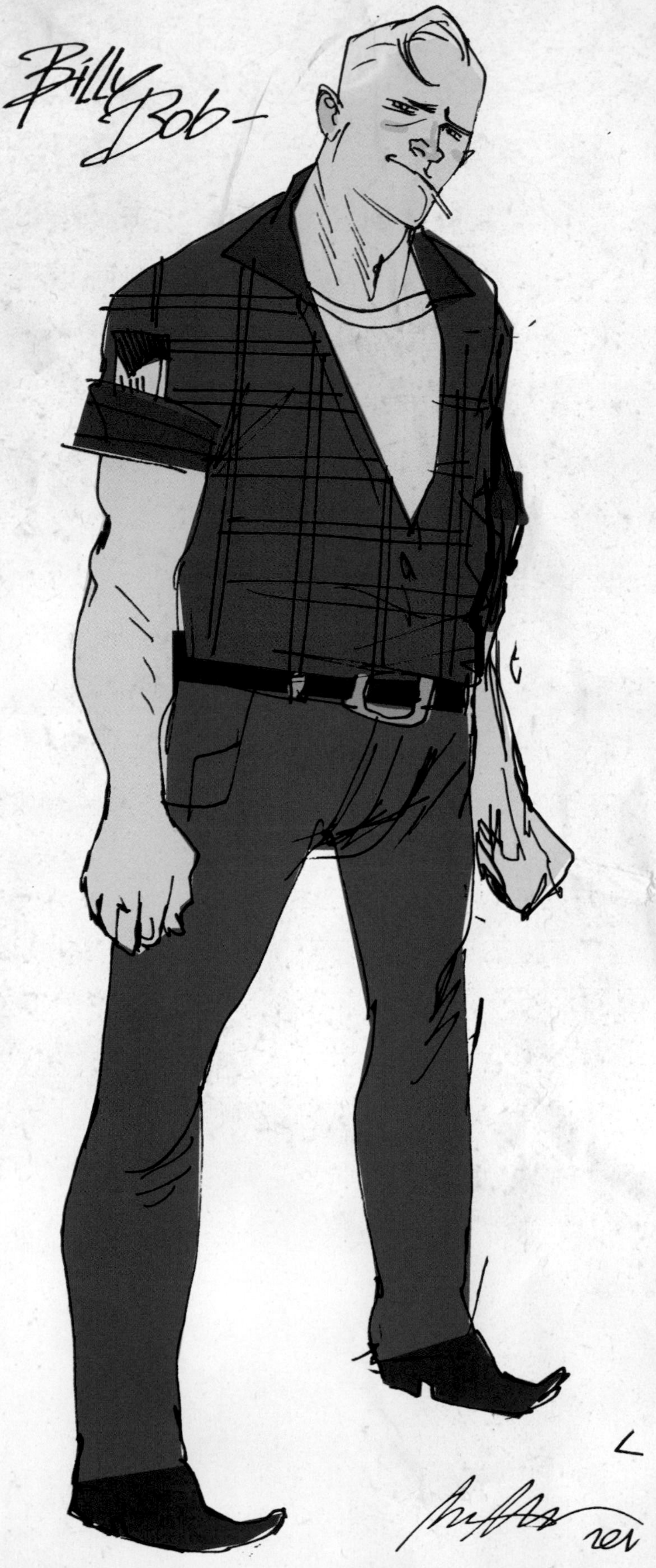
Billy Bob-

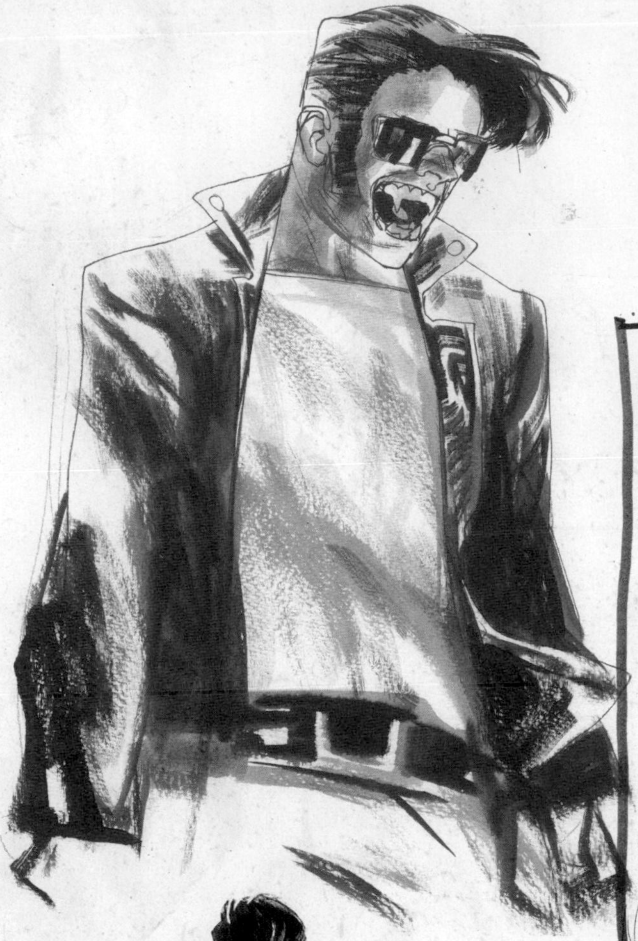

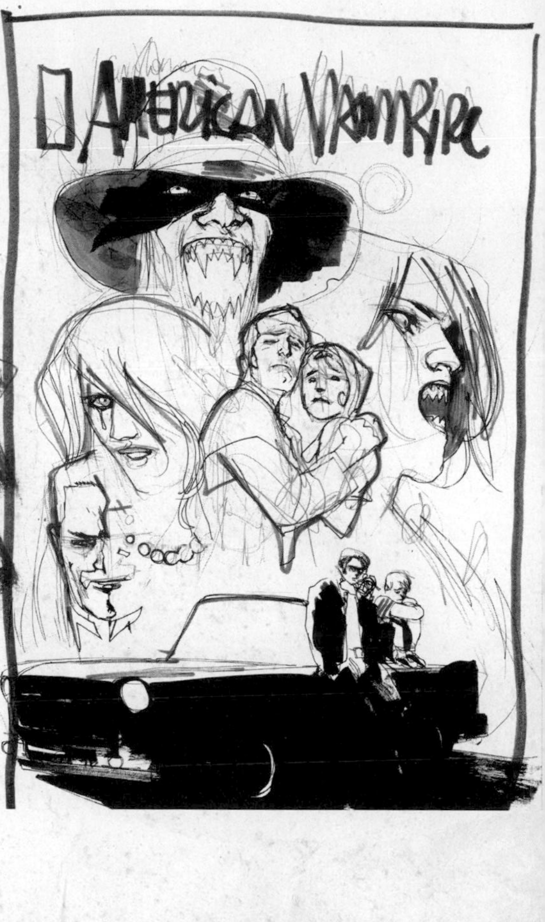
AMERICAN VAMPIRE

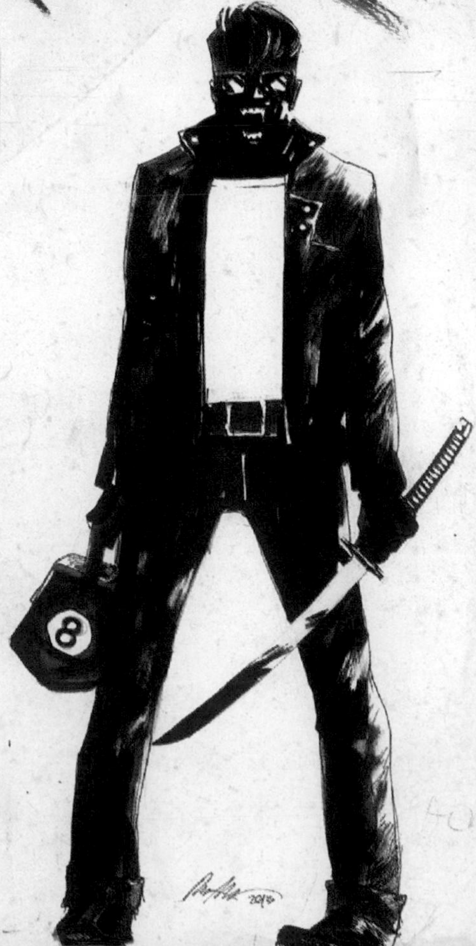

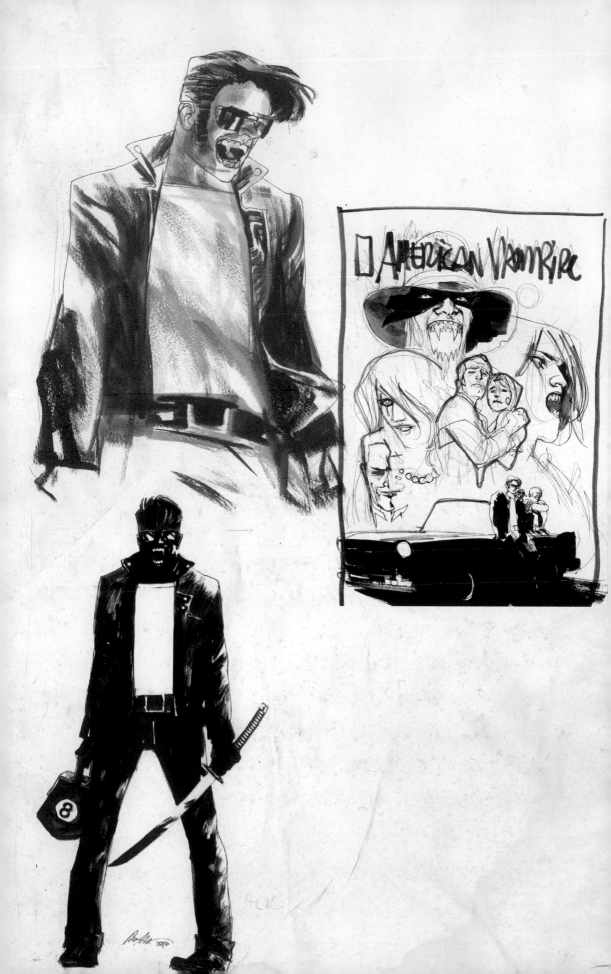

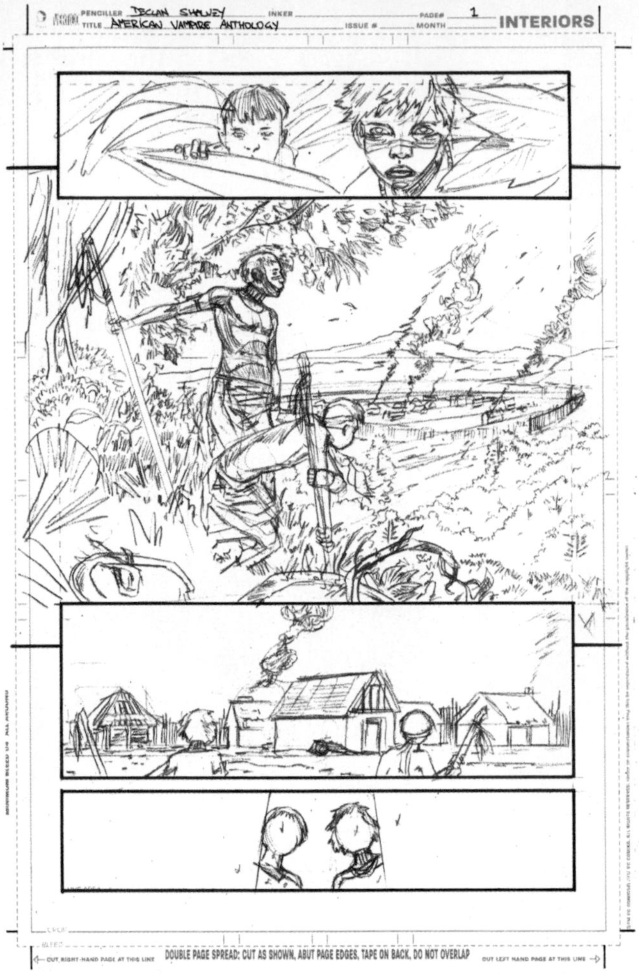
PENCILLER DECLAN SHALVEY
INKER
PAGE# 1
INTERIORS
TITLE AMERICAN VAMPIRE ANTHOLOGY
ISSUE #
MONTH
DOUBLE PAGE SPREAD: CUT AS SHOWN, ABUT PAGE EDGES, TAPE ON BACK, DO NOT OVERLAP

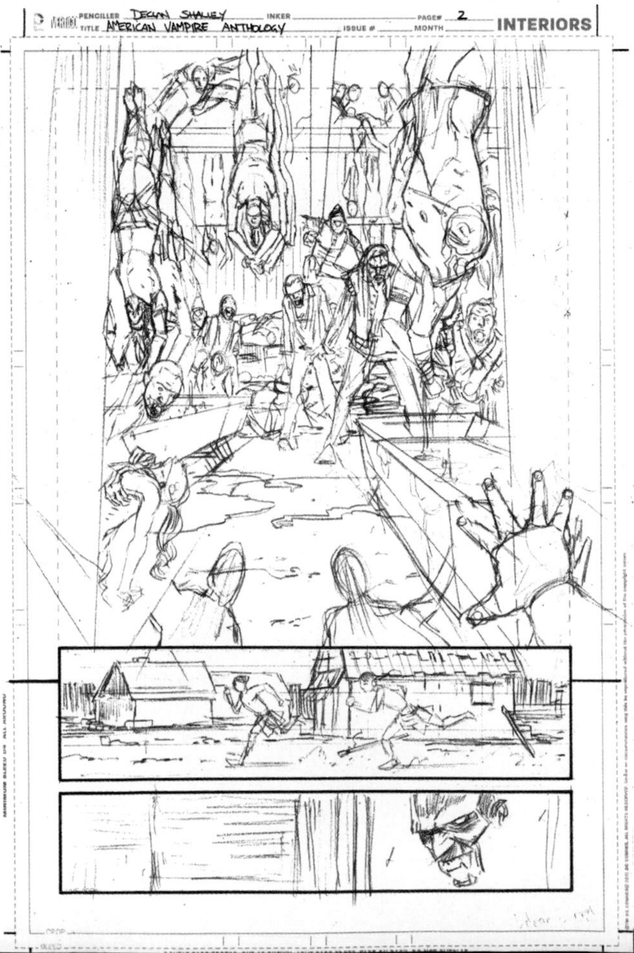
PENCILLER DECLAN SHALVEY
INKER
PAGE# 2
INTERIORS
TITLE AMERICAN VAMPIRE ANTHOLOGY
ISSUE #
MONTH

LAYOUTS
AND
DESIGN
BY
DECLAN
SHALVEY

DECLAN

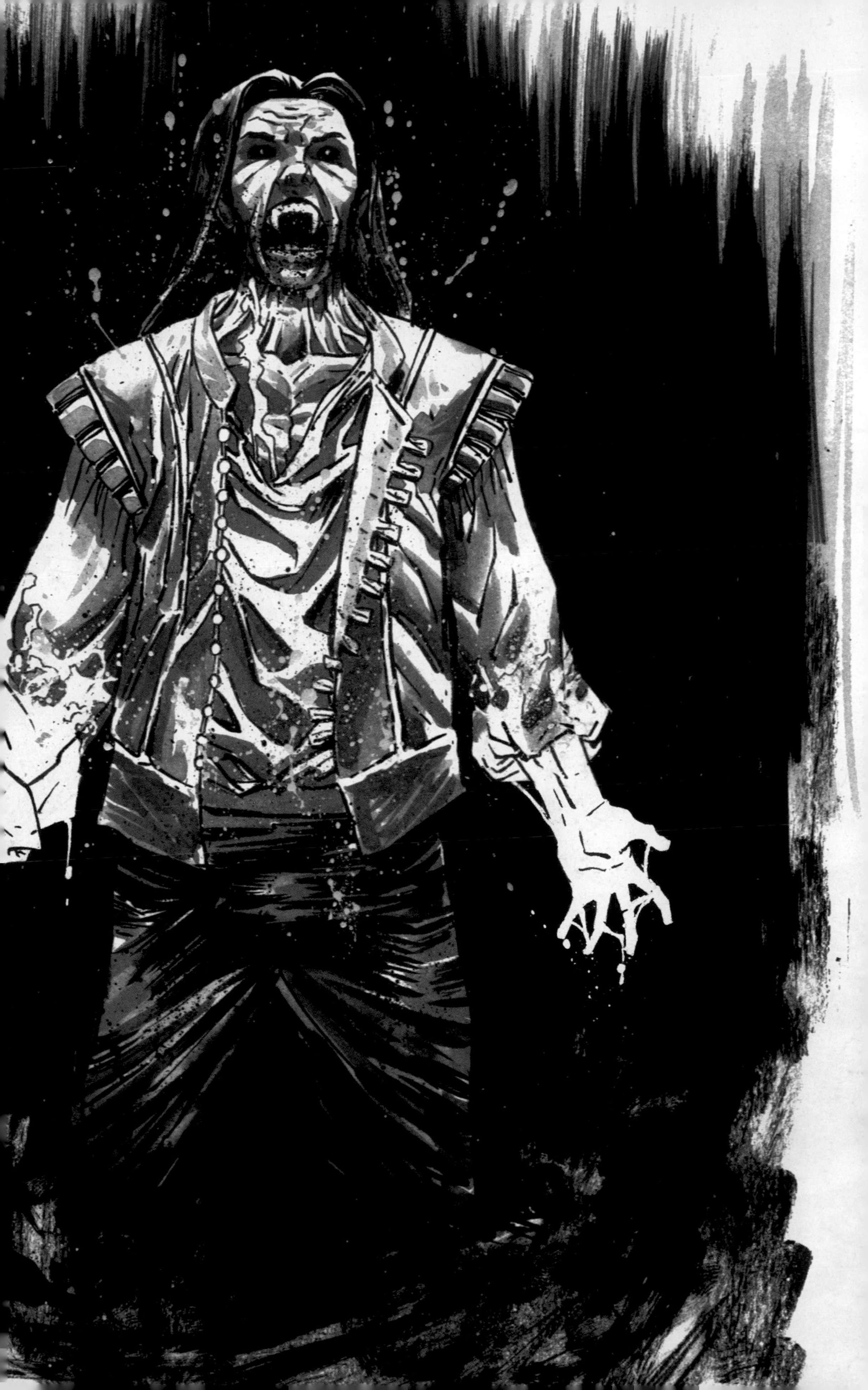

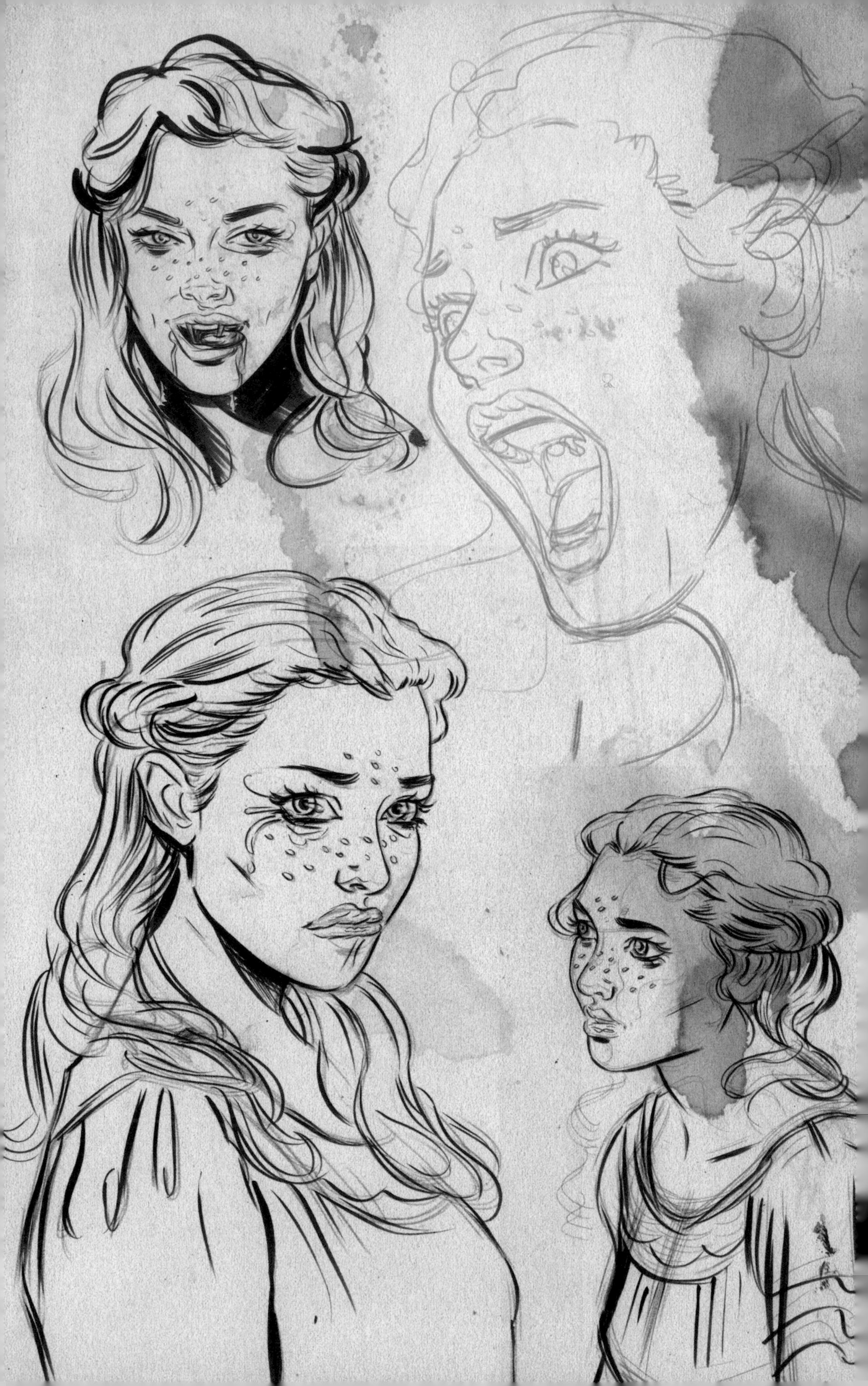

DESIGNS BY TULA LOTAY

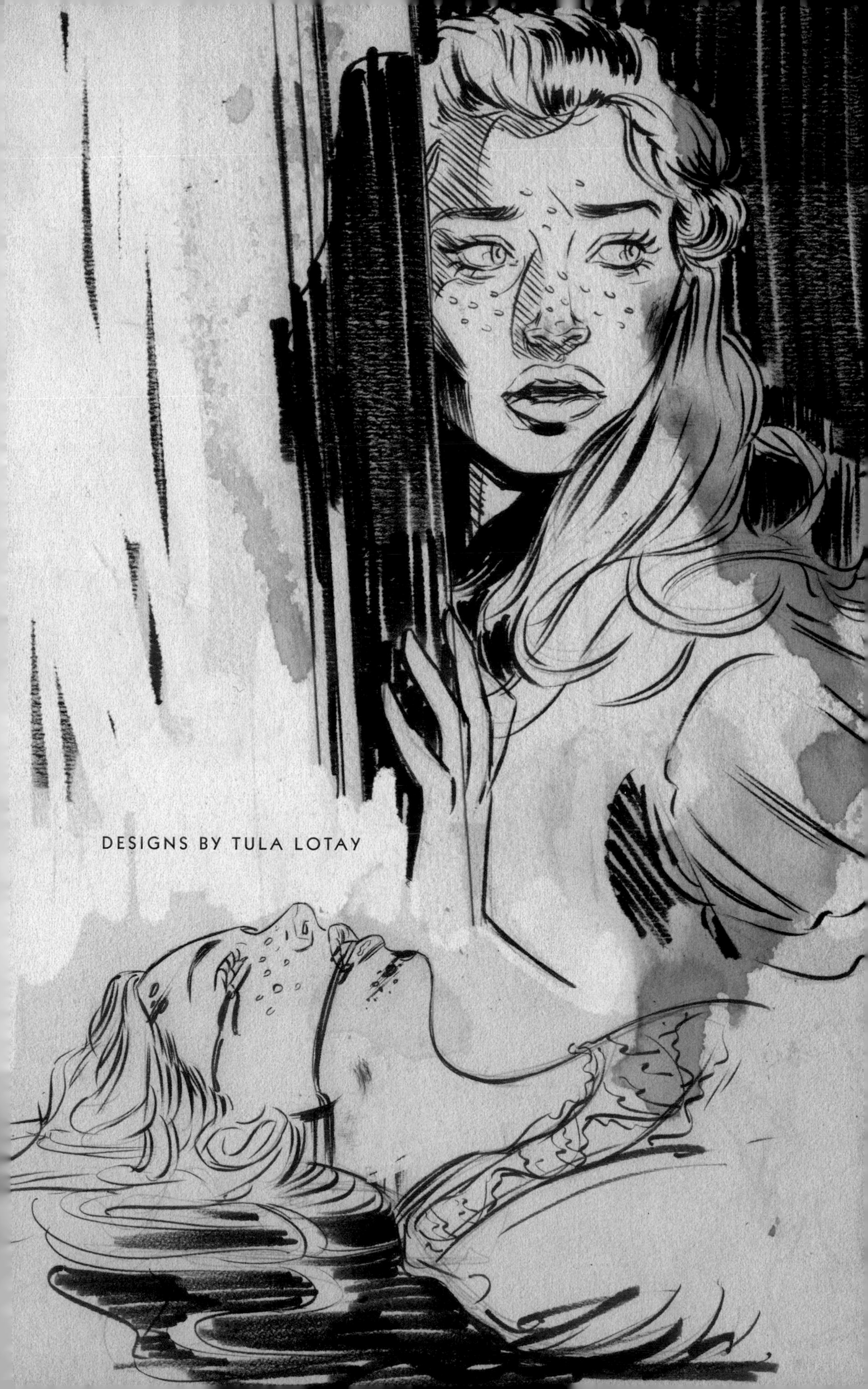

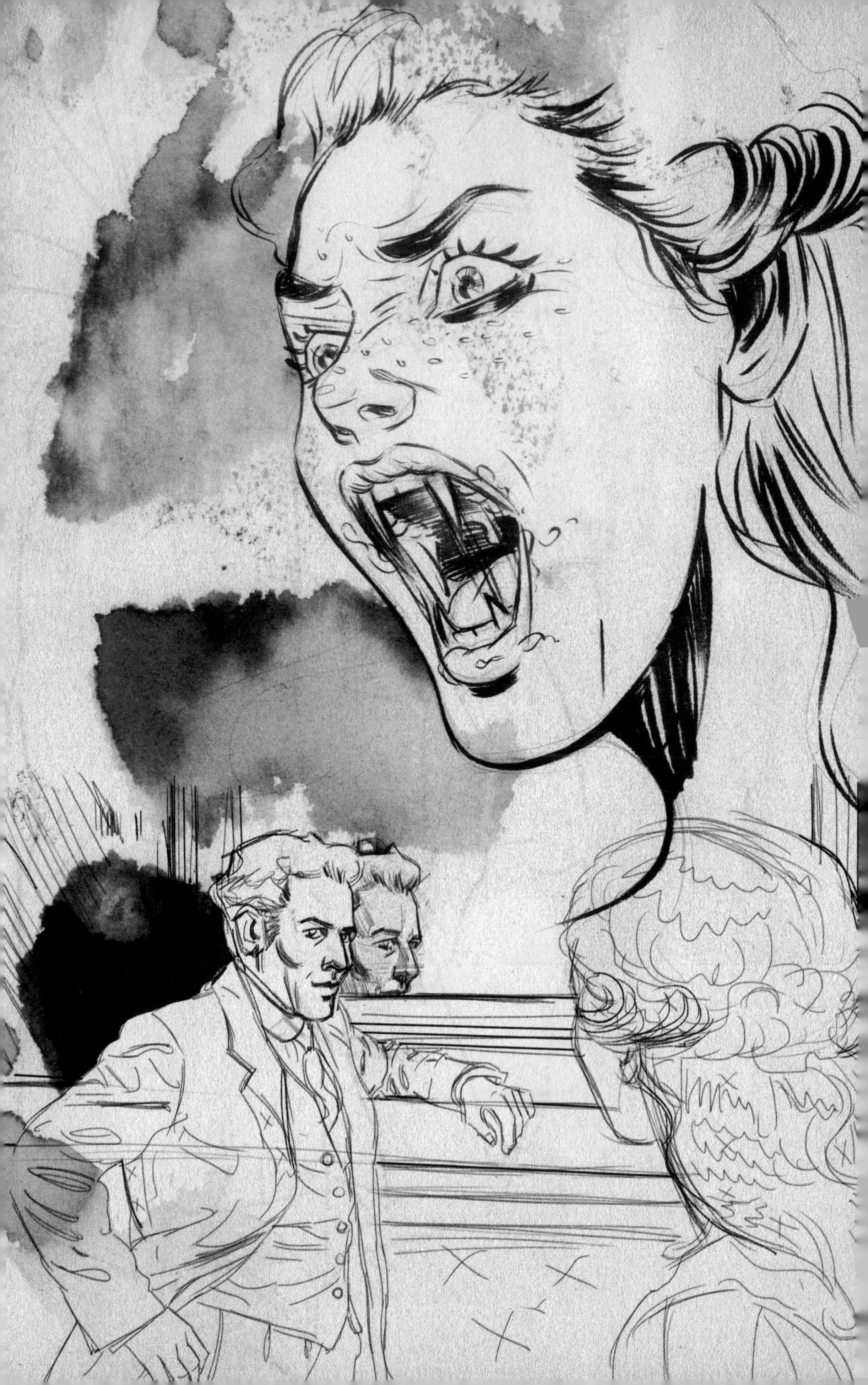